Christians for Biblical Equality
122 West Franklin Avenue Suite 218
Minneapolis, MN 55404-2451
Ph: 612-872-6898 Fax: 612-872-6891
Email: cbe@cbeinternational.org
Website: http://www.cbeinternational.org

Women Caught in the Conflict

The Culture War between Traditionalism and Feminism

Rebecca Merrill Groothuis

Foreword by Kenneth S. Kantzer

WIPF & STOCK PUBLISHERS

790 East 11th Avenue Eugene OR 97401

1997

Women Caught in the Conflict
by Rebecca Merrill Groothuis
Copyright© 1994 by Rebecca Merrill Groothuis
ISBN: 1-57910-048-1

Printed by  1997
790 East 11th Avenue • Eugene OR 97401

To my husband, Doug,
whose loving encouragement
and intellectual discipleship
have made this book—
and so much more—
possible

_____

Contents

Acknowledgments

I owe the existence of this book to a handful of people who encouraged me to begin and/or to continue writing it. Many thanks to Paul and Jean Merrill, Kin Millen, Allan Fisher, Catherine Clark Kroeger, Wanda Fisher, and, of course, Doug Groothuis (already in the dedication!). A special note of gratitude goes to Jean Merrill, my mother, who patiently read various versions of the manuscript and offered much invaluable advice (most of which I dutifully heeded). Whatever grace or equanimity now characterizes the book is due largely, I am sure, to her input. I am also grateful to Linda Triemstra for her diligent oversight of the editorial and publication process.

Foreword

by Kenneth S. Kantzer

In recent years few issues have produced more heat and less light than the role of women in home, church, and society. It is the role of women in the church that creates the greatest dismay on the part of committed evangelicals. By definition, an evangelical is one who takes the lordship of Jesus Christ seriously and finds guidance for his thought and life from the teaching of the Bible.

On this issue, more than most, evangelicals have proved unfaithful to their own deepest convictions. Probably a majority have exegeted two or three passages from the Bible. There it is: Women are to serve men; in public worship, women must be silent and must never teach or rule over men. What more needs to be said? Then they proceed to set their feet down hard—and I would add, promptly close their minds and shut their Bibles.

On the other hand, many evangelicals—especially women, outraged that all other areas of society are more considerate of them as human than is the church—vent their spleen on male leaders of the church, reject this judgment that condemns women to second-class status, and sad to say, often turn away from both the church and the Bible. Unfortunately, few are either capable (past theological education being what it was) or concerned to dirty their fingers in the mucky task of careful, meticulous exegesis of crucial biblical passages, discovering the overall teaching of Scripture regarding the role of women in the home and church. They have opted instead for what they consider the "logical" concomitance of true feminine equality. In doing so, they sometimes opt for "equality" with the worst features of the male role in Western culture. Many feminists, in fact, have simply departed altogether from biblical teaching.

Here is where Rebecca Groothuis comes to our rescue with *Women Caught in the Conflict: The Culture War between Traditionalism and Feminism*. First, as a committed evangelical, she recognizes the authority of Scripture and insists that any right view on this issue must begin with scriptural authority. Second, she lays down appropriate hermeneutical principles to enable us to get at the real meaning of Scripture. Third, she insists that we must found our doctrine on the whole of Scripture—not excluding any passage, particularly passages that fail to fit our preconceived or traditional notion of what the Bible teaches. Fourth, she points us to a wealth of solid exegesis from the last century that cannot be simply disregarded as "feminists building a case." And last, she warns against the unbiblical and often antibiblical conclusions of contemporary feminists who are constructing a theology on their own apart from the Bible.

In short, Rebecca Merrill Groothuis has much to say that is highly relevant to this troublesome issue, and she says it without rancor or meanness of spirit, as any good Christian should.

Introduction

These are contentious times. Social change is catapulting through culture, frequently running smack up against the stone wall of tradition. Generally, neither the old nor the new is being evaluated objectively on its own terms; each is simply being reacted to. Liberals defy tradition, and conservatives back off from change. People are labeled according to the bandwagon on which they ride, and each bandwagon trumpets a fixed ideology, running the gamut of political and religious concerns. "Misfits" who cannot adhere to the entire ideological agenda of any one bandwagon are nonetheless branded as riding on one or another. For example, someone who believes that preferential hiring is unfair and that morally offensive material should be removed from the public airwaves is deemed a conservative and a champion of all things traditional. Yet, if that person also believes women are being unjustly denied equal status with men in the church, the home, and the workplace, she is labeled a radical feminist who hates men, devalues the family, and believes in something called abortion rights. It is not easy to come up with a reasonable viewpoint in an age when slogans and bandwagons have largely replaced the use of logic and common sense. It is even more difficult to communicate a viewpoint that cannot be reduced to a battle cry or a campaign motto.

When I was just beginning to write this book, I was bold (or perhaps foolish) enough to attempt to explain to a friend why I felt the need to undertake such a project. It was a painful but illuminating conversation. I said that I was concerned that women whose callings lead them outside the traditional woman's role are often discouraged by other Christians from pursuing those callings and developing their gifts for the good of the church and the glory of God. I said that because this is such an inflammatory and easily misunderstood issue I was exerting a great deal of effort to steer a course of moderation and balance between the extreme positions at either pole. I also spoke of my growing awareness of the need to receive grace from God for a humble and forgiving heart in the midst of controversy and misjudgment.

The first response of this Christian woman (who happened to be a full-time homemaker) was that she had few opinions about and even less interest in the subject of women and careers. Then she thought for a minute and announced that she would hazard a comment after all. She declared it to be her view that it shouldn't matter what society decrees a woman should do; what really matters is that each woman do what God wants her to do. And, she added, what God wants a woman to do could be almost anything, because God made everyone so different.

I wanted to shout, "Bravo!" I couldn't have said it better myself. But then she suddenly offered more opinions. She said that what I had told her about my motive for writing this book made me sound no different from all the other women's libbers who have been loudly insisting for years that women have the right to do anything a man can do. She doubted that there was any need for such a book as mine, because she had never seen any evidence of prejudice against women. She also said that she had had enough of the women's movement; it has been so successful that now men are being discriminated against.

I was astonished. This friend had heard me say one thing and had understood me to be saying something else entirely. She had pegged me as a flaming feminist, when in reality she and I were essentially in agreement on the issue of what a woman should do with her life! When I finally explained that I did not advocate reverse discrimination or the other extreme measures proposed by today's secular feminists, and that she herself had beautifully stated what I believed to be true concerning women's roles, we came to understand each other.

Any discussion of the issue of gender roles is fraught with many pitfalls. This particular conversation ran afoul of four of the biggest of these. The first pitfall lies simply in the fact that *every* person has strong feelings on this subject, regardless of whether or not these feelings have ever been articulated or thoughtfully considered. Even a person who professes not to have given the matter much attention is nonetheless likely to hold some very definite views. The second pitfall is the alacrity with which so many people label as obnoxiously feminist any idea that deviates at any point from what is considered the "traditional" view of gender roles. A third pitfall is to underrate the need for any kind of defense of women's equality. A person who is not aware of a problem will be impatient with any effort to find a solution. A fourth pitfall is the tendency to overrate the "success" of secular feminism. (Actually, modern secular feminism seems to have succeeded in doing what it ought not to have done and failed to do what it ought to have done—but I get ahead of myself.)

So it happened that my very effort to explain why I wanted to write this book illustrated the reason for it. What is desperately needed in the evangelical feminist/traditionalist debate is the willingness to hear and understand other people's views for what they are. Instead, we find an over-eagerness simply to peg them for what they *appear* to be. Disagreement is probably inevitable on this issue, and, if it results from views expressed graciously and with accurate comprehension of the "opposing" positions, it is healthy. Further, when mutual understanding is reached, combatants may realize that they are on the same side after all—as happened in the conversation I had with my friend—and disagreement may melt away. However, disagreement mixed with condemnation and based on caricature and misunderstanding is not only unhealthy but unfitting for those who profess the name of Jesus Christ.

In negotiating the conceptual terrain in this subject area, how can we avoid the pitfalls? First of all, we can submit emotional reaction to reasonable reflection and become informed concerning actual ideas and issues, rather than rely on caricatures thereof. Much of the fuss and furor in the current culture war over gender roles is fueled by the "bandwagon mentality," whereby any differing viewpoint is labeled according to the most extremist ideology, and the issue comes to be perceived as a forced choice between two antithetical extremes. Such a battle strategy succeeds only in perpetuating the conflict and precluding a resolution.

For example, if some should determine a particular traditional belief to be unhelpful or inaccurate, they are likely to be viewed by traditionalists as having boarded the radical bandwagon wherein all social change is deemed good and all tradition bad. But simply rejecting some aspects of tradition entails no obligation, either moral or logical, to jettison *all* that has traditionally been valued. It is quite possible to question some traditional ideas and yet to affirm truly noble and biblical traditions such as the permanence of marital commitment, the value of all human life, and the responsibility of parents to care for their children.

Rather than succumbing to the bandwagon mentality, let us learn to evaluate each change and each tradition according to biblical standards, which are neither changeable nor necessarily traditional. All aspects of social change need not be rejected simply because they appear to have originated outside the church. We can reject those traditions and social changes that are unbiblical and accept those that do accord with biblical principles.

Any argument for any position that is not based on or compatible with scriptural teaching is useless and dangerous. The Bible—not tradition, not modern society—is our only authoritative, inerrant guide. A great deal of what is touted today as "women's rights" must be flatly rejected as unbiblical. On the other hand, an unbiased consideration of the principles taught in the Bible can turn on its head some of the "traditional" teachings concerning the biblical roles for women and men. In this book I will be criticizing some of these traditional teachings, but I hope readers will understand that my purpose is not to discredit the character or impugn the integrity of those Christian traditionalists who hold these views. Rather, my intent is simply to clarify what I believe to be errors in their understanding of not only the biblical parameters of male/female roles, but also the actual views of those evangelicals who advocate biblical equality.

Another strategy by which we can avoid the conceptual pitfalls in the evangelical feminist/traditionalist debate is to be aware and wary of our own prejudices and "preunderstandings." Theologian Millard Erickson explains that "we all bring to the study of the Bible (or of any other material) a particular perspective which is very much affected by the historical and cultural situation in which we are rooted. Without being aware of it, we screen all that we consider through the filter of our own understanding (or 'preunderstanding')."[1] But how can our approach to Scripture and to cultural issues be unbiased by our own preconceptions, prejudices, and expectations? "One way to do this is to study the varying interpretations held and statements made at different times in the church's life. This shows us that there are alternative ways of viewing the matter. It also makes us sensitive to the manner in which culture affects one's thinking. . . . Observing how culture influenced theological thinking in the past should call our attention to what is happening to us."[2]

Although complete freedom from personal bias is probably not possible, an important step in the direction of clear thinking and fair-mindedness is to try to look at an issue with the objectivity that comes from refusing to be limited to a subjective, personal perspective. As Millard Erickson points out, knowing the history of a theological concern will often shed light on our own culture-bound opinions and presuppositions on the subject. This book will attempt to offer a new perspective on the evangelical feminist/traditionalist debate by putting each position into its historical and cultural context, and then evaluating it in light of that context.

The goal of this book is not to analyze the competing viewpoints in depth[3] but simply to step outside the familiar rhetoric of "women's equality" versus "traditional family values" in an attempt to obtain a view of the Big Picture. In order to do this, we must ask (and answer) some new and discerning questions. What are the historical roots of what is called traditionalism? What is the history of evangelical feminism? Under what cultural circumstances, with what motivation, and for what purposes did each movement originate? These same questions must then be asked of modern secular feminism before addressing the question of whether modern secular feminism and evangelical feminism are *fundamentally* or merely *superficially* different from one another.

Having gained a new awareness of these belief systems by inquiring from history not only *what* happened but *why* it happened, we must then try to understand the culture war over gender roles. Observing the polarizing tendencies of the extremist rhetoric that ignores all middle ground and assigns every viewpoint either to one bandwagon or another, we will try to discern the cultural dynamics and the inarticulated prejudices and preunderstandings which have created this ideological battlefield.

The aim of this inquiry is a clearing of the conceptual atmosphere. I hope it will point the way toward a more instructive and accurate understanding—and perhaps even some resolution of discord—among evangelical Christians caught in the conflict concerning the biblical view of the roles of women and men.

The first ten chapters of the book are intended for a general readership. The final three chapters pursue in greater detail some of the logical and theological dynamics of the debate; these chapters may be of more interest to those readers with an academic bent. The nineteenth-century roots of today's traditionalism and evangelical feminism will be explored in chapters 1 through 4. Chapters 5 through 7 will discuss and critique various types of contemporary feminism, especially secular radical feminism, and then contrast evangelical feminism with other views on gender roles. Chapters 8 through 13 will explore the cultural dynamics operative in the conflict between evangelical feminists and traditionalists.

How Traditional Is Traditionalism?

For nearly two millennia, the approach of the Christian church toward the role of women usually has been to sanction the view current in mainstream secular society, decreeing it to be the "biblical" role for women. If the role of women changed in society, it would change in the church as well. This typically has been the determining factor in the stance of the church toward women—with two notable exceptions. First, as a result of the example and the gospel of Jesus Christ in whom there is "neither male nor female" (Gal. 3:28), women in the New Testament church found their status elevated above their social position in the patriarchal cultures of that time.[1] And second, ever since the 1970s, the church by and large has refused to conform to social norms; but this time the situation has been reversed. Women in the church are being denied the kinds of opportunities for leadership and equality that women now enjoy elsewhere in society.

Because the church has failed to develop a biblically-based doctrine of sexuality, it has been at a loss to understand the implications of biblical principles for gender roles. Given this "fundamental level of historical confusion" regarding the Christian view of womanhood,[2] it is not surprising that the church historically has looked to secular culture for guidance. Nor is it surprising that the current evangelical debate on this subject tends to generate so much more heat than light.

During the church's history, one feature of the woman's role has remained constant: her subordination to male authority. But the social institution of patriarchy (the rule of men over women, especially within the family) did not originate with the Judeo-Christian tradition. It has prevailed both within and without the church, in virtually all cultures through all recorded history.

Other normative Christian beliefs about the family—although not as culturally pervasive or historically persistent as male authority—have also had a long tradition. Unlike the tradition of male authority, traditional moral standards of sexual behavior that prohibit sexual relations outside of marriage and define marriage as an exclusive and permanent covenant between one man and one woman are a direct product of biblical theology. With such traditions we can have no quarrel.

The "Traditional" Family

Traditionalists believe that their understanding of biblical gender roles is corroborated by church tradition, and that all "feminist" thought is a direct reflection of modern culture and ought therefore to be resisted. However, that which is culturally contemporary is not necessarily opposed to biblical truth, nor is the traditional necessarily in line with it.[3] But this is not the only problem with an antifeminist argument that pits tradition against modern culture. Much of what is billed today as traditional is not really traditional at all. The agenda of those who espouse "traditional family values" does include the traditions of male authority and biblical standards of sexual behavior. But the traditionalist agenda promotes just as vigorously the features of a family model that did not develop historically until the nineteenth century.

According to this model, the husband works outside the home and provides sole financial support for the entire family. The wife has no role in earning income; she attends to the household and cares for the children. The wife is dependent on her husband for her financial wherewithal and her personal identity and social status. Motherhood is deemed the primary calling of every woman and is regarded as essential to the preservation of the social order. Being a wife and mother is viewed as a full-time occupation; if a woman has her own career, it will deprive her husband and children of the attention they require for their well-being and proper function in society. Children receive a great deal of nurture and attentive care from their mother, who is their primary caretaker. Women's delicacy and fragility are contrasted with men's virility and physical strength; women are regarded as the opposite sex, different from men in every way. The home is viewed as a private haven, a retreat from public bustle, an emotionally safe oasis, a place of nurture. The woman of the house, drawing on her "feminine" moral purity, is the maker and provider of these benefits of the home for the family members. Childbearing is the woman's sole means of production, her chief creative contribution to human society, and is therefore essential to her sense of achievement and self-worth. The woman's role as homemaker is not only her own identity; it also identifies her husband as a masculine (i.e., financial) success. A wife who stays at home is a man's status symbol. When women do venture into public life, their sphere of activities and responsibilities is separate from men's.

These features of family life, which developed in middle-class Victorian society and were revivified in the suburban domesticity of the 1950s, are anomalies in history. In clinging to this model of gender roles and dubbing it the "traditional" biblical ideal, the contemporary church is misunderstanding the message of history; it is also deviating from the church's "tradition" of accommodating to current cultural norms concerning a woman's place in society. But the church *is* still looking to secular culture for guidance—that is, to the culture of Victorian society as "reincarnated" in the American society of the 1950s.

Family Life and the Industrial Revolution

The change in family structure that occurred in nineteenth-century American society is largely attributable to the development of industrial capitalism in the Western world at that time. The most notable social effect of the Industrial Revolution was the separation of the home from the workplace. This ramified in at least two areas: the roles of women and the role of the church in society.

Seventeenth-century Puritanism had elevated marriage and family to a place of centrality as the loci of both morality and industry in church and society. Then industrialization removed the center of industry from the home to factories outside the home; men's sphere of activity followed industry away from home and into society at large. The home remained the center of morality and church-related concerns; these then became women's work. "Unanticipated by the Puritans, home became not a center of morality *and* industry, but a retreat, a shelter from the world." The marriage relationship itself was similarly bifurcated. After industrialization, the Puritan "idea of marriage as an economic and spiritual partnership, sweetened by love, bit the dust. The 'love' part alone remained, and became the fragile romantic ideal prized by later centuries as the supposed basis of marriage."[4]

The Industrial Revolution divided the world into a private sphere (the home, where women belonged and with which the church was concerned) and a public sphere (society, where men belonged). The public sphere— man's world—was the sphere of significance, of cultural development, and of social activity. In becoming privatized, the social roles of both women and the church became trivialized; they were cut off from the sphere of significance. The cultural irrelevance of the church today is rooted in this dichotomy of the sacred and the secular and was, no doubt, exacerbated by the association of church life with the sphere of women and the home. The Freudian credo that women's domains were "Kinder, Küche, und Kirche" (children, cooking, and church) summed up the nineteenth-century Victorian mentality that developed as a result of the social effects of the Industrial Revolution.

For centuries prior to the nineteenth century, the home served as an economic unit of both production and consumption. Women worked at home, but so did men; and their work, though different, was comparable. The usefulness and necessity of women's work as well as the skill required for it was equal to that of men's work. The duties of the much-acclaimed woman of Proverbs 31 exemplify the work that women have traditionally done at home. While such work has not entailed public leadership roles, it has involved a great deal more skill and versatility than is required of the modern homemaker.[5]

Not only did women work alongside their husbands before the Industrial Revolution, but the children were put to work at an early age. Neither mother nor father had time to coddle their children; in fact, children were often mistreated and neglected. "Life was a struggle for all family members. Children were brutalized as much by the daily routines of life as by outbursts of parental rage—beatings, sexual abuse, and abandonment were not at all uncommon."[6] Many children died before adulthood, and little energy was spent on family sentiment or affection; parents were not inclined to become attached to someone who was likely to live only a few years. Marriage was more a practical, economic arrangement than a romantic relationship. Mothers as well as fathers had economically necessary work to do, so mothers were not occupied primarily with childcare. Children were cared for by older children and members of the extended family. "Women did not organize their lives around their children to any great extent. The definition of motherhood as a full-time job did not exist."[7] This model of the family can be said to be more traditional than that which is currently billed as traditional, since its "features have characterized family life for a much longer period in Western history than they have not."[8]

With industrialization, the home was no longer essential to economic production and the woman was no longer economically essential to the marriage. Woman's role was therefore redefined in order to fill the vacuum created by the privatization of the home. Marriage as an economic partnership was replaced by marriage as a romantic ideal. The home was reconceptualized as a private haven that provided emotional nurture and personal fulfillment for family members, and as such provided also the moral foundation of society. The role of "mother" was redefined to encompass a woman's entire mission in life. No longer depicting merely a relationship, motherhood became a full-time occupation that entailed bearing sole responsibility for the daily care of the children. The premise of the woman's new role in the home was the idealization of her character. She was placed upon the proverbial pedestal, thus beginning the cult of the True Woman.

The Nineteenth-Century "True Woman"

In past centuries—particularly within the Judeo-Christian tradition—woman had often been scorned, feared, and ruled by man because of the supposedly evil, seductive, and morally and rationally inferior "animal" nature of the female. But by the nineteenth century, the belief in man's "right" to rule woman was apparently so well entrenched that the old rationale was no longer necessary. In fact, it suited the new gender roles to bill woman as morally and spiritually inclined and man as the one with the "animal" nature. This was no loss to man, because he retained his corner on rationality and superior intellect—which, since the Enlightenment of the seventeenth and eighteenth centuries, had generally come to be valued more highly than spirituality or morality.

The "True Woman" in nineteenth-century middle- and upper-class Victorian society was an innocent, delicate creature. Her fragility demanded that she not soil her hands with work but lounge decorously about the home; her moral superiority equipped her for her role as moral guardian of society. Woman's function as civilizer of man set her apart from man as his opposite in every way. The relationship of female to male was perceived in terms of dichotomies. Her purity compensated for his wickedness. Her frailty was protected by his energy and industry. Her religious sentimentality was offset by his superior rationality. Her private role did not encroach upon his public role.

Men and women occupied such totally separate realms in society (befitting their supposedly totally opposite natures) that they remained quite a mystery to one another. So it was that an early suffrage leader declared that no man could understand woman's need for emancipation. "Man cannot speak for us—because he has been educated to believe that we differ from him so materially, that he cannot judge of our thoughts, feelings and opinions."[9] Empathy and communication become virtually impossible between people who live in totally different worlds and are believed to have totally opposite natures.

It was widely believed in the nineteenth century that "while sinful man was controlled by his brain, delicate woman was controlled by her reproductive organs."[10] Women had wombs that were used for physical creation; men had brains that were used for mental creation. Women were not considered to have brains any more than men were considered to have wombs. The womb was a female organ and the brain was a male organ. From this belief derived not only the notion of woman's irrational, unpredictable, and mysterious "feminine" nature, but also the idea that childbearing was every woman's ultimate fulfillment while intellectual pursuits were the fulfillment of the masculine nature. A woman who pursued intellectual activities therefore assumed for herself a masculine nature; such women of the nineteenth century were often accused of being "hermaphrodites in mind."[11]

Much was made of the supposed smaller size of the female brain and the dire effects (everything from disease to insanity) that would befall a woman who undertook to receive a "man's education." Education for women was feared, lest it induce women to abandon their divinely-ordained profession of motherhood. The term "strong-minded, which had formerly been used to praise men who had vigorous and determined minds, began to be used in the 1850s to describe women who, because of their vigorous and determined minds, were not really women. . . . A strong-minded woman was the opposite of a true woman, who was weak-minded."[12]

But when Victorian women began to go to college and prove themselves as healthy physically and as capable intellectually as men, the notion of the True Woman was severely strained. Men in positions of leadership gradually began to realize that women had brains just as men did. Vassar Female College opened in 1865 because, said Matthew Vassar, "It occurred to me that woman, having received from her Creator the same intellectual constitution as man, has the same right as man to intellectual culture and development."[13] Alice Freeman Palmer, a former president of Wellesley College, argued that women's capacity for intellectual and physical vitality was considerably greater than had been supposed. She pointed out in 1897 that "the standard of health is higher among the women who hold college degrees than among any other equal number of the same age and class."[14] Palmer had no patience with "the old notion that low vitality is a matter of course with women; that to be delicate is a mark of superior refinement, especially in well-to-do families; that sickness is a dispensation of Providence."[15] "Nothing breaks down a woman's health like idleness," she declared, thus turning on its head the popular notion that the True Woman must remain idle *because* of her delicate physical constitution.[16]

Despite their insistence on the female potential for physical and intellectual vigor, Alice Freeman Palmer and others who campaigned for women's education and health reform nonetheless espoused the prevalent belief that the chief cultural responsibility of a woman was to refine and civilize society through the performance of her domestic duties. A good education, Palmer maintained, was toward the end that "the profession of woman *par excellence*"—that is, being "a companion to her husband and children"—might be performed all the better.[17] These reformers maintained that it was against woman's nature to venture into "male" roles in public life. "What they hoped was that the new female vitality would be channeled into traditional functions, and woman be made a more efficient homemaker rather than a rival of man."[18]

Alice Freeman Palmer adhered to this ideology in her own life. Upon marrying in 1887, she retired from her position as president of Wellesley College. She wrote of her decision:

> At a crisis hour
> Of strength and struggle on the heights of life
> He came, and bidding me abandon power,
> Called me to take the quiet name of wife.[19]

When she was a college president, she had her own vocation; when she was a wife, her entire vocation was to help her husband in his vocation. As a result of the Victorian idea that being a wife is in itself a full-time occupation, the career orientation of students in the women's colleges led many of them not to marry. In 1895 only 33 percent of graduates over the age of twenty-five had married; a majority entered the teaching profession. Also, many graduates of women's colleges found that the foreign mission field offered them a freedom and equality that was denied women in American society.[20]

The woman's role as mother was seen to equip her to be the moral guardian of society. "By the middle of the nineteenth century, motherhood had emerged as a full-time vocation and it was exalted in the culture accordingly. . . . 'Good mothering,' an invention of the period, had become the moral standard for all women of standing, the significance of which was the reform and perfection of the entire social order."[21] The moral fate of the nation was seen to be in the hands of mothers whose patriotic duty it was to instill moral virtue in their sons and daughters (but especially their sons) for the next generation.

Yet the culture over which women were in actuality allowed influence was the private, superficial world of social and religious convention. (Palmer speaks of a woman's role in connection with "dainty and finished ways of living" and the "higher graces of civilization."[22]) In placing women in charge of morality and religion, men not only divested themselves of responsibility for their own moral rectitude, but also trivialized the religious agenda as something for just the women to worry about. Men tended to view the women's world of moralistic, religious sentiment as limiting and irrelevant; it was for weaklings. The mixed message concerning the Victorian role for women was reflected in the extreme courtesy which men habitually offered women in public—as though women's superiority earned them certain privileges and preferences. But perceptive critics of the time recognized that chivalry merely offered women "indulgence as a substitute for justice."[23] The True Woman was not placed upon her pedestal, she was chained to it.

The contradictions inherent in the prescribed role for nineteenth-century women set the stage for a women's rights movement. It proved unrealistic to give women responsibility for the moral virtue of the country and to allow them the opportunity to be healthy and well-educated— a historical first, incidentally—and still to expect all women to remain quietly at home with their children. As we will see in chapters 3 and 4, women in nineteenth-century reform movements broke out of the limited, privatized role of inculcating moral purity in the home and applied themselves to reforming *public* morality. This, of course, shook up the status quo considerably; but these women were, after all, only acting on the basis of what their alleged social and moral responsibility should logically demand. The increase in the number and social acceptability of women preachers later in the nineteenth century would seem also to be a logical consequence of the moral superiority women were at that time said to possess (just as the ban on women preachers had traditionally been justified by women's supposed moral inferiority). The image of the Victorian lady characterized by fear, dependence, and feeblemindedness was significantly challenged by the educated, public-spirited, reforming women of the late nineteenth century.

Economic Aspects

Fundamental to the social change that brought about the historically unique Victorian home was the fact that the financial wherewithal for the family was earned solely by the husband working outside the home. All other aspects of Victorian home life were accommodations to this central socioeconomic fact. This was the "Victorian heritage," historian Andrew Sinclair observes, "that a man's work alone should support his family, and that the self-respect of his wife should depend upon *his* status, not upon her own. This idea was, in fact, a new one in terms of human history—that one sex should support the other entirely."[24] This arrangement did not come about from a chivalrous concern to relieve women and children of arduous labor; it happened simply because of the economic necessity created by industrialization. Once it occurred, however, it became a point of pride to men that their women be idle. "The curious fact about the Victorian lady was that her husband was prepared to work himself almost to death to support her." American men were eager to keep up with "European society, where the rich man was judged by the uselessness of his dependent women."[25] As Alice Freeman Palmer noted, "It is the regular ambition of the chivalrous American to make all the women who depend on him so comfortable that they need do nothing for themselves."[26]

But Palmer was concerned about the detrimental effects to women of "wealth and comfort, and the inherited theory that it is not well for the woman to earn money." She spoke of "the undermining influence which men also feel when occupation is taken away and no absorbing private interest fills the vacancy." Women, after all, are not so different from men that they have no need for a sense of purpose in life higher than "the wearisome monotony" of "the daily doing of household details."[27] A woman, in fact, needs an education more than a man does, for a man's work is such that it is "in itself a means of growth, of education, of dignity. He leans his life against it. . . . And that is the reason why men . . . have grown old better than women. Men usually retain their ability longer."[28] The danger of the unemployed woman is that she will not grow in character, because her work will not require her to do so. Palmer's vision for women's work was that women take initiative and use their leisure for the good of their own minds and of society.

Because women no longer had the responsibility to help provide the family livelihood, they were given instead the responsibility for providing a morally pure home environment. This included devoting a great deal of time and energy to mothering their children, training them in the moral standards of which women were the social guardians. The restriction of woman's work to child bearing and caring resulted from the fact that this was all that remained for women to do after industrialization took away the work traditionally performed by women at home.

But the Victorian agenda of full-time motherhood obtained only for the bourgeois or middle-class families. Women who did not have husbands who could support them financially were obliged to work for low wages in factories. Some women found these wages so inadequate that they resorted to prostitution, which was a well-paid and popular "service." The wife who was a True Woman was expected to have a dim view of sexual relations for purposes other than procreation; her husband therefore—with social sanction on account of his licentious male nature—might seek recourse with prostitutes. At a time when the womanly ideal was that of unemployed homemaker and prostitution was the only lucrative work available for women outside the home, the term "working woman" acquired a particularly pejorative connotation. Even if a woman were a factory worker rather than a prostitute, she would be scorned and pitied as a woman who had failed to find her true calling in a life of domesticity.

With this threat of character assassination hanging over her, the middle-class Victorian wife often went to great lengths to appear unemployed when, in fact, financial necessity compelled her to work behind the scenes. One such woman wrote:

> We women did more than keep house, cook, sew, wash, spin and weave, and garden. Many of us were under the necessity of earning money besides. . . . We worked secretly . . . because all society was built on the theory that men, not women, earned money, and that men alone supported the family. . . . Most women accepted this condition of society as normal and God-ordained and therefore changeless. But I do not believe that there was any community anywhere in which the souls of some women were not beating their wings in rebellion.[29]

That which is seen to be true today has to a certain degree always been true. If for no reason other than financial necessity, the family model whereby men earn all the money while women care for the children at home cannot always be translated from ideology to reality. Unfortunately, since Victorian times, female breadwinners have been saddled with two jobs, while male breadwinners have had but one. Financial necessity and expanding vocational opportunities for women have conspired in today's society largely to dispel the Victorian myth of the man as sole financial provider. But still society clings to the nineteenth-century myth of motherhood—that childcare and household management are woman's sphere of responsibility. This mindset prevails despite the obvious objection that if women are to share in the "male" responsibilities, this should be balanced by men sharing in the "female" responsibilities.

But when tradition collides with social change, some traditions are rejected while others are retained. The process of determining which traditions are kept and which are abandoned is governed primarily not by reason but by complex cultural dynamics; the resulting social customs are often both unquestioned and unreasonable. Illustrative is the approach of traditionalists such as James Dobson. In one of his "Focus on the Family" broadcasts devoted to finding ways to help support mothers who are financially constrained to find employment outside the home, no one even mentioned the possible solution of husbands or older children shouldering their share of household responsibilities; and this broadcast included a panel of half a dozen employed mothers. Even women accept their "second shift" without question and try to find strength to bear up under the load.[30]

Today's Traditionalism

With some modifications, the family model of the Victorian middle class held sway over mainstream American culture through the 1960s, enjoying an especially notable upsurge of popularity in the 1950s and early 1960s. Writing in 1965, Andrew Sinclair declared, "We are the new Victorians. . . . Victorian traditions still rule the proper place of women in business and in the home."[1] At the present time, this model remains normative only in evangelical marriage and family manuals and in the remnants of traditional social custom which are yet scattered throughout modern culture—despite earnest feminist efforts to ferret them out. Many of these anachronistic conventions show up when women attempt to combine a career with motherhood. Employment situations with long, inflexible working hours, for example, are still structured according to the assumption that the employees all have wives at home to tend to the children and household—even when the employees are women!

Twentieth-Century Variations
on a Nineteenth-Century Theme

The transition from the pre-industrial view of the family as a practical, working cog in the socioeconomic system, to the modern view of the family as a setting for the individual fulfillment of its members, did not happen all at once. James Hunter characterizes the twentieth-century "traditional" family as a "hypersentimentalized" version of the nineteenth-century Victorian family, which itself was more sentimental than the pre-industrial family.[2] Women and children were sentimentalized in the nineteenth century. In the twentieth century, the role of the man in the family became sentimentalized in the sense that his patriarchal authority was modified and qualified by the expectation that he be emotionally expressive and intimate with his wife and children.

The woman's role also underwent further alterations in the twentieth century. When the helping professions became a booming business and the governmental welfare system took responsibility for the economically disadvantaged, women were left without the one "public" function of charity and social reform that had kept many of them socially involved in the nineteenth century. Sociologists Brigitte Berger and Peter Berger note that "the women, celebrated as mothers, wives, and 'homemakers,' were thrown back upon themselves into a kind of social vacuum. This was especially the case in the new, middle-class suburbs, where women were separated geographically as well as socially from the non-'homemaking' activities of their husbands and frequently experienced a sort of cage effect."[3]

In addition, contraceptive technology was developed that, for the first time in history, was fairly reliable. Fewer children resulted not only in fewer years in which women were occupied with childcare, but in increased health and a longer lifespan for women. Due to various modern household appliances and services, women also found housework considerably less demanding and time-consuming. Because of these social changes, the twentieth-century "Victorian" woman had even more time to devote to "good mothering" than her nineteenth-century prototype. Even as the definition of motherhood had expanded in the nineteenth century to fit the increased time available for it, so the "traditional" responsibilities of the homemaker were broadened and redefined in the first half of the twentieth century.

Another important change that the twentieth century wrought in the "Victorian" woman was in the area of her sexuality. While the nineteenth-century True Woman denied her sexuality, the twentieth-century woman was primarily sexual. This was her identity; she was a "sex creature" whose destiny in life was entirely determined and encompassed by her sexuality, her femininity. Her role as a wife now included a physical relationship with her husband which should preclude the interest a nineteenth-century husband was permitted to have in prostitutes. The twentieth-century woman was expected to find her destiny in meeting *every* personal need her husband might have. Fulfilled womanhood consisted mainly of having a man to wait upon. All of the women's magazines and marriage advice literature in the 1950s propounded this modernized and sexualized Victorian view of femininity—which Betty Friedan aptly dubbed the "feminine mystique" in her 1963 book by that title.

It became more important for a woman to be a woman than for her to be a person with a unique, individual identity or vocation. Being a woman was a career in itself. Any need or activity that did not directly pertain to a woman's sexual role was considered irrelevant and off limits; such non-feminine concerns were handed over to the men. This hyper-feminization of woman's nature and purpose was the justification for her mandated "career" as a full-time wife and mother. While vocational homemaking emerged in the nineteenth century for economic reasons, it was perpetuated in the twentieth century for cultural and ideological reasons.

Early twentieth-century feminism did encourage a number of women to embark on careers other than vocational motherhood. But because of the cultural mindset that developed in the 1940s, most women did not follow through on these options. Careers came to be considered unfeminine. The fact that prior to World War II most women with careers had been unmarried, along with the fact that family experts in the 1940s and 1950s decried such career women as "masculine," led women to believe they had to choose either marriage or a career. They overwhelmingly chose marriage and made it their career.

Although women made up one-fourth of the labor force during this time, they did not occupy career positions. Discouraged from entering the "male" professions, women in the first half of the twentieth century—just like their nineteenth-century prototypes—often labored behind the scenes in menial jobs for low wages out of financial necessity. During World War II the employment situation was temporarily altered, with many women working in defense plants and other factories. But these jobs were not careers; when the men came back, the women were obliged to return home and allow the jobs to go to the men.[4]

By 1959 there was a smaller percentage of women in college and the professions than there had been in 1929.[5] In the late 1950s, only 10 percent of doctorates were awarded to women, down from 17 percent in the 1920s and 1930s.[6] Women's relatively high representation in the professions in the 1930s coincided with a low point in the national birthrate.[7] By the 1950s, women had fled the professions and were concentrating on professional motherhood. More than ever, women were told (and believed) that their sole significance in life was in bearing children. The population growth in America during the 1950s was phenomenal (referred to now as the baby boom)—four times that of Great Britain and nearly matching that of India.[8]

The New Victorians of the 1950s

Why did this wholesale retreat to a century-old lifestyle occur in the late 1940s and 1950s? By 1945, America had gone through two world wars and a major economic depression in the space of three decades. War had highlighted the traditional gender role distinctions, with men fighting for their country on the battlefield—work that called for the "masculine" traits of courage, strength, and intellect—while women did the back-up, support work on the home front. After the war, people were tired, frightened, and lonely; they wanted to go home. Men were worn out from fighting; women were worn out from worrying about the men. Both men and women had been afraid that the war would deprive them of a home and family. So, in the wake of a war and under the shadow of communism and the nuclear bomb, people hurried home to the suburbs for safety and security.

America's unparalleled economic prosperity during the fifties made it economically possible for many women to give up their wage-earning responsibilities and to rely entirely on their husbands for financial provision. Both the economic and the social climate of this period conspired to assign the vocation of homemaking to all married, middle-class American women. Family experts and social commentators during this time regarded this gender role as normative, rather than as a specific historical phenomenon. The idea that women and employment are by nature not meant to mix became the ethos of the decade.

Freudian ideas were intoned with the certainty and solemnity of religious conviction during these years. They were, in fact, used to "prove" far more than Freud would likely have thought possible. The Freudian notion of "penis envy" was enlisted with enthusiasm to caricature and condemn the unfortunate, unfeminine career women of earlier decades. The new Freudian social religion effectively recapitulated the Victorian emphasis on totally separate social and economic spheres for men and women. All the authority of psychoanalysis was invoked to label as psychologically maladjusted any deviation from the prescribed pattern. "Women were to find their mission at home, as mothers and as the intelligent, emotionally sensitive companions to their husbands—and if they did not accept this mission, the psychologists were ready to treat this reluctance as a neurotic ailment."[9] So while post-war nostalgia sent women home, pseudo-Freudian psychologizing kept them there.

Observing the "new Victorians" of the fifties and sixties, Andrew Sinclair wrote, "Through psychological language, as once through the language of romanticism, women have become more conscious of being women than of being human beings; but they are worse off than the early Victorians, for their bodies have been exalted at the expense of their minds."[10] Betty Friedan reported in the early sixties that editors of women's magazines studiously avoided printing anything that would exact mental effort from their readers. "Whole pages of women's magazines are filled with gargantuan vegetables," Friedan complained.[11] Finding themselves, as Sinclair put it, "frightened at the hard work and uncertainties of improving the mind and the spirit,"[12] the leisured women of the fifties tended to occupy themselves with the mundane, domestic details of life.

The Freudian-inspired fear of women becoming like men, and the resultant atrophying of the female mind, gradually overtook the philosophy of women's education. Alice Freeman Palmer's vision of college education serving as a means to ennoble housework and to "make drudgery divine"[13] did not seem to be working out. Just as Palmer had prescribed, women were indeed going to college primarily with one career goal in mind: motherhood. But rather than enhancing their household duties, a college education seemed only to frustrate many homemakers. Educators and family specialists then began to say that when women are given the same type of education that men receive it educates women to be like men, and this throws women out of sync with their destiny as housewives. A woman's career, after all, is determined by her body, not her brain.

Therefore, a woman having difficulty "adjusting" to the homemaking role should simply renounce her "masculine" college education and celebrate her uniquely feminine qualities—those abilities which she possesses and men do not.[14] The solution, in other words, lay in defining womanhood as consisting solely of those characteristics that are absent in manhood. Such thinking renders *woman* equivalent to *child bearer,* and strips from a woman's identity all that is not part of her sexual identity as man's sexual opposite.

The Traditionalist Backlash

Since the advent of modern feminism in the 1960s and the 1970s, many evangelicals and social conservatives have argued earnestly and insistently for a return to the "traditional" family model of the 1950s. Sociologically, this traditionalist movement "must be seen as essentially a backlash phenomenon."[15] The backlash has occurred not only in the evangelical church but also in the conservative sectors of society at large—although its effect has been felt with the most force within evangelicalism. The event that galvanized the backlash was the 1973 Supreme Court ruling that rendered abortion legal in all states. It was during this time—when mainstream feminism was in its most militant phase—that those in the traditionalist camp formed enduring convictions about the inevitable evils of feminism.

The traditionalist movement was in large part goaded by the belief in a causal connection between feminism and the breakdown in society of Christian moral values and sexual norms. Brigitte and Peter Berger note:

> As with most cultural or ideological movements, it is difficult to determine to what extent feminism *caused* changes in behavior or merely *legitimated* changes that were happening anyway. Thus divorce, pre- and extra-marital sex, and abortion are phenomena rooted in broad societal changes for which the feminist movement cannot be (as the case may be) blamed or praised. Clearly, though, many people *perceived* feminists to be responsible for these changes, and this perception contributed to the genesis of the neo-traditionalist alignment.[16]

If the modern feminist movement, which gained momentum in the 1960s and the 1970s, had not endorsed the immoral, anti-family values of the sexual revolution, perhaps the traditionalist backlash would not have gathered and maintained such strength. As will be seen in the next two chapters, the evangelical church's response to feminism in the late nineteenth century—when women's liberation was identified with pro-family rather than anti-family values—was by no means as virulent as it is today.

As an antidote to the perceived evils of feminism, traditionalists have advanced the "Victorian" family of the 1950s, billing it as the biblical ideal that prevailed throughout history until it ran afoul of modern feminism. Traditionalists have overlooked or perhaps are ignorant of the fact that "the family type they envision is 'traditional' only in a limited sense. What is in fact at stake is a certain *idealized* form of the nineteenth-century middle class family: a male-dominated nuclear family that both sentimentalized childhood and motherhood and, at the same time, celebrated domestic life as a utopian retreat from the harsh realities of industrial society."[17]

It is striking how the marriage advice literature in evangelical bookstores today reflects that of the entire society in the 1950s. For example, the Easter 1954 issue of *McCall's* proclaimed: "For the sake of every member of the family, the family needs a head. This means Father, not Mother."[18] *McCall's* did not support this proclamation of husbandly headship with a Scripture reference. This type of thinking in the fifties was not derived from Bible verses but from purely cultural values that exalted the home as a haven, the woman as its keeper, and the man as its chief executive.

The anxiety fueling the traditionalist movement seems at least in part to be due to the fact that, for the first time, the possibility exists for women to be economically independent from men. Society has moved from a pre-industrial situation in which both men and women worked at home, to an industrial situation in which men worked outside the home, to a post-industrial situation in which both men and women have the option of working outside the home.

In both pre-industrial and industrial societies, a woman was financially dependent on her husband, who was in some sense financially in charge—whether as the "boss" of a home-based business in which his wife was "employed" or as the family's sole wage-earner. In today's technological, post-industrial society, the potential exists—at least in terms of employment opportunities—for men and women to be equally financially dependent on their respective employers, and equally financially independent of one another. In other words, a woman no longer needs to be married (or lodged as a maiden aunt in the home of relatives) in order to find financial provision.

The traditionalist response to the modern economic situation has been to lobby vigorously for continued wifely dependence upon husbandly provision. Perhaps traditionalists fear that if women no longer need to be married in order to be provided for financially, they will no longer bother to remain married, and this will unravel the family, especially the institution of full-time motherhood. Although it may well be true that women who are unhappily married are more likely to divorce their husbands if they have some means of earning their own living, it is also true that marriage need not be financially necessary in order to endure. While the Victorian economic roles may keep couples married perforce, a union based on mutual respect and affection will keep them married by choice.

The traditionalist backlash has resulted in the polarization of the issue of gender roles. Those who don't buy into twentieth-century Victorianism are identified with the advocates of "abortion rights" and sexual "freedom." Kari Torjesen Malcolm sums up the situation nicely:

> Just as the feminine mystique was a reaction against the war years, so the backlash against women's liberation was society's way of reacting against the unknown changes that feminism might bring. With the tension between the two sides, evangelical Christians found themselves trapped in a corner between two bad choices. Should they join the radical feminists or the anti-feminists? Many did not realize that both groups were inspired by human culture, not Christianity.[19]

The analogy between the post-war backlash and the present-day backlash against feminism is helpful. Both were impelled by similar motives. As all of America felt in 1945, so the evangelical church has been feeling in recent decades: under siege by social change and nostalgic for days gone by. Because many of today's traditionalist leaders came of age in the 1950s—a time of national stability and prosperity—there is a natural tendency to enshrine the family values of that period with an aura of sanctity and security.

Non-Traditional Evangelical Traditionalism

When, after World War II, evangelicals began "to outline the sexual hierarchy in stricter terms—and with greater insistence,"[20] they were simply continuing in the "traditional" church practice of agreeing with whatever secular society decreed concerning the role of women. But when evangelicals began in the 1970s to reassert—with still greater insistence—a subordinate role and a separate sphere for women, they were, for the first time since New Testament days, rejecting secular society's designated role for women.

The traditionalist movement breaks with church tradition in other ways besides its rejection of the prevailing social norms regarding women's roles. It is also historically unique in that it invests the "traditional family" with supreme, symbolic significance. "The so-called traditional family has generated tremendous passion, and its survival in the modern world has become perhaps the highest priority on the Evangelical social agenda." As a result, James Hunter notes, "the programs given to the articulation of what the Christian family should be and to the defense of this 'traditional family' are almost numberless."[21] The traditionalist insistence that every family abide by a strictly stipulated pattern is premised on the notion that this family order is ordained by God. Adherence to these rules and roles is therefore a matter of the utmost gravity; one must not tamper with what God has decreed.

Larry Christenson's *The Christian Family* is representative of the ideological underpinnings of evangelical traditionalism. Here we see what Hunter calls the "mythic qualities"[22] of the "traditional" family: "The family belongs to God. He created it. He determined its inner structure. He appointed for it its purpose and goal," which is "to bring glory and honor to God."[23] According to Christenson, the "inner structure" and "Divine Order" for the family entails a situation wherein "the burden of caring for the support of the family lies upon the man,"[24] while "a wife's primary responsibility is to give of herself, her time and her energy to her husband, children and home."[25] Besides invoking the "Divine Order," Christenson justifies these gender roles with the quaint notion that the burden of financial support is "too heavy" for the wife to bear. "Stronger shoulders are given to the man; he has a greater natural strength of mind to enable him to stand up under the pressure of these cares. The heart of a woman is more easily discouraged and dejected. God has made her that way."[26] The image of the nineteenth-century True Woman looms large. As in Victorian society, so in "the Christian family": a woman's innate weakness and fragility require husbandly protection and provision in every area and render her fit only for the limited domain of the "domestic virtues."

"Traditional" gender roles are based not only on the nineteenth-century definition of womanhood, but also on the nineteenth-century litmus test for successful manhood, which consisted of a man's ability to provide all that was financially necessary to keep wife and children at home. From this the nineteenth-century man derived the "masculine identity that . . . gave him a sense of pride and accomplishment in his manhood."[27] Holding up this Victorian value system as an ideal model which should be followed today, traditionalist James Dobson goes on to say,

> One of the greatest threats to the institution of the family today is the undermining of this role as protector and provider. This is the contribution for which men were designed, physically and emotionally. . . . I have worked hard to provide necessities and a few luxuries for [my family]. . . . My identity is inextricably linked with that family commitment. If my role as protector and provider had been taken from me, much of the joy in family life would have gone with it.[28]

In the traditionalist mind, the male identity is linked with the "male" role of sole financial provider, which in turn is linked with the man's position as the authoritative head of the household. Proof of the man's authority is generally understood by traditionalists to reside in the male role of financial provider and the corollary female role of household helpmate.

Important as male authority is to traditionalists, it has nonetheless been qualified and modified in the twentieth century, probably in response to legitimate feminist complaints regarding oppressive male domination in the home. The traditional view of male authority had been grounded in the notion of female inferiority and resulted in an emotionally distant autocrat who ruled both wife and children. Because such a view would be totally unacceptable in today's society, it needed to be adapted in order to gain any hearing. So it is now said that male leadership does not imply male superiority. Furthermore, men are not to use their authority to tyrannize their families but rather to serve them; men must be sensitive and emotionally intimate with their wives and children and treat their wives with respect, as "equals."

While the idea of the man as the ruling patriarch of the household is very traditional indeed, the conceptualization of his leadership as entailing sensitivity and servanthood is a modern modification. James Hunter deems this recent adjustment to the male role "an unusual kind of doublespeak." He explains,

> To maintain final authority and to carry out the form of strong leadership normative for centuries past, a clear difference in status from other members of the family was required. Patriarchy, in other words, required the husband to maintain social distance from the rest of the family. That social distance though is significantly reduced if not eliminated altogether by the normative expectation of sensitivity and intimacy. In this sense his authority becomes purely theoretical and abstract.[29]

The end result of all this tinkering with the patriarchal role has been a historically unprecedented and logically inconsistent definition of the husband's role. He is to take ultimate control of and complete responsibility for his wife and children as their God-ordained leader, all the while treating his wife as an equal and relating to his wife and children with emotional warmth and intimacy.

The woman's role prescribed by modern-day traditionalists is likewise of rather recent origin historically. The simple fact that full-time motherhood was a cultural invention of the nineteenth century stands in stark contrast to the traditionalist contention that until the modern feminist assault on the family, motherhood had always been a full-time job. James Dobson argues for vocational motherhood and homemaking as an "honorable occupation," which women have held "since the beginning of human existence." He deplores the "revisions of age-old behavior patterns" in gender roles which have occurred in the last twenty to thirty years. "Everything understood to identify womanhood for thousands of years has been held up to ridicule and disdain," partially as a result of "the incessant bombardment by the media on all traditional Judeo-Christian values."[30]

Apparently, the claim here is that the gender roles that held sway prior to the 1960s were those which had consistently obtained since the inception of Judeo-Christian values, and that any deviation from these gender roles constitutes deviation not only from the tradition of time immemorial, but also from the mandate of God himself. There appears to be no acknowledgment of the fact that prior to industrialization, both parents—along with their children—were occupied running the family farm or business, and women simply did not have the time to make a career of caring for their children. For traditionalists, the ideal family model—by which modern society is judged and to which it ought to conform—is found, without reservation or qualification, in nineteenth-century middle-class society and its 1950s reincarnation.

In *The Christian in an Age of Sexual Eclipse,* Michael Brown describes the mother's role that he maintains has been women's "for centuries": "The mother's role has been preserved by the concept that the father would provide the necessary material support that would enable the wife to remain at home giving primary care to the children. The first responsibility of the mother was to provide day by day, hour by hour nurturance and guidance for the children."[31] Presumably, society's departure from the ideal of full-time motherhood has contributed to a historically unique "sexual eclipse."

Here also is the common traditionalist worry—straight from the nineteenth century—that woman's role as a full-time mother "is the crucial pivot—the foundation—upon which both family and society revolve."[32] The fear is that if women do not devote their lives exclusively to "good mothering," the entire social order will collapse. While it is true that modern society is suffering from a sexual eclipse of severe proportions, this situation cannot justifiably be blamed on the fact that—unlike the limited period of history from the nineteenth century to the mid-twentieth century—mothers are generally unable to provide "hour by hour" care for their children.

Although traditionalism continues with the tradition of male authority, its teachings are untraditional at several key points. First, today's traditionalism breaks with the church's historic practice or "tradition" of simply endorsing current cultural views of women. Second, it invests the family with a historically unprecedented symbolic significance, reinforcing the traditionalist-specified "order" and "roles" with which every Christian family is expected to comply. Third, though the idea of authority as a male prerogative is undeniably traditional, the traditionalist reconceptualization of it in response to modern cultural trends is not. The customary view of male authority has been modernized and mollified at the hands of today's traditionalists. Fourth, the traditionalist-prescribed woman's role as homemaker or "full-time wife and mother" is not the role historically occupied by women, but is a cultural invention of the middle class in nineteenth-century Victorian society.

Conclusions and Clarifications

"The ideal family celebrated by Evangelicals (especially its ministers and specialists) is claimed to be both traditional and biblical. This is the family of the Judeo-Christian heritage—an ideal inspired by the divine; its qualities, timeless." Yet this "ideal Christian family," Hunter observes, is "largely foreign to Christianity before the modern age."[33] Clearly, the "traditional family" cannot be defended on the grounds that it has been the biblical model, the heritage of age-old Christian tradition.

The real issue, of course, is not whether the gender roles prescribed by traditionalists are truly traditional, but whether they are beneficial and prescribed by God. Certainly it is far better to nurture and care for children than to neglect and mistreat them as was the general custom in traditional, pre-industrial families. But is it best to have children cared for almost exclusively by their mother? In *Gender and Grace,* psychologist Mary Stewart Van Leeuwen makes a strong case from the social sciences that children are better off when mother and father share parenting responsibilities more or less equally. Boys especially suffer from being overmothered and underfathered.[34] In *A Time for Risking,* Miriam Adeney offers a cross-cultural perspective which also suggests that children benefit from the care of other family members—older siblings, aunts, uncles, cousins, grandparents, and so forth.[35]

The idea that child neglect is the only alternative to full-time motherhood is a false dilemma put forth by today's traditionalists. Apparently, a home cannot survive and thrive unless it is tended by a full-time woman. But this belief from the nineteenth century that all is lost unless children receive full-time care from their mother is not only a historically narrow view but a rather narrow-minded view as well. Although it may not be easy or even always possible for other family members to share with the mother the responsibility for childcare, it is certainly a viable option that ought not be dismissed as a failure to adhere to the Christian ideal.

But traditionalists are not the only ones with false dilemmas. Feminists sometimes say—less frequently now than in the 1960s and 1970s—that the role of full-time mother/homemaker is *so* mindless and boring that no woman with any self-respect should bother with it. So, for some feminists, the choice for a woman seems to be that she either pursue a career, even if it is at the expense of her family and home, or completely forsake all social status and personal identity and become just a housewife. Here, too, the middle ground needs to be acknowledged and explored.

It would be far more helpful to begin, not with either the traditionalist or the feminist false dilemma, but with the premise that because God made each person to be special and unique, each person's vocation should be tailored to match his or her individual situation. There is no reason why Alice Freeman Palmer's vision of the educated homemaker should not be admirably suited to many women. Vocational homemaking does not have to be a demeaning, mind-numbing experience; for many women it can be combined with and energized by the "hard work and uncertainties of improving the mind and the spirit."[36] But since women are not all alike, it is counterproductive to try to corral them all into a homemaking career or to drive them all out of the home and into a professional or business career. But whatever options are chosen in regard to careers and childcare providers, the only thing that is not optional is that children receive the care that they need to grow safely and happily to maturity.

When the prescription for the biblical home becomes rigid and formulaic and its symbolic significance assumes "mythic" proportions, then deviation from the prescribed, so-called biblical ideal is seen as tantamount to sacrilege. Worse yet, when the "traditional" family is romanticized and idealized as both a personal haven in a heartless world and the moral foundation upon which all civilization stands or falls, it has been blown up out of all proportion; it has become a modern idol. Families are important; families are ordained by God. But it is the family of God bought by the blood of Christ and destined to rule and reign with him that is the hope not only of this life but also of the one to come.

Not only is the "traditional" family unworthy of the claims made as to its cosmic significance and universal applicability, but certain aspects of its structure may well be less than ideal. Evidence is accumulating that the traditional home wherein the husband holds the reins is more likely to be the setting for abuse than is a home structured along equalitarian lines. After alcoholic families, "the next highest incidence of both incest and physical abuse takes place in intact, highly religious homes. The offending fathers in such families . . . often espouse 'old-fashioned values' to the point of rigidity and stuffiness. They emphasize the subordination of women, sometimes to the point of believing that they 'own' their wives and daughters."[37] David Brubaker states that "one of the most accurate predictors of incestuous conduct [is] highly authoritarian and/or paternalistic power relationships in the family system. . . . Hierarchical, authoritarian systems that disempower many or most members tend over time to become pathological."[38]

Of course, not all or even most traditional families degenerate into an abusive situation. A hierarchical family structure does not in itself cause abuse in the home, but it would seem to offer opportunity for an abusive situation to develop. The success of the traditional family is largely dependent on the moral rectitude of the man who is in charge of it (that the man is in charge is ironic in view of the Victorian belief that men are morally weaker than women!). When the man falls short of that which is morally demanded of him as the one holding the reins of responsibility and authority, the risk of dysfunction is higher than when husband and wife are equally accountable to one another. The traditional family in which the husband always has the last word and the wife is economically dependent on him offers no system of checks and balances whereby a man who is getting out of hand can be brought back into line. Such a situation can offer opportunity for a man who is cruel or emotionally unbalanced to wreak considerable damage on the family members who are under his authority.[39]

Traditionalists maintain, however, that such practices of male domination are simply examples of sinful abuses of God-given male authority and do not render male authority per se sinful. The husband's authoritative headship is deemed essential for the biblical integrity of the family. Traditionalists deny that absolute authority placed in the hands of the husband necessarily diminishes the wife's integrity or identity. The husband's "servant leadership" is said always to work for the wife's benefit.

What are the implications of male authority for the woman? In recent years there has been a great deal of emphasis on "proving" the innate and therefore presumably God-ordained differences between men and women—differences that are said to entail a masculine aptitude for leadership and a feminine capacity for receiving and affirming that leadership. Although we are told that male authority does not reflect male superiority exactly, it does seem to be justified by the belief that men are better equipped to lead—usually by virtue of their "natural" male ability to think logically and objectively. The woman's role of compliant helpmate is in turn justified by her supposed nurturant, emotional nature. Yet, traditionalists maintain that this gender difference does not imply that men are superior, nor does it militate against women's equality. Women are subordinate but equal, less rational but not inferior. There is a curious kind of doublespeak at work with the traditional role prescription for women as well as for men.

But as long as the definition of woman's difference entails the need for her to come under the protective guidance of a man and to gear her entire life around helping that man as he leads her, the implication of her inferiority and inequality will be very real indeed. She is not "different" in any neutral sense. She is, whether by in-built incompetence or by arbitrary fiat, not able to make her own decisions and control her own life—as is expected of any grown man. She is, quite simply, more child than adult.

Although traditionalists insist that they do not deny women equality with men, the equality which they grant women is a "spiritual" equality, not a functional or practical equality. Traditionalists maintain that women are equal before God in worth, value, and salvific status, but not before men when it comes to who is in charge of things. However, if tradition decrees that whenever a man and a woman work together in the church or home the man should be the one to take authority and decide how things are to be done, the assurance that the woman is nonetheless somehow "equal" has a hollow ring. Equal but subordinate is not only a logically contradictory category, it is virtually impossible to live out in practical reality. A man who exercises male authority (unearned authority granted him by virtue of his sex) will not be encouraged to regard as his equal a person whose sex denies her the right even to *earn* a comparable level of authority.

In actual practice, the conflict between the elements of hierarchy and equality in the traditionalist model is usually resolved by neutralizing either the husband's authority or the wife's equality. The resolution chosen will depend largely on how a man views his wife. Perhaps part of the reason why many traditional families do not degenerate into dysfunction is that a man who truly loves his wife will be likely to view her as an equal; that is, he will see her as a person who is more like than unlike him, a person who also has needs for self-determination, identity, and creative use of her gifts. If he recognizes her gifts for what they are—even if they range outside the bounds of traditional femininity—and allows for her personal growth in these areas, then his authority will become an administrative technicality and their marriage a functional equality.

If, however, the husband views his wife as destined by God and/or inherently suited only for an ancillary role as his "helpmate," then although he may do all he can to protect and provide for her and to make her helping/homemaking tasks as undemanding as possible, he will not acknowledge any need she may have to do anything beyond her designated role as domestic helper. If she is unhappy or discontent with this role, he will explain it as a rebellious refusal to accept and adjust to God's will for her life, regardless of how differently she may (but probably won't) explain her discontent.

So it seems that traditionalist tinkering with gender roles has resulted in an inherently contradictory role for the woman as well as for the man. The peculiar place in which the "traditional" man and woman find themselves is a result of the effort, on the one hand, to placate the feminists who object to woman being deemed unequal and inferior and, on the other hand, to retain traditional male authority over her.

The Victorian image of woman as delicate and decorative often serves as the traditionalist counterpart to male leadership. In itself, of course, there is nothing wrong with a woman looking sweet and pretty; it is certainly to be preferred to her looking mean and ugly. But the problem with the romanticized, idealized Victorian image of femininity is that it is reductionistic. Woman tends to be seen as *only* delicate and decorative. Her entire being is reduced to her external appearance and the purpose that external appearance serves (which is to please men). It is essentially a view of woman as witless and helpless. By virtue of her helplessness and pleasing appearance, she appeals to the protective instinct in men. This image results not only in a vacuous view of women, but in rather vacuous marriages as well. A man who marries a woman because she makes him feel all romantic and protective is soon going to tire of the game and begin to view her more as a ball and chain instead. Romance without relationship invariably wears thin. Relationship consists of two persons working together on a common project with mutual respect and affection, and it is not possible as long as the woman is there only for decorative purposes.

As a concluding observation, it should be noted that "advocates of the 'traditional' family in Evangelicalism . . . are not somehow unique in the cultural landscape in America. They merely represent the Evangelical component of a larger group of social pathologists who have, for over a century, made the family a social cause."[40] The general impression people receive as a result of the onslaught of family experts' how-to manuals is "that couples, parents, and families are incompetent to run their lives in the private sphere and that commonsense knowledge is not good enough."[41] Married couples must be assigned their roles by the experts; they cannot be trusted to work them out themselves. Just as the structure of the traditional family meets the need for security and stability in a rapidly changing society, so the plethora of marriage and family rule books meets the needs of people who are tired of questions without answers and who want only to be told what to do next.

When people no longer recognize the need to think for themselves, common sense becomes very uncommon indeed. "Functional rationality" replaces theoretical rationality. Peter Berger describes functional rationality as one of "the elements of modernity derived from technological production"; it entails "the imposition of rational controls over the material universe, over social relations and finally over the self."[42] It is ironic that those who tout tradition as the biblical ideal do so by means of the modern techniques of the modern helping professions, emphasizing rules over relationship and functional rationality over the far more "traditional" common sense.

Evangelicalism and the Rise of American Feminism

In the nineteenth century, the political ideas of classical liberalism interacted with the religious zeal of the Second Great Awakening to energize numerous social reform movements in the quest of a godly society of free individuals. Many of these reform efforts were led and supported by Christian women and men.

Women and Slaves

The first women to become public advocates of abolition were Christians. In 1830, Angelina and Sarah Grimké began speaking and writing against slavery, and soon other women followed suit. The cause of abolition provided "activist women with an ideology, a methodology, and the occasion" which led them formally to organize a campaign for women's rights.[1] The ideology of anti-slavery was equality and independence for all human beings; many abolitionists became feminists when they realized that the principle that "all men are created equal" applied as well to women as it did to slaves. The methodology was activism, organization, and communication through public leadership. The occasion that clarified the need for a women's movement came in 1840 when the American women delegates—many of whom were orthodox Quakers—were refused seats at a world anti-slavery convention in England. The first women's rights convention was held eight years later in Seneca Falls, New York.

The similar state of women and slaves prior to the reform movements is particularly notable. The eighteenth-century English common law of William Blackstone—which early America inherited from England—upheld the "civil death" of women who married. Blackstone asserted in his

Commentaries: "By marriage, the husband and wife are one person in law; that is, the very being or legal existence of the woman is suspended during her marriage, or at least, is consolidated into that of her husband under whose wing, protection and *cover,* she performs everything."[2] Even as he owned his slaves, so a man owned his wife. Andrew Sinclair notes,

> Early American women were almost treated like Negro slaves, inside and outside the home. Both were expected to behave with deference and obedience towards owner or husband; both did not exist officially under the law; both had few rights and little education; both found it difficult to run away; both worked for their masters without pay; both had to breed on command, and to nurse the results.[3]

In early America, neither women nor slaves had rights as individuals. Both were under the legal cover and control of their male masters.

The early feminists' objection to legalized domination of wives by husbands led some couples publicly to renounce such laws upon their marriage. Before John Stuart Mill married Harriet Taylor in 1851, "he wrote out a 'formal protest against the law of marriage' for conferring on the husband 'legal powers and control over the person, property, and freedom of action of the wife'; and he made a 'solemn promise never in any case or under any circumstances' to use such powers."[4] At the wedding ceremony of evangelical abolitionists Theodore Weld and Angelina Grimké, Weld disclaimed any right that the law gave him to own and control his wife's person or property. Their marriage of mutual love and equality served as an example to others, particularly to Henry Blackwell who diligently courted suffragist leader Lucy Stone for some time before she agreed to marry him. In his letters of persuasion to her, he wrote concerning Angelina and Theodore Weld, "If ever there was a true marriage it is theirs—Both preserve their separate individuality *perfectly.*"[5]

Blackwell also wrote, with remarkable insight, "I believe nineteen women out of twenty would be unhappy with a husband who, like myself, would repudiate supremacy." He explained that this was because "the great majority of people, in endeavouring to imagine a contrary state of things, conceive of the woman as the *leader* and the man as the *subservient.*"[6] This misconception haunts us still. The idea of equality and mutual submission is rarely considered as a possibility. Only two options are recognized: either a man dominates his wife, or he is dominated by his wife. Because the idea of a man being dominated by his wife is particularly repugnant to most people, his "right" to dominate her is retained. But Henry Blackwell saw through this false dilemma and promised Lucy that he would "repudiate the supremacy" of either woman or man in marriage. "Equality for me is a passion," he wrote to Lucy. "I dislike equally to assume, or to endure authority."[7]

The minister who married Henry Blackwell and Lucy Stone commented, "I never perform the marriage ceremony without a renewed sense of the iniquity of . . . a system by which 'man and wife are one, and that one is the husband.'"[8] He was very pleased indeed when Lucy and Henry included in their marriage vows a renunciation of all laws of marriage that "refuse to recognize the wife as an independent, rational being, while they confer upon the husband an injurious and unnatural superiority."[9]

Because of the blatant injustice of the law toward women, early feminist efforts were directed toward equalizing marriage and property laws. Also promoted, however, were women's rights to education, to decent working conditions, and to public speaking and leadership. As American feminists were successful in legal reform, "it allowed American lawyers to boast of the superiority of their legal system to those of European countries, most of which now possessed a version of the Code Napoléon that was based on his dictum, 'Woman is given to man to bear children; she is therefore his property, as the tree is the gardener's.'"[10]

Women's suffrage was slower in coming than other legal reforms. The idea of women having the right to vote struck at the very heart of male authority by presupposing that women had minds of their own, that they had thoughts and opinions independently of their husbands, and that the ideas of female minds should be counted equally with those of male minds in determining the laws and leaders of the country.

Nineteenth-Century Liberalism

The application of the principle of equal rights for all people—regardless of race, sex, or economic class—is characteristic of classical (premodern) liberalism. The legal rights that were traditionally granted only to free men began to be extended to slaves and women in the nineteenth century. This advocacy of the rights of the individual was part of a trend in Western society toward abandoning the traditional practice of ascribing roles to people solely on the basis of the circumstances of their birth—their sex, race, socioeconomic status, and father's vocation. The pattern in Western society has been an increasing awareness that these characteristics ought not determine a person's role in life and that the only valid determining factor should be each individual's competence to perform a given role or job.

The classical liberal understanding of justice and equality for everyone demands that each individual be judged as an individual, according to his or her own unique constellation of interests and abilities. The opposite of this basis of judgment is pre-judgment, or prejudice, whereby a person is judged as a member of a group rather than as an individual, and is assumed to possess the personal traits that are supposedly inherent to all members of the group to which that person belongs. This is the essence of racism and sexism. When, for example, blacks are assumed to be lazy and ignorant and women are deemed weak and irrational, then the social subjugation of women and blacks will follow from these pre-judgments, and they will be denied justice and equality.

John Stuart Mill's *Subjection of Women,* published in 1869, gave logical coherence and persuasive power to the cause of classical liberal feminism. He pointed out that, at that time in Victorian England, women were the only group of people who, by virtue of "a fatality of birth which no exception and no change of circumstances can overcome," were denied access to "the higher social functions," regardless of their individual capabilities.[11] Employing the incisive intellectual tools of a philosopher, Mill developed the logical case for equal legal rights for women and exposed the illogic of women's lawful subjection. Mill observed that when "women are declared to be better than men" (as was the custom in Victorian society), it is "an empty compliment which must provoke a bitter smile from every woman of spirit, since there is no other situation in life in which it is the established order, and quite natural and suitable, that the better should obey the worse."[12] Mill argued forcefully that mutual affection in marriage usually forestalled husbandly cruelty, but women were legally slaves of their husbands and had no recourse should their husbands choose to exercise their legal rights. Moreover, Mill observed, a man's virtually unlimited power over his wife "evokes the latent germs of selfishness in the remotest corners of his nature . . . [and] offers to him a license for the indulgence of those points of his original character which in all other relations he would have found it necessary to repress and conceal."[13]

Abolitionism and the Church

The anti-slavery impetus did not come only from nineteenth-century political ideals. Christian abolitionists believed the abolition of slavery to be in obedience to biblical principles. Most of the exegetical arguments of northern Christian abolitionists went along the lines of Presbyterian minister Albert Barnes's 1846 publication, *An Inquiry into the Scriptural*

Views of Slavery. He upheld that "The principles laid down by the Saviour and his Apostles are such as are opposed to Slavery. . . . the spirit of the Christian religion is against it; . . . *it is an evil, and is displeasing to God.*"[14]

The pro-slavery faction in the church responded by firing a volley of proof texts against the abolitionist appeal to biblical principle. Texts used in support of slavery included Leviticus 25:44–46, Matthew 8:9–13, Luke 17:7–10, 1 Corinthians 7:20–24, Ephesians 6:5–8, 1 Timothy 6:1–2, and 1 Peter 2:18–21. But "Christian abolitionists rested their hermeneutical case not just on what decontextualized, individual passages of Scripture said but on their perceptions of where scriptural revelation in its entirety was heading."[15] As theologian Cornelius Plantinga explains, "Despite what Paul says to slaves about obedience, despite what Peter says about obedience even to bad masters, the bigger historical-redemptive line of Scripture tells us that humans made in God's image cannot be owned by anyone but their maker . . . and especially, that Jesus Christ came to set at liberty those who are oppressed."[16] Those abolitionists who "learned to defend the egalitarian and liberationist 'spirit' of the Bible against status quo literal interpretations found that the same arguments could be used in support of the women's movement. Even Galatians 3:28 seemed to conjoin the issues by declaring that 'There is neither Jew nor Greek, there is neither bond nor free, there is neither male nor female: for ye are all one in Christ Jesus.'"[17]

The pro-slavery proof text assault rested on the assumption that the apostles Paul and Peter simply accepted existing social institutions as God's order for society. Christian abolitionists, on the other hand, contended that, "for the sake of advancing God's kingdom in a given time and place, temporary compromises can and often must be made with the societal status quo."[18] Hence, a biblical command to cooperate with a particular cultural institution does not necessarily constitute an endorsement of that institution as God's ultimate will for society. Christian abolitionists believed that biblical texts commanding slaves' obedience to their masters were examples of just such a compromise, by which God's perfect will was accommodated or applied to imperfect human society. A biblical principle—or, in Plantinga's words, "the bigger historical-redemptive line of Scripture"—is unchanging; but its application to culture changes according to cultural conditions. The way in which a biblical principle was applied in biblical times is not in itself to be our rule and standard of conduct; rather, we must appropriately apply the biblical principle to our own time.

But, as both anti-abolitionists and antifeminists have learned, the power of the proof text is considerable. As long as someone has an arsenal of proof texts, he or she can make the sort of accusations that a pro-slavery university professor uttered in 1860: "the history of interpretation furnishes no examples of more willful and violent perversions of the sacred text than are to be found in the writings of the abolitionists. They seem to consider themselves above the Scriptures: . . . they put themselves above the law of God."[19] Pro-slavery Christians had no patience with the notion that the Bible merely tolerated slavery rather than advocated it—any more than traditionalists accept the biblical feminist contention that biblical revelation accommodated itself to patriarchy but was not itself patriarchal.

Similar to the antifeminists of today, nineteenth-century anti-abolitionists grounded the practice of slavery in the order of creation, or the God-ordained order of things. African people were viewed as designed by God for poverty, hard labor, and subservience.[20] Slavery was rationalized by the belief that the subjugation of certain classes of people to other classes of people is somehow built into the hierarchical order of the universe.[21] Also seeming to echo today's antifeminists, advocates of slavery claimed that the Christian equality of slave and free (as stated in passages such as Galatians 3:28) referred to "spiritual equality" only and did not obtain in any practical social sense.[22] God, they said, had ordained slavery even as he had ordained the subordination of women. In the biblical case for slavery, proof texts were exalted to the status of universal applicability, and fundamental biblical principles such as the equality of all believers in Christ were qualified and conditioned by cultural preunderstanding—the precise antithesis of the procedure that would normally occur in unprejudiced biblical interpretation.

In addition, anti-abolitionists claimed that because Old Testament law allowed slavery and because people in both the Old Testament (Abraham) and New Testament (Philemon) owned slaves and the Bible contained no specific rebuke of such activity, slavery was God-ordained. As one Reverend Frederick Ross of Alabama put it, "Abraham lived in the midst of a system of slaveholding, exactly the same in nature with that in the South—a system ordained of God." Ross did have one qualification, that being that the southern master "has slaves of an inferior type of mankind from Abraham's bondmen."[23]

The assumption here is the same one that seems often to be made by antifeminists today: any aspect of the culture of biblical times that was not specifically condemned or prohibited in the Bible must be God-ordained. But by such a hermeneutic, a proponent of gang rape could justify his position by the story of the man who, while in the Benjamite city of Gibeah, gave his concubine to be gang-raped (Judg. 19). There was no outrage expressed by either the narrative or the characters in the story at the fact that this woman was handed over matter-of-factly to the rapists in order to spare the man who owned her. The man in the story became outraged only after he learned that the rapists had *killed* the woman who was his concubine, and his outrage was apparently only because of the destruction of his property, not out of concern for her person. It was evidently not an uncommon procedure in Old Testament times for a man to offer his womenfolk to be raped in order to protect himself or a male guest in his house. A similar offer was made by Lot of his virgin daughters (Gen. 19:8). But not even the most traditional traditionalist would attempt to apply this hermeneutic to these biblical passages and conclude that the violation of defenseless women is God-ordained simply because it was reported without indication of biblical censure. Rather, such instances are rightly viewed as examples of cultural evil.

Highly indignant, emotionalized rhetoric was another defensive strategy used against the abolitionists. The antifeminists of today have nothing on Josiah Priest, who wrote in his *Bible Defense of Slavery* in 1853 that abolitionism was "a withering blighting curse, a pestiferous excrescence . . . begotten by the father of lies, born of the mother of harlots . . . its breath is pestilences and death, its practical operations the destruction of all domestic tranquility and social order."[24]

The anti-abolitionists became so vehement in their "biblical" defense of slavery that some, such as zealous abolitionist leader William Lloyd Garrison, became convinced that they were right and that the Bible really did sanction slavery. He responded by forthwith rejecting the Bible's authority.[25] Again a familiar note is sounded. Most of what is termed "feminist theology" today is based on the assumption that the Bible, in at least some places, advocates the patriarchal subjugation of women. Theologically liberal feminists, convinced by the antifeminists that the Bible is patriarchal, have rejected its authority.

The correlation between the abolitionist cause and the feminist cause was not missed by the anti-abolitionists, who further defended their position by pointing out that if slaves were freed, women would most likely be next, and this, of course, would never do. Albert Bledsoe declared in his pro-slavery treatise that for women to "come forth in the liberty of men" and to take up roles of public leadership would be in "studied insult to the authority of God" and would result in "a country . . . from which all order and all virtue would speedily be banished."[26] Such are the quirks of tradition's legacy that today the proof-text hermeneutic is still applied by evangelicals to the question of women's roles but the broader hermeneutic of biblical principle is applied to the issue of slavery.

The traditionalist tendency is always to assume that tradition rests on Scripture and that any new or contrary idea is therefore a violation of biblical authority. Martin Luther exhibited this tendency when he wrote in support of slavery in his day, employing all four weapons of the anti-abolitionists: the example of the culture of biblical times, the proof texts commanding slaves' obedience, emotional rhetoric, and an appeal to the God-ordained social hierarchy: "Did not Abraham (Gen. 17:23) and other patriarchs and prophets have slaves? Read what St. Paul teaches about servants, who, at that time, were all slaves." The idea of freedom for slaves, therefore, "absolutely contradicts the gospel. It proposes robbery, for it suggests that every man should take his body away from his lord, even though his body is the lord's property. . . . A worldly kingdom cannot exist without an inequality of persons, some being free, some imprisoned, some lords, some subjects."[27]

In propounding the biblical doctrine of justification by faith, the Protestant Reformers were able to counter elements of false theology in church tradition. Nonetheless, they were blinded by tradition when it came to defending not only slavery, but male supremacy, the divine right of kings, and a geocentric universe. When Copernicus advanced his theory of a heliocentric cosmology in the sixteenth century, Martin Luther found biblical grounds for disapproving of that "upstart astrologer" in the fact that "sacred Scripture tells us that Joshua commanded the sun to stand still, not the earth."[28] John Calvin demanded, "Who will venture to place the authority of Copernicus above that of the Holy Spirit?" Puritan leader John Owen deemed the Copernican theory "a delusive and arbitrary hypothesis, contrary to Scripture."[29]

The lesson to be learned from such historical misuses of Scripture to support tradition is not that traditional biblical interpretation is always or even usually wrong, but that in some cases it can be wrong, and we ought not assume that the traditional is always the biblical. Neither may we assume that any traditional biblical teaching may be evaded simply by dismissing as proof texts those references which support that teaching, and by claiming allegiance instead to some overarching biblical theme or principle to the contrary. In the first place, there are objective criteria for determining which texts are culturally specific (i.e., applicable primarily to biblical cultures) and which texts are universally applicable. These criteria must not be dismissed in favor of personal preference. In the second place, those texts which seem to contradict a clear biblical principle and are rightly deemed culturally specific nonetheless mean something for us today, and that meaning must be determined by understanding the biblical author's reason for writing the passage to that specific culture.[30]

Suffrage and Temperance

After the cause of abolition had been won in 1865, the cause of temperance drew the enthusiastic support and leadership of many Christians, including Jonathan Blanchard and A. J. Gordon, founders of Wheaton College and Gordon College, respectively. Evangelical reformers Blanchard and Gordon "also championed the legal recognition of the rights of women."[31] Evangelical minister Frances Willard was president of the Women's Christian Temperance Union (WCTU) from 1879 until her death in 1898. After the WCTU officially endorsed suffrage in the 1880s, Willard began working with evangelical minister and medical doctor Anna Shaw to enlist the support of churches by stressing the benefits of suffrage and temperance for moral purity and the home. By 1902 clergy support for women's suffrage had reached a ratio of six to one.[32]

From 1900 until the passage of the Suffrage Amendment, the National American Woman Suffrage Association (NAWSA) was under the leadership of Anna Howard Shaw and Carrie Chapman Catt, who "both believed the Bible was an infallible guide for all Christians. Shaw, an ordained minister in the Methodist Protestant Church, stressed the consistency between modern Christian ethics and women's rights."[33] Shaw was also instrumental in NAWSA's official disowning of *The Woman's Bible,* a work that was prototypical of modern liberal feminist theology in its rejection of biblical authority and "offensive" texts.

If women are supposed to be the guardians of social morality, the suffragists reasoned, then giving them opportunity to exert their influence through the vote would help elevate the moral standards of society and safeguard the home and family from evil. This rationale for women's rights was present in the movement since its inception. Elaine Storkey notes that "'Votes for women and purity for men' was one of the earliest suffragette slogans!"[34] The "Declaration" adopted at the first women's convention in 1848 resolved that "in regard to the great subjects of morals and religion, it is self-evidently her [woman's] right to participate with her brother in teaching them, both in private and in public."[35]

Despite the suffragists' tradition-friendly rationale for women's right to vote, the suffrage movement drew considerable traditionalist fire. Biblical texts that are used today to keep women subservient to men in the

church and at home were used one hundred years ago to keep women subservient to men in the political arena as well. It was said that allowing
women to vote would destroy society and the Christian home and render
women immoral and unfeminine. Horace Bushnell went so far as to predict that, among other dire effects, women's brains would become heavier
if they voted (indicating, no doubt, a deplorable increase in intellectual activity among females).[36]

After women's right to vote was legally acknowledged in 1920, traditionalist Christian leaders were obliged to regroup; they redoubled their efforts to keep women subservient in the spheres over which they still had
control—a project which in some denominations extended even to denying women the right to vote in church elections. Today, of course, few if
any traditionalists believe that women ought not be granted the right to
vote in public elections; it is assumed instead that the biblical texts are intended to place women under male authority only in the church and the
home, and to silence women only in the public worship service. There are,
however, some conservative denominations that even today prohibit
women from voting on matters of church governance.[37]

Evangelical Reform Movements

While abolition, suffrage, and temperance were broad movements that
drew followers from both within and without the church, the extent to
which these movements were fueled by the evangelistic and reformist zeal
of the Second Great Awakening (1795–1840) should not be underestimated. Concerning the early nineteenth-century social reform campaigns, religion historian Sydney Ahlstrom comments that "church leaders of one sort or another frequently provided the initial impulse, ministers
and dedicated laymen were often active agitators, and nearly all the campaigns were pervaded by appeals to 'Christian principles.' If the collective
conscience of evangelical America is left out, the [reformist] movement
as a whole is incomprehensible."[38]

Charles Finney was a principal leader behind evangelical social concern. In an issue devoted to North American spiritual awakenings, *Christian History* magazine notes that when Finney "propelled the awakening
onto center-stage in America" its "side-effects became more widespread
than ever before: out of it came power for the antislavery crusade, women's
rights, prison reform, temperance, and much more."[39] Although Finney
did not identify himself as a feminist, his insistence on women's freedom
to testify and pray aloud in mixed gatherings flew in the face of the tradi-

tional silencing of women in church meetings. But Finney's "new measures" regarding women were not without precedent. In 1825 Theodore Weld had urged women to speak and pray in public meetings, and a number of women had responded, confessing their sin of being "restrained by their sex."[40]

The refusal of revivalists such as Finney to consign women to silence and inactivity in church affairs served as an important first step for the nineteenth-century evangelical women's movement. Ahlstrom notes that "one breakthrough [for women's rights] resulted from the revivals, especially in the West . . . notably by Charles G. Finney's new measures."[41] Another Yale historian, Paul E. Johnson, comments on the most controversial of Finney's new measures, that women be encouraged to pray publicly in "promiscuous" or mixed meetings. "Traditionalists considered Finney's practice of having women and men pray together the most dangerous of the new measures, for it implied new kinds of equality between the sexes. Indeed some harried husbands recognized the revival as subversive of their authority over their wives."[42]

Not only did Protestant church membership increase from one in fifteen Americans in 1800 to one in seven by 1850 as a result of the Second Great Awakening,[43] but thousands of evangelical societies for social betterment were formed during this time—to which "the support of local women's groups came gradually to be almost essential."[44] "The combination of concern for revival and creation of reform societies led to . . . significant 'Christianization' of the culture."[45] It also led to women taking an active, influential, and public role in society, as early feminist leader Lydia Child noted in 1841:

> In modern times, the evangelical sects have highly approved of female prayer meetings. In the cause of missions and dissemination of tracts, they have eloquently urged upon women their prodigious influence and consequent responsibility, in the great work of regenerating a world lying in wickedness. Thus it is with those who urged women to become missionaries, and form tract societies. They have changed the household utensil into a living, energetic being; and they have no spell to turn it into a broom again.[46]

Finney and other revivalists and preachers helped women "to achieve an attitude of self-confidence and a sense of mission that infected many of their later activities. Surely it is no coincidence that the areas where Finney's revivals and women's religious education flourished . . . were early centers of women's reform work and feminism."[47]

According to the *Dictionary of Christianity in America*, "The rise of

American feminism had its roots in the Christian reform movements of the 1830s and 1840s that were in turn generated by the Second Great Awakening. Following the Civil War, as the women's movement increasingly focused on the suffrage issue, the traditional link with Christian thought remained strong."[48] George Marsden notes that the "ministries [of prohibition and women's rights] were a part of the wider holiness revival," which followed the Second Awakening later in the nineteenth century.[49]

As sociologist David Lyon points out, "A simple correlation of feminism with secularism is hard to square with nineteenth-century evidence. . . . What may appear to some today as the permeation of 'secular' ideas into the churches has a nineteenth-century precedent which was quite the other way round! The 'secular' movements were initiated or boosted by the 'religious.'" Lyon notes, "Of course, these feminisms were pro-family—a far cry from some contemporary counterparts (not of Christian origin) which doubt the necessity of any formal heterosexual relationship for the nurture of children."[50]

Nonetheless, antifeminists today persist in the conviction that feminism has always been motivated by anti-Christian convictions. George Grant's historical survey of the pro-life movement is illustrative. First, he says that in the nineteenth century, *"even* the most ardent feminists *had to* rally under the pro-life banner."[51] The assumption here seems to be that any pro-life rhetoric from feminists could not be sincere; it *must* have been forced upon them by social consensus. Grant also includes the suffragettes with other turn-of-the-century groups which, he claims, were "intent on the utter decimation of the Christian vision of life, liberty, and the pursuit of happiness."[52] And this when evangelical suffrage leaders Anna Shaw and Frances Willard were laboring to gain women the vote *for the sake of the home and family*!

In a speech to the National Council of Women in 1891, Julia Ward Howe showed how the cause of women's suffrage was conceptually tied in with the comprehensive aims of Christian social reform.

> We can work for peace and for temperance, for social purity, for civil service reform, without calling ourselves suffragists. . . . And yet, I believe that the principle which is slowly bringing the political enfranchisement of women is identical with that which we recognize in the accepted measures I have just named. It and they are only features of that better state of society towards which we are not drifting, but marching. The whole new Christian scheme holds together.[53]

In short, evangelicalism in the early nineteenth century set into motion numerous social reform campaigns, including that of women's rights. "Out of these currents flowed a stream of feminism that engulfed much of Evangelicalism by the end of the century."[54]

1920–1960: The Decades Between

Feminism began to fall out of favor after 1920 as reformist zeal waned in both church and society. The slaves had been freed, women had gotten the vote, and prohibition was in full swing. Suffragists and other reformers believed there was nothing more to do after the legal battles had been won, so they gave up the fight for social reform. With feminist fervor run aground and the stereotype of the "flapper" of the 1920s serving as society's image of the liberated woman, the tide of public opinion began to turn against equality for women. Women, for their part, did not take advantage of the legal freedoms that had been won for them. Succumbing instead to the prevailing cultural climate, they retreated from the public arena and sank back into retiring domesticity.

Feminists had assumed that once women were granted equal opportunity under the law everything would turn out as it ought. But it did not. The hidden force of patriarchal social custom prompted a cultural return to female subservience. Legal inequity had long been recognized and resisted by advocates of women's rights. The more subtle yet more powerful inequity of patriarchal tradition continued to go unacknowledged and therefore unresisted. Its increasing effects on American culture between 1920 and 1960 were thoroughgoing and monolithic.

Traditionalists contend that women and men had been perfectly content with the gender role prescriptions of the 1950s until feminism came along to unsettle and disturb everyone. But there is evidence that change had been on the way for some time prior to the cultural revolution of the 1960s. One indication of brewing discontent in the fifties was *Playboy* magazine's persistently negative depiction of parasitic wives who were forever demanding financial success from their husbands. Aside from the injustice of this complaint—it was, after all, the men who pushed the women from their income-producing jobs after World War II—it does reveal the incipient dissatisfaction of both men and women in their traditional roles.[55]

Betty Friedan's *Feminine Mystique,* which recharged a fading feminism in 1963, recounted numerous social indications that an exclusively domestic role was proving to be psychologically unhealthy for many women. Friedan's insights into the culturally entrenched stereotype of womanhood also served as a transition from early feminism to modern feminism. The groundswell that developed in the wake of *The Feminine Mystique* instigated a wide variety of feminist thought, from a revival of the evangelical and classical liberal ideas of early feminism to the fairly recent woman-centered ideology of radical feminism. As is apparent from the following comparison of early and modern feminism,[56] today's evangelical feminism belongs more in the tradition of early feminist thought than in the current of modern, secular feminism.

Comparing Early and Modern Feminism

Both early and modern feminism developed in a general cultural milieu of social discontent and reformist idealism. Social concern for the rights of African-Americans (the anti-slavery movement beginning in the 1830s and the civil rights movement beginning in the late 1950s) served as a catalyst for both feminist movements. When women began to fight against racism it did not take them long to become aware of the ways in which sexism violated their own civil rights. Their awareness of discrimination against themselves was hastened by their systematic exclusion by the male leaders of the movements: in 1840 women were denied seats at the anti-slavery convention, and in the 1960s women who were active in the civil rights movement "increasingly became conscious that they were not included in any of the decision-making processes but were instead saddled with domestic and ancillary chores."[57]

Although the women's movements in both centuries have been diverse, with internal squabbles and factions, they hold in common an insistence upon the idea of woman as an individual, as her own person, who does not need to be dependent on a man for her value and identity. Fundamental to any feminist agenda, therefore, is that woman's personhood and equality be established, verified, and protected through social change wherein inequitable laws and social customs are made equitable.

As a corollary to the ideal of woman's individual personhood, both early and modern feminists have evidenced a strong resistance to the traditional notion that woman's only complete fulfillment is in motherhood, that her place is in the home where she is under the rule of her husband, and that in the public sphere she is to be silent and subservient. There is a conviction that woman's silence and subservience unfairly restricts her from important spheres of activities. Feminism has therefore encouraged qualified women to take part in political, social, or church leadership.

While feminists in both centuries are alike in what they want women to be liberated *from*, they are unlike in what they want women to be liberated *for*. Both early and modern feminists have recognized and objected to the double standard of sexual behavior for men and women. But while the early feminists sought to hold men accountable to the high moral standards to which women themselves were obligated, the modern feminists have sought to level the moral landscape by allowing women the same sexual license that convention has traditionally allowed men. Modern feminists, of course, have been more successful in their campaign than the early feminists. It is always easier to allow sin than it is to enforce righteousness.

Nineteenth-century feminism testifies to the fact that sexual license is not inherent to the idea of women's rights. The accusation that evangelical feminism is an offshoot of modern feminism and therefore intrinsically endorses sexual immorality betrays historical and cultural ignorance. The evangelical denominations at the turn of the century that were most committed to women's equality were part of the holiness movement—which could hardly be said to be promoting sexual promiscuity. The only motivation of these groups to "liberate" women was the desire to open up all the channels through which God wanted to bless the church. The notion of using liberation to engage in a lifestyle of sexual irresponsibility could not have been more alien to the convictions of early evangelical feminism.

Modern feminists (especially during the 1970s) have also been more intent on beating men at their own game than on using women's increased social power as a tool for the moral betterment of society. Unlike that of the early feminists, the modern feminist's agenda is likely to center on achieving personal fulfillment as an individual woman rather than on employing her talents for the good of others.

Just as the focus has shifted from improving society to improving the self, so it has shifted from home and family to the marketplace. In modern feminism, home and family are all very fine, but peripheral; for both men and women, modern life is defined primarily in terms of work done apart from the context of the family. But early feminists campaigned to make home and family values central to the lives of both men and women in both the public and the private spheres. "Indeed, nineteenth-century feminism hoped to reform the world according to the model of home and family. Domesticating the marketplace, not commercializing the domestic realm, was the central focus of much early feminist thought. Thus, the current identification of home and family as the source not of woman's strength but of her weakness stands as a sharp departure from earlier feminist traditions."[58]

While nineteenth-century feminism was not composed entirely of Christians or supported by the entire evangelical church, its goals and motives were in line with biblical principles. A significant percentage if not a majority of those involved in the suffrage movement were Christians or at least "God-fearing." There was enough accord in early feminism between evangelicals and non-evangelicals that both were integrated into the same movement; there was not the distinction—indeed, contradiction—that there is today between evangelical feminism and modern, secular feminism. The anti-Christian element was a minority one in the nineteenth century, whereas today it characterizes the secular feminist movement. The evangelical support for women's rights in the nineteenth century is apparent in the fact that a significant number of evangelical institutions encouraged women to be pastors and evangelists.[59] This situation can hardly be said to prevail today!

Nineteenth-century feminists—both Christian and non-Christian—rightly viewed abortion as an instrument of male oppression rather than as a means of women's liberation. Specifically, it was seen as an act that devalued women and enabled men to evade responsibility for the children they fathered.[60] The ways in which abortion serves to subjugate rather than liberate women will be discussed in chapter 5.

New Age/pagan spirituality and "homosexual rights" were not linked to the cause of women's rights in early feminism either, whereas they are stressed in certain sectors of modern, secular feminism.

Modern feminists differ from early feminists also in the premise or base from which they have fought for women's rights. The roots of early feminism are in the evangelical efforts of social reform following the Second Great Awakening, as well as in the premise of classical liberalism that "all men [including women] are created equal." Early feminists understood inequality as a function of inequitable laws, so the solution was perceived in legal terms.

The roots of modern feminism are in the social upheaval and political leftism that characterized the 1960s. (This fact in itself has induced many conservatives to perceive leftist political ideas as intrinsic to feminism and therefore to disavow all notions of women's rights.) Observing that sexism remained even after most of the legal inequities had been removed, modern feminists have focused on the force of traditional social convention that views women as essentially—even if no longer legally—the property of men. In view of this vestigial patriarchy, feminists are now putting more energy into changing discriminatory social structures.

In this respect the feminist movement has seemed to follow a pattern roughly similar to that of the black civil rights movement. In the nineteenth century, the goal was to secure equal *legal* rights for both blacks and women. The slaves were emancipated in 1865, and black male citizens received the right to vote in 1870. Women's legal emancipation came more gradually and culminated in their right to vote in 1920. But getting the right laws on the books did not end systemic social discrimination for either blacks or women. The 1960s saw blacks fighting to realize their constitutionally guaranteed legal equality by protesting the segregation customs of the South. Following the inception of the civil rights movement by about a decade, women began to organize resistance to patriarchal custom. While legal reform continued as an element in both movements, both women and blacks were realizing that there was something deeper than law which accounted for their social subjugation. It was a deep-seated attitude, a cultural mindset that even new legislation would not budge. Members in both movements tended to respond with belligerence and anger to this intangible, ineluctable creation of culture called prejudice.

There grew factions in each group that went further, claiming not just their equality but their superiority over their oppressors. In this sense, they became *like* their oppressors, pre-judging and discriminating against members of the "other" group. Revenge is had by reversing the double standard: whites and males can now be maligned in ways that blacks and women cannot. The classical ideal of justice and equality—wherein *every* person is judged as an individual rather than as a member of a group—seems to have given way to an ethic of retribution. Prejudice against blacks and women is indeed a powerful and painful reality. But the solution lies in true equality, not in simply directing discrimination back upon the original perpetrators of it.

Evangelical Feminism: A Two-Century Tradition

Having surveyed the rise of and the reasons for American feminism in nineteenth-century society, I would now like to take a closer look at women's ministry in the evangelical church in the nineteenth and early twentieth centuries.

Women's Missionary and Reform Societies

Women's ministry in the nineteenth century initially took the form of evangelistic, missionary, benevolence, and reform societies founded and led by women. Numerous such organizations thrived from 1810 until 1920. In their zeal to involve women in ministry outside the home, these groups—without officially sponsoring feminism as a cause—were simply doing the things that evangelical feminists declare every woman should have the opportunity to do.

Frances Willard recognized the benefit these associations offered Christian women. She stated in 1892 that, because the male church leaders wanted "to keep the dimes and distinctions to themselves," they allowed women members to be nothing more than "hewers of wood and drawers of water."[1] Only in their own organizations, Willard argued, could women have the opportunity to develop and use their gifts of leadership and ministry.

The women's societies provided financial benefit to the denominations with which they were affiliated. The presence of these organizations was also in accord with the prevalent notion that women were of a more religious nature than men and therefore had the special mission of safeguarding social morality. The fact that women were thereby in some sense exercising leadership in the church was overlooked in view of the benefits and cultural acceptability of the practice.

Beginning in 1861, the influence of women's organizations expanded to the foreign mission field. Women's mission boards sent out a host of unmarried female missionaries; in less than fifty years there were two women for every man on the mission field. Women found far greater opportunity for ministry in foreign lands than they had found at home. Ruth Tucker comments that "the women's missionary movement was unique in that for the first time in history women could take up leadership positions in evangelistic outreach on a large scale."[2] Criticisms against women missionaries assuming such leadership roles as church planting and pastoring were largely swept aside in view of the need for competent workers in the mission field—a need women quickly proved themselves more than capable of filling. In fact, according to missiologist J. Herbert Kane, "the more difficult and dangerous the work, the higher the ratio of women to men."[3]

Tim Stafford observes that the successful ministry of women missionaries in the late nineteenth century

> ought to put to rest some fears about the blurring of roles in the church. Women have done everything overseas, and it has not led to disaster. On the contrary, it has produced both remarkable women and remarkable results. The transformation of the church from a European phenomenon to an international, transcultural movement is perhaps the most notable fact of church history during the past two centuries. Could it have been done without these women's leadership? That is very doubtful indeed.[4]

By the 1920s women's organizations began to disintegrate as revivalist and reformist zeal flagged and as their leaders were integrated (at nonleadership levels) into denominational administration. Women were comfortable exercising leadership in their own autonomous organizations, but in the men's world of church denominations they lost their confidence. When the women's domain was merged with the men's, women as individuals were subsumed under male leadership.

Because a pattern had been set up whereby men had their sphere of influence and women had theirs, the practice of maintaining separate women's groups persisted in the churches. But these groups have come to serve as little more than structures for female socializing. Whereas previously women and men were separate but somewhat equal, now they are separate but no longer equal.

Nineteenth-Century Evangelical Feminists

A number of Christian women were active in both evangelical ministry and the women's movement during the nineteenth century. Of these we can mention only a sampling here.[5]

As Angelina and Sarah Grimké began to speak and write against slavery, they came under fire not only for their anti-slavery views but for their public speaking. This created a need for them to defend the right of women to have a voice in the public sphere. In 1837 Sarah Grimké wrote the first scriptural defense of women's right to speak, entitled *Letters on the Equality of the Sexes*. In this work she described the parallels between woman's condition and the condition of the slave, stating, "in all ages and countries, woman has more or less been made a *means* to promote the welfare of man, without regard to her own happiness, and the glory of God, as the end of her creation." As for what the Bible had to say about women, Grimké said she was "willing to abide by its decision," but she protested the "false translations of some passages by the MEN who did that work."[6] The basic tenets of evangelical feminism appear in seed form in these conclusions of Sarah Grimké: the motive behind the cause of women's rights is to allow women to glorify God to the fullest extent that God enables them, and the prerequisite of women's liberation is an unprejudiced translation and interpretation of the biblical passages that have traditionally been used to keep women in subjection.

Evangelist Theodore Weld, whom Angelina Grimké married, developed a biblical argument against slavery and also supported women's rights. Converted in 1826 during one of Finney's revivals, Weld and his supporters helped build Oberlin College into "a center of both evangelical revivalism (Charles Finney came as the professor of theology in 1835) and Christian social action."[7] Oberlin College was also the first college in the world to become coeducational. In fact, its first president, Asa Mahan, was so pleased with this achievement that he said he wished to be remembered as "the first man, in the history of the race who conducted women, in connection with members of the opposite sex, through a full course of liberal education, and conferred upon her the high degrees which had hitherto been the exclusive prerogatives of men."[8]

Oberlin College also had the distinction of graduating from its three-year graduate theology course a woman who later became the first officially ordained woman in America and probably in the world. But it seems that, although Oberlin was all for educating women, when Antoinette Brown graduated in 1850 the college was reticent about women using their education for a non-traditional vocation. Oberlin did not formally acknowledge Brown's theological degree until many years after she had completed it. In 1908, the college awarded her an honorary Doctor of Divinity degree.

Antoinette Brown was ordained in a Congregationalist church in 1853. Luther Lee, a Wesleyan Methodist pastor, preached the ordination sermon with Galatians 3:28 as his text. "If the text means anything," he said, "it means that males and females are equal in rights, privileges and responsibilities upon the Christian Platform."[9] This sentiment echoed Adam Clarke's statement in his influential nineteenth-century commentary that "under the blessed spirit of Christianity, they [women] have equal *rights,* equal *privileges,* and equal *blessings,* and let me add, they are equally *useful.* "[10] By the end of Antoinette Brown's life, sixty-eight years after her ordination, there were over three thousand women ministers in the United States.[11]

Antoinette Brown was also supportive of the women's movement and was a close friend of feminist leader Lucy Stone—which association was made even closer when Antoinette and Lucy married brothers Samuel and Henry Blackwell in 1855. After her marriage, Antoinette had six daughters, wrote ten books, and continued to preach. From the beginning of the women's movement, Brown was an outspoken advocate for the view that the Bible upheld women's rights and that an anti-Bible stance would be counterproductive to the cause. She, along with other Christian feminists, encouraged the suffrage association to repudiate the theologically liberal *Woman's Bible.*

Frances Willard is especially notable for her involvement in both ministry and the women's movement. In her view, the same God called her to both, as she herself reports:

> While alone on my knees one Sabbath, as I lifted my heart to God crying, "What wouldst thou have me to do?" there was born in my mind, as I believe from loftier regions, this declaration. "You are to speak for woman's ballot as a weapon for protection for her home." Then for the first and only time in my life, there flashed through my brain a complete line of arguments and illustrations.[12]

As a Christian, Willard defended traditional morality and family-oriented values, and her leadership of the Women's Christian Temperance Union reflected these convictions. Willard referred to the WCTU as the "largest army of women inside the realm of conservative theology."[13] This two-million-strong army served to promote not only temperance, but also women's suffrage and other reform causes—always for the sake of "God and Home and Native Land."

When Dwight L. Moody asked Frances Willard in 1877 to work with him in his evangelistic campaigns, she was happy to oblige. Moody was not concerned about conservative reaction to her public speaking or her views on suffrage, but encouraged her to continue with both.[14] In fact, Willard was such a gifted preacher that she even won over some conservative evangelicals who were otherwise against women's rights. "Apparently Willard's preaching alone did much to cause Evangelicals to reconsider appropriate roles for women."[15]

Frances Willard wrote a defense of women's ordination in 1888 entitled *Woman in the Pulpit.* In it she carefully showed the inadequacies of the biblical exegesis of those who opposed public ministry for women. She also made a plea for the use of inclusive language in church services, complaining that preachers speak only to the men of the congregation and disregard the women. Like Free Methodist founder B. T. Roberts, who wrote *Ordaining Women* in 1891, Willard rejected the idea that the subordination of the wife in marriage is taught in Genesis.

Methodist lay evangelist Phoebe Palmer was the principal figure in the Third Great Awakening, or "holiness movement," which occurred between 1857 and 1859 and which gave birth to a number of denominations at the turn of the century. Assisted by her husband, Dr. Walter Palmer, she led revival services in the U. S., Canada, and England. During her work as a traveling revivalist, Phoebe Palmer wrote *Promise of the Father* to counter the attacks against her for having a "traditional male ministry" and to encourage other women to heed the call of God on their lives as well.

The Lord did use Phoebe Palmer to encourage Catherine Booth, who was moved by Palmer's preaching to repent of her own reluctance to speak and to acknowledge God's call for her to preach. It was well that Catherine Booth obeyed God's call on her life; "with her bright mind and powerful speaking abilities, Catherine Booth emerged as one of the most influential women in modern religious history."[16] She began her ministry traveling with her husband, "General" William Booth, but soon was in demand as a preacher in her own right. "In intellect she far excelled her husband's modest gifts; in preaching she exceeded his power of persuasion. . . . Many agree that no man of her era, including her husband, exceeded her in popularity or spiritual results."[17] Catherine Booth's role as cofounder of the Salvation Army served to establish in that organization a supportive stance for women in ministry; in 1934 her daughter Evangeline was elected to the highest office of general. Echoing many of Phoebe

Palmer's arguments, Catherine Booth wrote her own booklet in support of women's public ministry, entitled *Female Ministry.*

Amanda Smith, a woman who was born a slave, preached around the world during the holiness revival. She made a singular impression on Methodist Episcopal bishop J. M. Thoburn in India, who said, "During the seventeen years that I have lived in Calcutta . . . I have never known anyone who could draw and hold so large an audience as Mrs. Smith."[18] He also claimed to have learned more from her about Christian truth than from any other person. Despite the double-barreled prejudice she received as a black woman, Amanda Smith was faithful to God's call on her life, serving as a witness to the biblical truth that in Christ there is neither slave nor free, male nor female.

Evangelical Feminism at the Turn of the Century

The primary publication of the holiness movement, the *Guide to Holiness,* frequently upheld the rights of women in its pages. Characteristic was its objection to the conventional woman who "contents herself with shining, like the moon, with borrowed splendor, as the mother, sister, or wife of the great so-and-so. . . . She has left her talent in its napkin while she has been obeying the world's dictum by helping to make the most of his."[19] With convictions such as these and with leaders such as Phoebe Palmer, Catherine Booth, and Amanda Smith, it is not surprising that the denominations that grew out of the holiness revival began with a firm commitment to the right of women to preach. Early records of the Church of the Nazarene and the Church of God (Anderson, Indiana) indicate that twenty percent of the ministers were women. The original constitution of the Church of the Nazarene specifically allowed for women to be preachers.[20]

Seth Cook Rees, founder of the Pilgrim Holiness Church, was also strongly supportive of women's ministry. He wrote in 1897, "Nothing but jealousy, prejudice, bigotry, and a stingy love for bossing in men have prevented woman's public recognition by the church. No church that is acquainted with the Holy Ghost will object to the public ministry of women. We know of scores of women who can preach the Gospel with a clearness, a power, and an efficiency seldom equalled by men."[21] Early records of the Pilgrim Holiness Church indicate that in some sectors women constituted thirty percent of the ordained ministry.[22] Seth Rees's views on women did not preclude the denomination's identification in 1930 with the World's Christian Fundamentals Association, the principal organization of fundamentalism. This exemplifies the remarkable fact that, just a little over "half a century ago, a denomination could promote Fundamentalism while equally advocating women's public ministry."[23]

Seth Rees practiced what he preached and made a place for his wife Hulda as co-pastor and co-evangelist with him. Hulda Rees had been preaching since she was sixteen and was known as the "Pentecostal prophetess." Seth Rees's son, Paul, wrote of his stepmother, "Like Catherine Booth, she was a balanced soul in whom domestic virtues and platform gifts developed apace."[24]

A. J. Gordon, founder of Gordon College, published a treatise in 1894 entitled "The Ministry of Women," which supported women in public ministry.[25] Gordon based his argument primarily on the prophecy of Joel quoted in Acts 2 that "your daughters shall prophesy" (RSV). He believed that Pentecost signaled a new era of freedom in ministry for women. His emphasis on the ministry of the Holy Spirit was tempered by his insistence that any work of the Holy Spirit will always agree with God's inerrant Word. Gordon also noted the correlation that has occurred historically between spiritual awakening and an increase in the number of women in public ministry. Gordon's wife, Maria, was active in public ministry herself; she taught at the early Gordon Bible College and wrote her own defense of women's ministry.

A. B. Simpson, founder of the Christian and Missionary Alliance, also stressed the work of the Holy Spirit. In 1911 he wrote an article entitled "Our Mother God," in which he stated that "Jesus was not a man in the rigid sense of manhood as distinct from womanhood, but, as the Son of Man, the complete Head of Humanity, He combined in Himself the nature both of man and woman."[26] Such a view of Christ neatly disposes of one well-entrenched traditional argument against women in pastoral ministry, that only men can represent Christ as pastors because Christ was male. In rejecting the traditional notion that God is male or masculine, Simpson was not espousing a radical feminist goddess religion. He was simply pointing out that God is neither male nor female and can be likened to a mother as well as to a father. Simpson included women at every level of ministry in his organization. In 1887, women constituted half of all Christian and Missionary Alliance vice presidents.[27]

An important work defending women in public ministry, *God's Word to Women,* was written by Katharine Bushnell in 1919. Bushnell was a medical doctor and an evangelical reformer active in temperance and social work. When she felt the call of God to preach, she first began extensive research to determine whether or not the apostle Paul did in fact forbid women to preach. A scholar of Hebrew and Greek, she concluded after several years of study that male bias in translation and interpretation had yielded the traditional view that women were to be subordinate and silent in church.[28] Her scholarly, technical work was presented in a simplified, summarized form by evangelist Jessie Penn-Lewis in 1919, under the title *The Magna Charta of Woman*. Bushnell's study is prototypical of evangelical feminist biblical scholarship: it is grounded in careful study of the biblical languages and in the belief that the original manuscripts—not necessarily the English translations—of the Bible are inerrant and authoritative. As such, Bushnell's work has served as a model and inspiration for evangelical feminists today.

Lee Anna Starr, another scholar of Hebrew and Greek, published *The Bible Status of Woman* in 1926. An ordained minister with a doctorate in divinity, Starr was a local pastor and a temperance leader. The introduction to her book states that she was ordained by the Methodist Protestant Church, "a denomination which recognizes the mutual rights of men and women in the pulpit as well as in the pew, and whose ordination of Dr. Anna Howard Shaw . . . in 1880, gave to the Christian Church one of her most eloquent oracles. Dr. Starr occupies a place among the elect ladies of her denomination second only to that of Dr. Shaw."[29] *The Bible Status of Woman* makes a scholarly, biblical case for women's equality in both family and church. In her emphasis on Greek and Hebrew scholarship, Starr joined Bushnell in leading the way for later biblical feminist scholars to follow.

Around the turn of the century, both the Evangelical Free Church and the Moody Bible Institute were characterized by openness toward women's ministry—which appears all the more remarkable when compared with those institutions' views on women today. The original constitution of the Swedish Evangelical Free Church specifically provided for women preachers. Fredrik Franson, an early leader in this denomination, was an influential advocate of women in public ministry; he sent out women preachers and evangelists and wrote a defense of this practice in the booklet *Prophesying Daughters* (first published in 1890). Records of the early Evangelical Free Church of America list nearly fifty ordained women pastors and evangelists.[30]

At the turn of the century, the Moody Bible Institute (M.B.I.) accepted women as evangelists, conference speakers, and teachers of mixed groups. Female graduates of M.B.I. served as pastors in many different denominations. The official publications of M.B.I. routinely noted the work of these women. As late as 1929, women were allowed to graduate from the M.B.I. Pastor's Course. Catherine Booth preached twice at Moody Church. Although M.B.I. opposed the doctrine of healing of the Four-square Gospel Church's founder, Aimee Semple McPherson, it did not object to her role as pastor and evangelist.[31] As Janette Hassey notes, "it is obvious that Moody Bible Institute at the turn of the century trained and motivated women to publicly minister in Evangelical churches and applauded such efforts."[32] It was an example of "fundamentalist feminism"—a category that today would be considered an oxymoron but that a century ago was commonly accepted.

An article in a Moody Bible Institute publication in 1909 argued that a woman's highest call is Christian ministry, not the joys of motherhood.[33] The author objected to the common tendency of preachers "to emphasize that which is petty and small in woman's life" and to focus on "the effeminacy of woman rather than her humanity." Reminding her readers of the truth of Galatians 3:28, the author added, "it is eminently appropriate that I should say this from this platform, for if there was any thing for which D. L. Moody stood it was for this."[34] Clearly, today's *Moody Monthly* offers quite different fare for its readers!

A. T. Pierson, Presbyterian minister and close friend of A. J. Gordon, had similar ideas about woman's calling. He wrote in 1898 that he believed this to be "the day when godly women are first coming into real prominence as workers in the mission field at home and abroad, and when the sisterhood of the race seems to be for the first time mounting to the true throne of woman's influence and kingdom."[35]

Such writings from conservative evangelicals who consider woman's highest call and "true throne" to be Christian ministry rather than motherhood seem startling to those of us who are used to seeing the shelves in Christian bookstores crowded with how-to manuals instructing women to find fulfillment solely as wives and mothers. But Jesus himself—back in patriarchal Palestine—had ideas similar to these turn-of-the-century writers. Luke 11:27–28 records that a woman, full of the traditional belief that a woman's highest accomplishment in life is to give birth to an outstanding son, cried out, "Blessed is the mother who gave you birth and nursed you." Jesus corrected her, saying, "Blessed rather are those who hear the word of God and obey it."

The church at the beginning of the twentieth century, however, was not without its antifeminists who were so certain of the correctness of their interpretation of Scripture that they accused the feminist fundamentalists of denying the Bible's authority. But that accusation was as untrue then as it is today. Prior to and in the heat of the fundamentalist/modernist controversy (that is, the fundamentalist defense against modern biblical interpretation between 1900 and 1930), fundamentalist inerrantists could be found on both sides of the woman question. Although some feminists did deny biblical authority at that time—as some do today—the "fundamentalist feminists" did not. And neither do evangelical feminists today deny biblical authority. The issue today, as a century ago, concerns a difference in biblical interpretation, not a denial of biblical authority.

The Scofield Reference Bible, published in 1909 by one of the most adamant antifeminists of that era, acquired a stature among fundamentalist groups which rivaled that of divine inspiration. "Without a doubt, the attitude toward women's ministry expressed by . . . C. I. Scofield in his reference Bible notes directly influenced the Fundamentalist wing of early twentieth-century Evangelicalism."[36] The reverence for the Scofield Reference Bible continues even today.

Scofield held that, after the fall into sin, woman's condition was changed in the following ways: multiplied conception, sorrow in motherhood, and male rule. "The entrance of sin, which is disorder, makes necessary a headship, and it is vested in man," read Scofield's notes for Genesis 3:14–19. One consequence of this "headship," according to Scofield, is that women are to keep silent in church meetings.[37]

In grounding women's subordination in a view of the Genesis curse as normative, Scofield was fairly typical of traditionalist theologians prior to World War II.[38] Interestingly, this rationale for male authority has for the most part been superseded by the teaching that male rule was ordained by God at creation rather than at the fall. This more recent teaching is at once a stronger and a weaker case than the earlier one. It is stronger in that it grounds sexual hierarchy in the plan of God from the very beginning of creation. "The order of creation idea was clearly an intensification of the traditional notion of male and female spheres. Instead of basing women's status in the Fall and curse of Genesis 3:16, the newer theory rooted female subordination in creation itself. Thus, because they were created after men, women ranked below them in a divinely instituted hierarchy."[39] The weakness of the order of creation argument lies in the fact that there is no mention in the biblical text of male rule until after the fall.

Evangelical Feminism Then and Now

It should be clear to most observers that evangelical feminism does not enjoy the acceptance in today's fundamentalist and evangelical churches that it did in the churches of a century ago. "Of four institutions which mutually supported each other as well as women preachers at the turn of the century—D. L. Moody's Bible Institute in Chicago, A. B. Simpson's Christian and Missionary Alliance, Fredrik Franson's Free Church, and the Salvation Army—only the last today maintains its historical commitment to freedom for women in public ministry."[40] Donald Dayton laments, "What was no doubt the most massive effort to incorporate women into the life of the Christian church has faded away and today is not even remembered."[41] Even the Foursquare denomination, which was founded by a woman evangelist in 1921, has very few women in its pastoral ranks today. How easy it seems to be for the church to forget its heritage of evangelical women who took their places alongside men in pastoral leadership a century ago.

The reasons for this evangelical amnesia regarding women's role in the church are primarily cultural. As secular culture reverted to Victorian-era gender roles in the 1940s and 1950s, evangelicalism followed suit. "By World War II, *Moody Monthly* articles reflected the new image of God's ideal woman—no longer the Moody Bible Institute graduate who uses all her gifts for the kingdom, but the submissive, domesticated woman who knows her place."[42] Fifty years later, traditionalist evangelicals are holding firm to the conviction that a woman's "place" is in the home.

George Marsden notes that, at the end of the nineteenth century, a "sub-movement" in evangelicalism began to be male-dominated; evangelism came to be seen as a "masculine" activity and "was equated with power and action."[43] A concern grew over the numerical domination of female church members, especially in view of the belief that, as one writer put it in 1929, Christian orthodoxy is characterized by "a certain robustness which in its active aspect is essentially masculine."[44] Considerable discussion centered on the need for women to retire to the background and allow the men in the church to move to the forefront.

Strengthened by the growing cultural conviction of the 1930s, 1940s, and 1950s that the woman's role should be one of silent domesticity, this current in the church gradually overtook the attitude of openness to women's equality in ministry. The pastorate came to be seen as a man's job. A "masculine" church with a "masculine" God could only have male leaders, as John Rice declared in 1941.

> God is a masculine God. . . . God is not effeminate. God is not feminine, but masculine. . . . God did not intend a woman to be in authority over men. . . . Then do you wonder that in the modern sissified churches the average he-man will have no part? . . . [S]olid, masculine preachers with holy boldness and a

John the Baptist type of ministry, have no trouble getting a hearing among men today. The gospel is blood and fire and iron. . . . The pulpit is a place for the strongest men that we have.[45]

Rice echoed the sentiments of a number of evangelicals during these decades when he pronounced, "Feminism in the churches is a blight that has grieved God and made ineffectual his power. . . . [M]illions will go to Hell because of the unscriptural practice of women preachers."[46]

Whether or not women are granted equality with men in the church is often determined more by cultural and pragmatic considerations than by theological convictions. If men in the church perceive a need for women to serve in preaching and teaching roles, then women will be not only allowed but encouraged to preach. This is what happened in frontier America when revival's effects had not yet waned, preachers were in short supply, lay people were needed in active ministry, the work of the Holy Spirit was emphasized and respected as a validation of God's call, and denominations were in their formative stages. But when the demand for preachers diminished and church ministry became institutionalized, professionalized, and systematized, then women no longer had opportunity to fulfill their ministerial callings alongside their male counterparts. "The age of revival was gone, and with a return to 'business as usual,' the old prejudices against women began to surface."[47]

If women today were to assume pastoral leadership roles on the large-scale basis that they did eighty to one hundred years ago, it would upset the institutional apple cart. Most men in church leadership today perceive no need for women to preach the gospel. Along with all the emotional ties many men have to traditional gender roles—and the threat that shared leadership with women often poses to their sense of masculinity—there seems to be scant incentive for men to open the doors of the pastorate to women. The social climate in the evangelical church is simply not conducive to offering women equal status with men, and this in itself is sufficient to keep women silent and subservient. In determining who ends up on which side of the feminist divide, theology often takes a back seat to sociology.

The escalating internal contention in the contemporary church regarding points of legality on numerous issues—but especially the women's issue—seems to be symptomatic of a spiritual malaise. The body of Christ is like the body of a human being, in that its level of health can be measured by the degree to which it focuses on goals outside itself rather than on the functions and ailments within itself. Perhaps what is required to dissolve the dissension is less anxious arguing over exegetical technicalities and more earnest intercession for God to send revival again to his church.

History has shown that an outpouring of the Holy Spirit results in a church that is focused on the needs of the world and the sense of being called to meet those needs. A church in the midst of spiritual renewal has neither the time nor the patience for lengthy debates over which kinds of people should be permitted to respond to which kinds of calls to ministry. All are needed, and all who are called are sent. As Tim Stafford notes concerning the history of women's ministry in the nineteenth century, "Gender roles become less important whenever the church is outwardly focused. Few quibble about who does what when there is more work than all can do."[48] The connection between spiritual renewal and women in ministry was not lost on those evangelicals who were involved in the nineteenth-century revivals. A. J. Gordon wrote a century ago:

> It cannot be denied that in every great spiritual awakening in the history of Protestantism the impulse for Christian women to pray and witness for Christ in the public assembly has been found irrepressible. . . . Observing this fact, and observing also the great blessing which has attended the ministry of consecrated women in heralding the Gospel, many thoughtful men have been led to examine the Word of God anew, to learn if it be really so that the Scriptures silence the testimony which the Spirit so signally blesses.[49]

Would that "many thoughtful men" in the church today be led to do the same.

Traditionalism versus Evangelical Feminism: Two Traditions

Traditionalists criticize evangelical feminists for acquiescence to cultural conditioning; yet, as was discussed in earlier chapters, traditionalism is no less a culturally conditioned view than feminism. Few Christians, it seems, are aware of the impact of culture on their theology. Those who attempt to be "separate from the world" often end up only being separate from the contemporary world, while cultural values from the secular society of an earlier era are adopted without question.

The issue of traditionalism versus biblical feminism seems to many Christians to be so obvious as not to merit any further study: the traditional way is the biblical way, and biblical feminism is not biblical at all but a product of a contemporary secular movement. But an examination of these assumptions from a historical perspective shows that many elements of traditionalism are derived from nineteenth-century Victorian culture, while evangelical feminism is rooted in the evangelical revivals of the nineteenth century.

Antifeminists in the church today often speak as though the late twentieth century is the first time that the evangelical church has been influenced by feminism. They appeal to tradition as though prior to 1970 there had been an uninterrupted, monolithic evangelical consensus confining women to roles of subordinate domesticity. But as we have seen, the late nineteenth-century church's openness to women in preaching, evangelistic, and pastoral leadership ministries far surpassed that of the late twentieth-century church. Around the turn of the century, women in public ministry received support not merely from an individual here and there, but from entire institutions—and fundamentalist institutions at that.

It is clear that opposition to women's equality—especially women's right to preach and teach publicly—is *not* one of the historically unquestioned tenets of evangelicalism. It is also apparent that the church's move in the direction of evangelical feminism in the late nineteenth century was made feasible by the feminist movement in society at that time. Fueled by the Second and Third Awakenings and grounded in essentially biblical principles, this early feminist movement persuaded many in the evangelical church to reconsider the traditional role of women.

Today, when feminism is again encouraging some in the evangelical church to offer women equal ministerial opportunity, these evangelical feminists are being accused of corrupting the church with an anti-Christian, secular movement—a movement that dismisses biblical authority and traditional moral standards for sexual behavior. The antifeminist assumption is that any type of feminism must necessarily be fundamentally opposed to Christianity.

But the perspective from history should put the brakes on that line of argumentation. Although secular feminism is now largely anti-Christian, the basic feminist idea of equality for women is not *inherently* anti-Christian. Indeed, the secular feminism of the nineteenth century was as compatible with Christianity as late twentieth-century secular feminism is incompatible with it. Christians who believe in equality for women need not fear merely mimicking contemporary, secular culture. There is a sound, Bible-based, Spirit-led historical precedent for granting women equality with men, which included ordaining qualified women into public ministry in the evangelical church.

Early feminism laid the groundwork for understanding women's rights within a Christian context, wherein marriage is understood to be a monogamous, heterosexual, permanent relationship, and the two-parent family is viewed as the basic unit of society and the primary means of moral instruction to the young. In this respect, the theological roots of evangelical feminism are clearly in nineteenth-century evangelical feminism, born of the Second Great Awakening and grown to maturity in the burgeoning pastoral and teaching ministries of evangelical women at the turn of the century. For that matter, as historian Ruth Tucker notes, "well-reasoned books articulating Christian feminism have appeared since the Reformation. . . . Biblical feminism is not simply a by-product of secular feminism. It is deeply rooted in Scripture and has been publicly articulated for centuries."[50]

The theological similarity between the evangelical feminist biblical scholarship of today and that of the early twentieth century is one strong indication that evangelical feminism has a tradition dating back further than the 1970s. Contemporary evangelical feminism holds much in common with the aims of early feminism, but it shares very little conceptual ground with modern secular feminism. The charge that evangelical feminism derives from the largely anti-Christian modern feminist movement falls distinctly afield of the mark. The only causal connection that may legitimately be noted between evangelical feminism and modern secular feminism is in the fact that the late-twentieth-century cultural milieu of women standing up for their equality has provided opportunity and encouragement for evangelical women to do likewise.

A movement, of course, need not be consciously aware of its historical and ideological roots. In fact, the culture-shaping power of tradition characteristically goes unnoticed by those most influenced by it. Probably many evangelical feminists and most traditionalists are not aware of the historical origins of their beliefs.

If the roots of evangelical feminism go back at least to the nineteenth rather than merely the late twentieth century, then the roots of today's traditionalism—which are also in the nineteenth century—are no deeper. Except for its diligent preservation of the cultural heritage of male authority, the family model prescribed by today's traditionalists is no more worthy of the designation "traditional" than are the more flexible gender roles advocated by evangelical feminists. Both ideologies developed in newly industrialized nineteenth-century society in response to social conditions that prevailed at the time. Which, then, can best claim to be traditional—traditionalism or evangelical feminism? More to the point, which tradition is based on the ideas of secular society and which is based on biblical principles?

When we see the roles that culture, Christianity, and tradition have played in the historical development of these two views of gender roles, we see that evangelical feminism cannot be summarily dismissed as an off-shoot of the modern feminist movement, nor can traditionalism be automatically accepted as the model of family life espoused by the Christian church for centuries past. Reducing the issue to a simple conflict between biblical tradition and secular culture misconstrues the nature of the two views and deflects the discussion from actual ideas to superficial carica-ture. Keeping in mind a historical perspective on traditionalism and evan-gelical feminism should help us as we attempt to analyze the merits of ideas rather than emotionally react to the ethos of a "movement."

Modern Feminism: The Good News and the Bad News

The efforts of early feminism resulted in the removal of most of the legal inequities which had subjugated women for millennia. But some of the assumptions (prejudices) about women which had undergirded legal inequity have been retained in our social customs and in the thought patterns of many men and women. This seemingly inbuilt orientation toward oppressive inequality cannot be legislated away. Laws influence but do not determine social attitudes. There were, for example, a few exceptional couples in the nineteenth century who were committed to equality in marriage even though the law gave husbands the right to control their wives' behavior and property, just as there are some husbands today who control and dominate their wives even though they have no legal justification for doing so.

The Patriarchal Premise

The most helpful insight of modern (late twentieth century) feminism is that patriarchy—that is, culturally rather than legally instituted male domination of women—is at the root of women's traditionally subordinate place in society. Laws that favor men over women are themselves grounded in the cultural mindset that sanctions the rule of women by men. The belief that prejudice against women is based more on the patriarchal social system than on an inequitable legal system has set modern, radical feminism apart from earlier feminist thought.

Modern feminists have also pointed out that what is cultural is not necessarily what is natural. When traditionalists divide gender roles along lines of male leadership and female subordination, with men in the public arena and women in the home, they do so believing that such role divisions are *natural* and God-ordained and are the way things were meant to be. But feminists claim that such role divisions are based not on what is inherently natural for men and women, but on what has become *culturally normative*—and cultural norms have been determined by patriarchal social values.

The premise of patriarchy is that maleness is both normative and central in the human agenda; femaleness, by comparison to the male norm, is different and peripheral. Another term feminists use to describe the male-centered perspective of patriarchy is, appropriately enough, *androcentrism* ("andro" meaning male). A purely androcentric view of woman is reductionistic. A man needs a woman to do the one thing a man cannot do himself: bear his children. What only she can do, she must only do. This is woman's function; this is woman's only function. Few people overtly espouse such unqualified androcentrism. Most traditional ideas of woman's role are adaptations and modifications of the pure, patriarchal position. But the basic idea that man is primary and woman is secondary remains.

In keeping with the patriarchal premise, men traditionally have set the agenda for both men and women in society. A woman who falls in with this agenda will view her life as dependent on a man's and her identity as derivative from his. The feminist, however, refuses to accept, automatically and without question, the identity that patriarchal society has assigned to her. But in doing so she pays the price of being judged unwomanly or masculine. Such is the hold that the patriarchal premise still has over social attitudes—especially in conservative church circles.

Patriarchy is a self-perpetuating system, a machine that in operating generates its own power. Social supremacy is accorded men by society's male-dominated institutions of power. Men—like all humans—are sinners, and one trademark of sin is the mismanagement of power: once power is acquired, there is a strong tendency to guard it jealously, and with it to use powerless people for one's own benefit. People with power tend to interpret their power as self-deserved and to view the powerless as therefore undeserving of power—or of basic respect and dignity. The sinful urge to establish oneself as supreme is gratified by a system that continually rewards this bid for supremacy. Male prejudice against women is more tenacious than other bigotries because it is always being reinforced by the constant association of men with women, the social expectations attending that association, and the ingrained habit of many women to humor the male ego and to conform to male expectations. Traditionally, when men patronize or despise women they are socially rewarded for it.

Disagreement with most if not all of the radical feminist solutions to the problem of patriarchy should not prevent us from appreciating the insights that radical feminism offers concerning the nature of the problem. To acknowledge the patriarchal premise of traditional gender roles—and the inherent unfairness of these roles for many women—is not to subscribe to the reverse discrimination and the woman-centered ideology that many radical feminists propose as an alternative and that itself commits the same sins it seeks to redress in patriarchy. We can recognize the problem without accepting the feminist "solution" to it.

Patriarchy in Action

Patriarchy has been so pervasive throughout all of history and in nearly all cultures everywhere that it often and easily passes unnoticed. Like water to a fish, so is patriarchy to human culture. But a person has only to become aware of the patriarchal premise to see its multitude of effects in society.

A graphic example of the male-as-norm assumption can be found wherever a drawing of one person is used to depict a group of people. Invariably, that representative person will be male. Leonardo da Vinci's classic drawing of "man" is illustrative. The male is assumed to possess a sort of generic human identity, whereas the female has more of a sexual identity (probably because her primary function is seen to be her role in sexual reproduction).

The traditionally accepted generic use of male nouns and pronouns in our language serves as another example of the androcentric assumption. The word *man* can be used to represent all of humanity, both male and female, or it can be used to represent a specific male human. Yet, never can it refer to a specific female human. This in itself speaks volumes concerning the common assumption that the male human is representative of humanity in general, whereas the female is a sexual subspecies which deviates from generic "man."

Dutch theologian Abraham Kuyper views the Genesis creation account in this androcentric light. He says that Eve "embodied potentially all that is female," which he describes in terms of "dependence" and "susceptibility" to spiritual influences from both God and Satan (in other words, gullibility and vulnerability). But "Adam represented more. He embodied not only all that is male, but also all that is human."[1] Here in bold relief is the patriarchal assumption that the male is a human being and the female merely a sexual being, that the male is the standard model and the female somewhat deficient by comparison. To Kuyper's mind, the male-before-female order of creation serves as a paradigm that explains everything about the nature of men and women and the relationship between them. The sequence of first creation is not balanced by the observation that ever since Adam and Eve, man has come from woman—as Paul notes in 1 Corinthians 11:11–12. Nor is it balanced with the biblical teaching (Gen. 1:26–27) that woman and man are both created in God's image. Woman is not some less-than-human creature who derives from and depends upon man for her being; she too embodies all that is fully human. It is such teaching as Kuyper's to which secular feminists point accusingly when they wish to find something to blame for women's historically subordinate status in Judeo-Christian cultures. But the Bible itself cannot be blamed; rather, the error lies with the historically androcentric interpretation of what the Bible says about women.

My grandmother, a kind and devout Christian woman, wrote some wonderful memoirs of her childhood and family background. But the priority she gave to the men in her family is illustrative of the patriarchal premise she had unconsciously absorbed and internalized. She wrote more than ten pages about her father and grandfathers and their families. Embedded in the accounts of these men were a few remarks about their wives, which remarks together took up less than one page. The legacy of the Christian faith of her father and one of her grandfathers was noted with gladness, and the lack of faith in her other grandfather was deplored. But there was no word at all concerning the state of her mother's or her grandmothers' faith. In the patriarchal social system, the family is a father's legacy; as the old hymn puts it, our faith is defined in terms of the "Faith of Our Fathers." Women serve primarily as the means by which the family is perpetuated.

The patriarchal premise of the father's centrality loomed large in a Father's Day sermon I once heard. The pastor enumerated the characteristics of fathers which, when spiritualized, he said, provide a model of how both men and women in the church are to function in ministry. Topping the list was the father's reproductive function: fathers, he said, have the power of the seed, which is the power to beget life by depositing that seed in another person. This may be a good metaphor for what happens in spiritual ministry, but as an actual physical description of reproduction it is hopelessly archaic. Before twentieth-century studies in biology informed men otherwise, the widespread conviction—which served patriarchal purposes well—was that a woman's role in reproduction was merely to provide good "soil" in which the male seed could be "planted." The mother's equal genetic contribution to new human life was not acknowledged.[2]

This is compatible with the theme running through all patriarchal descriptions of gender roles—that it is the male role to create and the female role to nurture what the male has created. Despite its having been overturned by scientific fact, the old-fashioned understanding of human reproduction continues to serve as a paradigm for gender roles, even in the non-biological areas of life. The millennia-old myth that male power resides in the testicles[3] is evidenced in certain contemporary crass expressions used to describe the capabilities of men to accomplish a variety of feats unrelated to sexual reproduction. The male reproductive function is seen to afford man supremacy not only in reproduction, but in matters pertaining to every other area of human endeavor.

If fatherhood speaks of that which is active and life-giving, then the female role is clearly secondary and less significant by comparison. But—the preacher of the Father's Day sermon informed us—women can become fathers in a spiritual sense; they too can beget spiritual life in other people. A woman's spiritual goal, then, is to be like God made men to be. However, the idea that women must become like men in order to become more spiritual is not a Christian belief; it is, in fact, closer to Gnosticism.[4] The preacher of this sermon was not a Gnostic; he was simply a man who had not questioned the patriarchal culture in which he lived and had therefore assimilated cultural values that centralize men and marginalize women.

Medical research has exemplified this perception of women as peripheral. Although there is no denying the biological differences between the sexes or the fact that a medical procedure or drug may therefore have different implications for women's bodies than for men's, health researchers have nonetheless primarily studied men, preferring not to "complicate" their work with the more hormonally variable female body. But the judgment that women's bodies are complicated is based on the assumption that the male body is the norm. Women's bodies are considered complicated *as compared to* a "normal" human body. As one congressman observed, "It's not discrimination by intent, but it certainly is by result."[5]

This is the insidious nature of patriarchy. It affects us without our realizing it. The assumption of the-male-as-norm hangs in the cultural air we breathe. Like the pastor who preached the Father's Day sermon, we don't mean to discriminate; we just do it without thinking. Feminists have shown us that if discrimination and its effects are to be removed, it must be done so intentionally and with effort.

Now that the problem of male bias in medical research has been brought to light, a conscious and concerted effort is being made—spear-headed by women occupying top medical positions for the first time—to correct a situation that has potentially dangerous if not fatal conse-quences.[6] The problem has been made known, changes are being made, and women are in these top leadership positions precisely because mod-ern feminists have been so busy ferreting out areas of sexism in society and encouraging women to take places of leadership in the public sector. This is one result of modern feminism for which we can be grateful.

Faulting Feminism

Imagine radical feminism as a physician and society as a patient who throughout her life had been afflicted with a set of symptoms that greatly impaired her life and impeded her liberty. But because she'd had these symptoms all her life, she had simply adjusted to them unconsciously. Then her physician became aware of the symptoms, ran some tests, and diagnosed the patient's ailment. But the physician only partly understood the etiology of the disease, and all the patient's symptoms were attributed to a single cause. On the basis of this incomplete diagnosis the physician prescribed a remedy. However, the remedy was almost entirely wrong; so the patient, upon following the doctor's orders, found herself with a new set of symptoms that impaired her health and impeded her liberty also, but in a different way. Moreover, the newness of these symptoms made them much more difficult to cope with than the old, familiar symptoms. The pa-tient therefore found her physician to be deeply disturbing, first because the doctor pointed out an ailment of which the patient *had* been blissfully ignorant, and second, because the cure turned out to be scant improvement over the disease.

As traditionalists have been only too glad to point out, the cure that radical feminists have prescribed for the social ill of sexism has resulted in parents who are too busy with their own careers to care for their chil-dren, spouses who are too concerned with their own fulfillment to contin-ue to care for each other, legally mandated reverse discrimination (against men) in some instances, and a general disregard for the sexual norms with-out which no society can remain sane. We must therefore try to identify some of the strands of the rope in which our "liberated" society has en-tangled itself.

While early feminism failed to finish the job it began because it failed to recognize that the power of patriarchy was cultural as well as legal, mod-ern feminism has gotten off track by *overemphasizing* patriarchy's cultural power. Patriarchy has become the monolithic paradigm that explains all the woes of sexism. It alone is presumed to have set the entire course of social history. From the history of the world to the history of each individual woman, patriarchy's force is felt to the point of overriding all other formative factors. If there is any definition of sin in the radical feminist world view, it is patriarchy. Every social interaction involving both sexes is viewed through the lenses of male oppression. This position is simplistic, one-dimensional, and reductionistic. It is true, but it is not the whole truth. The element of male oppression is not operative in every situation, and when it is operative, it does not determine every outcome.

The radical feminist premise that patriarchy is the single foundation on which Western civilization has been built leads to the conclusion that Western civilization must therefore be forthwith overthrown. Again, the feminist diagnosis is only partially correct. Patriarchy *has* shaped the social structures of Western culture. But is patriarchy integral to the values and ideals of Western culture, or is it a persistent perversion of Western values and ideals? Perhaps prejudice has blinded Western society to the contradiction between its customs and its professed beliefs. This was the contention of the nineteenth-century feminists who sought to hold the legal system accountable to the idea that "all men are created equal." The Western ideal of individual equality has been instrumental, not only in America but in all of Western culture ever since the eighteenth-century Enlightenment, in establishing the notion of human autonomy and freedom. "Ironically, [modern] feminists tend to forget that the West, and the West alone, has evolved the standards of justice, equality, and individual autonomy by which they now measure their society, and claim to find it utterly wanting."[7] Western culture does not need to be overthrown; it needs to be set firmly back on its own track.

Patriarchy is indeed a force to be reckoned with. But other factors—social, intellectual, and spiritual—have helped form our society's good *and* bad aspects. Moreover, there are social and economic forces apart from simple prejudice that keep women out of the many traditionally male-dominated positions in society. Inequality of women's representation in certain fields is not always a simple result of inequality of opportunity.[8]

The radical feminist replacement of the classical liberal ideal of "equality of opportunity" with the modern ideal of "equality of outcome" is based on the assumption that sexism born of patriarchy is the *only* factor hindering women from having equal status with men in every social sphere. Because the problem is perceived as one-dimensional, so is the solution. If, for example, there are fewer women than men in certain occupations, it is assumed that this is simply because women are being discriminated against; the possibility that there might also be fewer women pursuing these occupations for other reasons is not considered. The solution proposed is therefore to legally mandate quotas of women employees in these positions. This so-called solution results in the passage of laws that, in attempting to remedy past prejudice against women, end up discriminating against men. Forcing equality in this way is premised on a simplistic analysis of the reason for inequality. It results in a perpetuation of discrimination (only now in reverse) as well as entirely new grounds for hostility between the sexes.

The cultural monolith of patriarchy is undeniably a factor in contributing to women's social subjection. But lobbying for governmentally-enforced equality of result as well as equality of opportunity is not the solution. Attitudes are the real problem, and attitudes cannot be legislated. To attempt to do so is to invite resentment, retaliation, and backlash; it is also to institutionalize injustice for those who are denied the "special rights" of the "oppressed."

The one-dimensional feminist diagnosis of prejudice caused by patriarchy has seemed to convince many women that, because they are victims of oppression, the world owes them compensation. They apparently believe the responsibility for their welfare lies with their oppressors, not with themselves. Victims are passive, defeated creatures. Even after they rise up in protest, they continue to acknowledge their oppressors' control of their lives by insisting that they can be liberated only if their oppressors liberate them. This victim mentality and the hostility it breeds undermines the struggle not only against sexism, but against racism and all oppressive prejudice. It changes the earlier feminist objective of women-as-equal-with-men to women-as-against-men. Women's rights are no longer seen simply as the rights of an individual in a free, nondiscriminatory society, but as the right of women as collective victim to exact recompense from the oppressors. Founding feminist Betty Friedan recognizes the imbalance in much of contemporary feminist thought. She believes it is time for feminism to "transcend sexual politics and anger against men to express a new vision of family and community. We must go from wallowing in the victim's state to mobilizing the new power of women and men for a larger political agenda on the priorities of life. We need to confront the polarization. We're at a dangerous time."[9]

In viewing male oppression of women as the one and only "sin," radical feminists discount the sinful human predisposition—common to both men and women—to engage in self-centered behavior when given the opportunity. Since women tend to be somewhat weaker than men physically and are especially at a physical disadvantage when bearing children, history has afforded them little opportunity to dominate men, while men have found and used much opportunity to dominate women. The bent state of the human condition ever since Genesis 3:16 targets woman as the victim of man's *rule*.

Radical feminism seeks to remove any and all opportunity for male oppression of women, including those opportunities which derive from biological differences in reproductive function. But because they have no true doctrine of human sin, these feminists have no explanation for *why* men nearly always have and nearly always will take advantage of the opportunity to gain supremacy over the women in their lives. Radical feminists simply believe that, in general, whether from cultural conditioning or congenital character deficiency, men hate women and are hopelessly power-hungry. There can therefore be no place for males in the feminist utopian agenda promoted at the radical fringes of feminism.

When radical feminists seek to replace androcentric society with a woman-centered social consciousness, it is clear that they have not acknowledged, much less repented of, the sin behind the sin of patriarchy—a sin to which both men and women are predisposed, and of which too many feminists seem to be guilty as they now try to establish dominance. Radical feminists have, to a large extent, politicized and institutionalized their resentment toward men. This is unfortunate for women as well as for men. "The welfare of one gender is linked to the welfare of the other. The exploitation and subordination of women has been a tremendous loss for men as well as for women, and the militant attack on men by women is a hollow victory."[10]

Dorothy Sayers spoke prophetically when she stated in 1938:

> It used to be said that women had no *esprit de corps*; we have proved that we have—do not let us run into the opposite error of insisting that there is an aggressively feminist "point of view" about everything. To oppose one class perpetually to another—young against old, manual labour against brain-worker, rich against poor, woman against man—is to split the foundations of the State; and if the cleavage runs too deep, there remains no remedy but force and dictatorship.[11]

It is clear that American society has done precisely what Sayers exhorted us not to do, and the foundations of this country have indeed been fragmented.

The Christian understanding of patriarchy posits not only a deeper cause—namely, human sin rather than male chauvinism—but a different cure than the secular view. Patriarchal prejudice can stop only when God—perhaps through the efforts of a dedicated minority—interjects his dynamic of grace, love, and forgiveness into the social system. Women must find encouragement in the Lord to realize their identity in Christ and their equality with men in Christ. They must then learn by the Spirit's tutoring to forgive the men who—whether wittingly or unwittingly—have prevented them from realizing that identity and equality. Men, for their part, must take a long and honest look at women and, with God-given empathy and love (the giving, not the desiring, kind), must begin to relate to women without condescension, preconceptions, or other behaviors of bigotry.

Modern Individualism

Much of the fault of modern feminism is not that it is feminist, but that it is modern. At the core of virtually all modern ideology is the creed of radical individualism. The individual—his or her rights, needs, desires, and so forth—is considered paramount and absolute. The individual's basic responsibility is seen to be to herself or himself, rather than to others. This consummate self-centeredness, in whatever sphere it is applied, inevitably results in the breakdown of friendship, marriage, family, community, and society. The problem inheres, then, not in the idea of women's rights per se, but in basing an understanding of women's rights on the humanistic world view of radical individualism.

The cultural trend in Western society has historically been toward free choice for the individual. This is justifiable in such areas as marital and vocational choice; people now can choose the marriage partner and the vocation to which they are best suited rather than having these choices made for them. As noted in chapter 3 with regard to nineteenth-century classical liberal thought, the goal has been to allow each individual the right to choose his or her life's agenda according to personal preference and aptitude. Social and economic opportunities should not be granted to one person and denied another because of race, sex, class, or family background, but rather because of a person's character and qualifications.

But classical liberal thought is a far cry from modern individualism, in which personal rights are lifted out of a social context and consensus and are accorded an omnipotence of their own. Modern society has shot way past—ironically, without ever fully attaining—the goal of simply removing prejudice from the list of factors determining an individual's station in life. Now, the individual—whether in radical feminism or in any other modern *ism*—has been cut loose from the moorings of universal moral law and exists instead in self-actualized autonomy in a relativized universe. The modern individual believes he or she has the right of unconstrained free choice.

When such thinking is applied to feminism, the will of the woman becomes the new moral absolute. Sociologist David Lyon observes that in modern feminism, "the sacredness of certain institutions is denied, and female human power is asserted as a new sacred."[12] This sacralizing of the feminine is seen most clearly in the radical feminist spirituality founded not simply on secular humanism but on the cosmic humanism of the New Age, which pantheistically declares the divinity of humanity—and, with a feminist twist, asserts the "divine feminine." But the absolutizing and deifying of female human power is reflected also in the "pro-choice" battle cry of mainstream secular feminism, which denies that modern woman has any claim on her life other than the mandate of her own fulfillment.

But personal choice is good only when it is justified; it is not an absolute good. When the right choice has been predetermined by universal moral principles, an individual's choice should be governed by those moral standards and not by personal whim. Both early and modern feminist thought are rooted in the conviction of the individual's right of free choice. But in appropriating the ideology of modern individualism, modern feminism makes personal choice an absolute good. The centrality of the individual woman's self-fulfillment overrides her responsibility for the consequences her choices may have for others. Indeed, part of the woman's right to choose is seen as her right to make choices that supposedly undo her earlier choices. So abortion and divorce stand by as ready options to "fix" the unhappy consequences of other choices made in woman's search for self-fulfillment.[13]

In asserting that whatever a woman wants a woman has the right to get, modern secular feminism "is itself the daughter of that male individualism which so many feminists are attacking."[14] As Elaine Storkey points out, "the desire for *self*-fulfillment, *self*-achievement, *self*-growth and *self*-service is what has produced chauvinism in men. For women to travel further down the same road can only make the situation worse."[15]

Not only has the situation indeed been made worse, undermining family and community, but a newly-created double standard has served to camouflage the real problem. Women are deemed selfish when they take time away from their families to pursue a career, but when men do the same they are socially rewarded for being "good providers." Yet those who pass these judgments fail to see that in many respects women have learned their "selfishness" from men who routinely push family responsibilities to the periphery of their lives. The problem is not simply that women have become self-centered, but that now there is a greater tendency for both women *and* men to put self-fulfillment before all else.

Sexual Liberation and Women's Liberation

In a sense, it is understandable that autonomous personal choice for women has been perceived as a woman's right to choose for herself everything men have traditionally had the right to choose. Since woman's position historically allowed virtually no choice over her own life, she has had only men to look to as models of free individuals. But the unlimited picking of fruit in the formerly walled-off garden of male prerogative is not an unmixed blessing. Some of the fruit is poisonous, most notably the practice of sexual promiscuity. Nineteenth-century feminists, for the most part, had the sense to realize that women's right to equality with men did not extend to the activities which were immoral and harmful for both men and women—and to which neither men *nor* women had any real right.

In "sexual liberation," modern women have simply asserted their "right" to sink to the same level of sin to which men have traditionally had the right to sink. This is equivalent to solving the inequity in educational opportunities for children by releasing them all from school. Yet nobody is foolish enough to regard the absence of the discipline of education as a privilege or a "right" for children; rather it is a deprivation for children to be allowed to wander about doing what they please and getting into trouble. Nonetheless, it is considered a liberty and a "right" for adults to be unconstrained by the discipline of sexual fidelity and to go about behaving as they please. No-fault divorce and legalized abortion are then required in order to cover the tracks of adults who are acting like children playing permanent hooky from school.

The modern ethic of "sexual liberation" has placed women in a position of even greater vulnerability to oppression and abuse by men. The availability of women for casual sex brings out the worst in men and offers the worst for women. Men at their worst view sex as an occasion for an ego-building assertion of male power and dominance, while women are more likely to view it as an occasion for love and intimacy. It is not difficult to see who gets hurt by this mismatching of motives. Clearly, "the 'dating game' as it is now played is rigged in favor of men."[16]

If men have abused women for millennia through the traditional practice of male promiscuity, then the solution is not for women to acquire that same vice. Practicing sexual sin is degrading and dehumanizing to all concerned, no matter who practices it upon whom. Feminists who advocate "sexual freedom" for women as well as men are simply playing into the hands of those men who seek irresponsible sex with any woman who is momentarily desirable. Now, women are still sex objects; they are simply more available than they used to be. Now, women as well as men—with the help of legalized abortion—are routinely denying responsibility for the children they unintentionally conceive. Now more than ever, a woman is a pawn in a man's world, a sex object whose use is dictated by the male rules of the sexual game.

Although the casual approach to sexual behavior may come more easily for men than for women, this does not mean that this is how men *ought* to think or behave sexually. It may be "natural," but it is an element of the male sinful nature, not the male nature that God intended at creation. So when women attempt to adopt the "male" style of predatory and licentious sexuality, they are behaving in a way that is not only unnatural for women, but wrong and harmful for *any*one, regardless of how easy or difficult it may be.

In order for the "sexually liberated" woman to mimic the traditional male idea of sexuality, she must, of course, have recourse to abortion on occasion. So the woman is doubly hurt; she is hurt by those men who are more interested in sexual conquest than sexual intimacy and responsibility, and she is hurt when she perceives as necessary the violation of her own body and the killing of her own offspring in abortion—simply to be like men sexually. The woman who does not resort to abortion may wind up with a brood of fatherless children who require her financial support; she too pays a higher price for her sexual "freedom" than is ever exacted from the "sexually active" male. In sexual liberation, only lust has been liberated; women have remained enslaved.

Why then has sexual promiscuity for women as well as men been hailed as liberating? Germaine Greer's *Female Eunuch,* written in the early years of the modern feminist movement, offers a clue. She observes that traditionally men have garnered to themselves the right and reputation of sexual initiation and desire and in doing so have "castrated" women. (It should be noted, however, that the tradition of the "female eunuch" is not longstanding. Prior to the nineteenth century, there was a strong historical tendency for men to view women as evil seductresses intent on consuming men with their lust.)[17] Greer further observes that men have acted out their corner on the sexual energy market by reducing women to sex objects, engaging in promiscuous sex, and viewing marriage as a means to furthering their own personal success.[18]

The interpretation Greer and other feminists have given to these observations seems to be that, because men behaved this way sexually *and* held the reins of society, male social power was derived from male sexual power. (Men at times seem to espouse this view themselves.) Women therefore had but to claim the sort of sexual power and prerogative traditionally exercised by men, and they would have in their hands the reins of society as well. But once modern women laid claim to their own sexual energy, they proceeded to misdirect and abuse it even as so many men traditionally have done, and with consequences every bit as ruinous not only for society in general but also for women as individuals.

It is no wonder that in the past decade many feminists have come to recoil in disgust from all sexual relationships with men. But these feminists have failed to discern the root of the problem. Instead of recognizing that modern, "liberated" male/female sexual relations are based on false assumptions about the nature and purpose of sexuality, they have declared that heterosexuality is inherently oppressive to women. But heterosexuality per se does not oppress women. Rather, irresponsible and self-centered heterosexual behavior—promoted by sexually "liberated" feminists—has itself sabotaged the feminist goal of liberty and equality for women and has replaced it with more oppression.

Choice, Equality, and Reproduction

Within a relatively short period of time, women's vocational options have gone from being unrealistically limited to being unrealistically open. No longer having only one option in life, women now supposedly have their choice of any and all options. Women's "right" to abortion on demand has achieved top priority in the modern feminist agenda because it is viewed as necessary if women are to have no limitations imposed on their vocational (or sexual) opportunities. It is the only surefire way to guard against a woman being unwillingly derailed from her vocational pursuits and eliminated from the competition in what is still a man's world—a world that offers no pause for pregnancy on the race track to success.

But both role prescriptions—whether of no vocational choice or of absolute vocational choice—are unfair to women because they do not comport with reality. The former role prescription denies the reality that some women are not suited to a vocation of homemaking. With reasonable adjustments in society and in their own families, such women ought to have opportunity to pursue their gifts and callings in the world even as—although perhaps not always to the degree that—men do.

The latter role prescription denies the reality that woman's childbearing function inscribes on her at times a bottom-line limitation. A woman who chooses to reproduce probably will have—at least initially—more constraints on her personal freedom and vocational options than will a man who chooses to reproduce. A woman who chooses to have sex without choosing to reproduce is taking a greater risk than a man who makes this choice. A woman who divorces is likely to be more financially encumbered and limited than is a man who divorces, because she is more likely to have custody of the children and less likely to be prepared to earn a living. Most significantly, the idea of a woman's right to unfettered personal and vocational choice (which abortion is seen to ensure) denies the reality that an innocent human being—such as an unborn child—has an automatic and absolute right to life, which right takes precedence over a woman's right to vocational choice.[19]

Modern feminism's apparent blindness to these bottom-line realities has marred the movement so significantly that many have decided that the entire idea of women having vocational options and equal rights with men is ridiculous. Their conclusion then is that we ought to return to the days when every woman had but one job—to tend to her home, husband, and children. However, the problem is not with the idea of equality for women, but with a misapplication of equality. Women *are* equal to men in many areas where they have traditionally been denied expression of that equality (such as intellectual pursuits and leadership), but they are truly unequal in one area in which modern feminism is striving to make them equal (namely, reproductive function). Choices for women ought to reflect the reality of where equality does and does not exist.

It should be noted, however, that to admit the "inequality" of male and female reproductive roles—in that these roles are not reversible but are inherently different—is not to assert the inferiority of one sex and the superiority of the other. In one sense, a pregnant woman, all other things being equal, will be "inferior" in her ability to compete in the "man's world" of work. In another sense, a woman's reproductive role is "superior" to a man's; the ability of her body to grow new human life is in fact openly envied by men in some cultures (and is probably secretly envied by most men in most cultures).

Traditionalists magnify woman's biological sexual/reproductive difference to such an extent that it becomes a paradigm for woman's entire life. The "baby maker" view of woman excludes her from other human activities for which she may be suited. Modern feminists, on the other hand, advocate the "right" to abortion (absolute reproductive control) in order to prohibit woman's biological difference from ever impinging uninvited on any woman's life. Modern feminists want to remove all biological limits. Traditionalists want to add cultural limits to the biological limits and to inscribe them with the created "givenness" of biology. Woman's cultural inequality then translates into her inferiority in that it entails her subordination to male rule. The truth of the matter, though, is that biology *will* impinge, but biology is not destiny.

"Pro-Choice" Is Anti-Woman

Not only is abortion immoral, its practice actually serves to undercut the feminist concern that women be treated with respect and integrity. Abortion does not equalize the unequal; it destroys the unequal. It destroys both women and unborn humans, as well as society's valuation of human life in general, and children's lives in particular. In making abortion the centerpiece of the agenda for women's rights, modern secular feminism has quite possibly been sowing the seeds of its own destruction, and not only because it has thereby set off a powerful, antifeminist backlash among people who are pro-life. Even more significantly, modern secular feminism is self-destructive because abortion is inherently demeaning to women. It does not free women, it keeps them subject to the androcentric agenda.

The modern feminist advocacy of "abortion rights" is self-defeating and logically inconsistent in many ways. For one thing, as noted in chapter 3, it deviates from the early feminists' belief that abortion serves as a means of male oppression against women and their children. Tim Stafford notes that, although most Protestant churches did not take issue with the increasing number of abortions in late nineteenth-century America,

> The rising feminist movement was against abortion. Not even the most radical considered abortion to be an instrument of freedom for women; on the contrary, abortion was understood to be an aspect of male domination, whereby (outside marriage) men tried to conceal the results of their seduction, or (inside marriage) women behaved tragically because of the terrible conditions of a home governed by a tyrannical husband.[20]

The general consensus of nineteenth-century feminists was that the practice of abortion allowed and encouraged men to perpetuate their abuse of women as sex objects.[21] This clear insight into the misogynistic aspect of abortion has been completely lost on modern, mainstream feminists, who nonetheless bill themselves as the faithful followers of those early feminists.

Moreover, abortion is undeniably an act of violence, and feminists, on the whole, deplore the "male" means of problem-solving whereby the powerful exact violence against the powerless. Yet mainstream feminists unhesitatingly advocate the violent destruction of the powerless unborn as a solution to the problem of an unwanted pregnancy. Many advocates of abortion rationalize that the unborn baby is not an individual with rights but is merely part of the mother's body—over which she has absolute right of ownership. Such an argument slides glibly over the distinction between being *part* of the mother's body and being *in* the mother's body; the latter does not necessarily entail the former. But even according to the (false) definition of the fetus as merely part of the mother's body, abortion must be seen as an act of violence that a woman perpetrates against her own body, bringing a brutal end to a natural bodily process that would otherwise bring new life to birth.

Abortion rights have in large part been advocated in order to compensate for the effects of women's sexual "freedom"—which, as we have already seen, devalues rather than liberates women in that it plays along with the way in which men have sexually used and abused women for centuries. The abortion/sexual liberation ethic effectively renders irresponsible sex more easily attainable and less problematic for men. Those men who engage in such behavior cannot help but be pleased. Not surprisingly, a 1990 Gallup poll showed single men to be more consistently pro-choice than any other group. Women, however, were more likely to be pro-life than pro-choice.[22] As one pro-life feminist points out, "The pornography industry's glorification of unfettered sexual satisfaction cannot be underestimated as a contributing factor in the repeal of laws protecting the unborn." So pleased have pornographers been with the abortion solution that they have become major financial contributors to the cause.[23]

When feminists declare that women's only hope for freedom and equality is to have the opportunity to abort all unwanted unborn babies, they are essentially giving in to the androcentric agenda that accords men the right to impregnate women but absolves them of the responsibility to care for their children. The abortion "solution" agrees that men are not responsible for the children they conceive and, moreover, declares that neither are women. Abortion not only kills innocent human life; it keeps the players in the male game playing. It is essentially women's white flag of surrender, saying, we can't beat them, so we have joined them.

Patriarchal society has long deemed the tasks of bearing and caring for children an exclusively female problem. Pregnancy may cause a woman to lose social or financial standing, but the father of the child is rarely affected adversely. After the child is born, the responsibility remains with the mother; the father's involvement is optional. The abortion agenda perpetuates these cultural assumptions by legally making the child entirely the property of its mother. This not only gives her the right to destroy her child, it entirely relieves the child's father from all parental obligation. If the father has no claim on or rights to his child *before* it is born, he can quite easily and logically abdicate responsibility for his child *after* it is born.

Insisting that every woman has a *choice* whether to continue or to terminate a pregnancy has the same effect. On this basis, the father of an unplanned-for, unborn child can disavow all responsibility to both woman and child other than to offer to pay for an abortion. If the woman refuses to abort her baby, then it is deemed entirely her choice to have the child and consequently entirely her responsibility to care for the child. The pro-choice argument subverts the feminist ideal of co-parenting, which is based upon the conviction that the father's duty to care for his children is no less than the mother's. Women will never enjoy equal vocational opportunity until men are willing to assume equal parental responsibility. Again it is apparent that the "abortion rights" agenda ultimately undermines the cause for women's equality.

Nonetheless, mainstream feminists doggedly insist that women have no hope of equality or justice unless they have the "right" to destroy their unborn offspring at will. Such thinking is a capitulation to a society structured according to the assumption that only those who conform to the traditional male lifestyle are really free to pursue their own desires and vocational goals. But to the extent that women measure their liberty according to how closely they are able to approximate this lifestyle, they seek a false equality. They seek to be like men where they are not like men, and such an endeavor can only injure women, because it denies part of their essential identity.

The abortion "solution" simply submits to the cultural assumption that woman's work is worth less than the work that men do; that, indeed, a woman's work is valued only to the extent that it mimics that which traditionally has been called men's work. And this, of course, leaves no room for the task of childbearing. Pregnancy is quintessentially woman's work and therefore not valued, supported, or rewarded.

A career woman who becomes pregnant must survive simultaneously in two worlds—the "man's world" of work and the woman's world of childbearing. The abortion option stands at the ready, not because she is a liberated career woman, but because—her womanhood being devalued— she is required to be just like a man in order to remain in the world of work. The people who determine whether she will be promoted or demoted, retained or let go, reason that because she *could* choose abortion, her pregnancy is entirely her choice, her problem, for which she and she alone must pay the price.

Because the world of work outside the home was initially designed to suit the lives of men with "full-time wives," and because such men are concerned with neither pregnancy nor childcare, there is simply no room in the system for women with these concerns. But room needs to be made. Thanks to the abortion mentality, women suffer today, not because they are not allowed into the system, but because they must deny their womanhood in order to be allowed to remain in the system. Women are not given opportunity to do their work as women, but only as surrogate men.

This is not liberation or equality. It is plain, old-fashioned sexism in a new guise, and the implementation of "abortion rights" is its primary proponent and perpetuator. Although this new sexism allows women to be the same as men where they are the same (in their ability to make valuable contributions to society in both private and public arenas), it does not allow women to be—or value them for being—different where they are different. The male is still the norm, and woman is still less than man. Her difference is her deviance—a "problem" that abortion "solves."

In the old sexism, women were encouraged to marry and bear children, but they were allowed *only* to bear children; their other abilities were denied, and they were barred from significant contribution to society in other respects. Their womanhood denied them equality. Now, "equality" has denied them their womanhood. Womanhood is still deemed less valuable than manhood, in that whenever its functions are operative a woman loses her "equality" and may feel she needs to resort to abortion, the final "solution" in a society that devalues both women and the human beings they bear.

The Oppressed Have Become the Oppressors

Two decades of legalized abortion have not succeeded in according women justice in society. Rather, the devaluation of human life that is basic to the abortion ethic—and, indeed, to all forms of bigotry and injustice perpetrated by one group of people against another—has increasingly poisoned every aspect of society. The rate not only of abortion but also of divorce, child abuse, rape, and other forms of violence committed by humans against other humans has been on the rise. This is the abortion culture, in which human life is devalued and therefore deemed disposable—able to be sacrificed on the altar of the needs and desires of the more powerful. The abortion agenda shares with sexism, racism, and all types of prejudice a profound lack of concern for the powerless, unprivileged members of society.

The objective of any legitimate movement for equality is to equalize an unjust (undeserved and unjustifiable) relationship of inequality between two classes of people by endowing the underprivileged class with the basic human and civil rights enjoyed by the privileged class. This inevitably results in the loss of many of the privileged class's privileges, because those privileges were maintained by the denial of equal rights to the underprivileged class. White people, for example, no longer have recourse to easily available and underpaid domestic help. This is because black people have been accorded some of the basic human and civil rights enjoyed by white people. The subjugation of all black people was too high a price to pay for the privileges it offered white people.

Feminists employ the same logic with regard to male privilege and female subordination. For example, a man whose wife is suited for activities other than childcare and household service ought to pitch in and contribute to these tasks so that she can devote some of her time to other concerns. This is considered a trade-off which helps equalize that which would otherwise be inequitable.

But mainstream feminists today have established, for the sake of their own privilege, a state of inequity between women and the unborn. The class of unborn humans has been stripped of all inherent rights, beginning with the most basic—the right to life. This class of humans is entirely at the mercy of the privileged class, in whose bodies they reside. If the privileged class wants them to live, they are cared for with the same respect and concern for their health and well-being that anyone on the other side of the womb receives. But if the privileged class does not desire them to live, they are poisoned and/or torn asunder. This is the worst sort of oppression any class of humans could possibly inflict on another class of humans. The idea of "abortion rights" is premised on the same principles of prejudice and oppression that "justify" the actions of any privileged class that devalues, for its own purposes, the powerless members of society. Yet it is done in the name of women's equality. The cause, purportedly, is justice and liberty for the oppressed.

Feminists object to the traditional valuation of a woman according to the desirability of her body or the usefulness of her services to some man;

rather, feminists insist, a woman has intrinsic value that exists independently of male approval. Yet most modern secular feminists judge the unborn by the same sort of standard with which men have traditionally judged women. The unborn child is "allowed to live or die on one criterion, its sentimental value to its mother."[24] Apart from its desirability or usefulness to its mother, the unborn baby is granted no value, no rights, no life of its own. The rationale behind a woman's right to abortion bears an ominous resemblance to the traditional rationale for male supremacy and female subjugation.

Pro-choice feminism also holds in common with ancient patriarchy the belief that one sex has absolute power to determine for both sexes which of their offspring should live and which should die. The male head of a household in ancient Rome, for example, had the legal right to kill unwanted or unhealthy infants in his own household.[25] Now modern feminism has secured for women absolute power over the life and death of their own young. The child is seen as belonging exclusively to its mother, not also to its father, to its grandparents, to God, or even to itself—just as the patriarchs were accorded the right of exclusive ownership of children born in their households.

The "abortion rights" agenda fights inequality of one form with inequality of another. In shooting at one double standard it uses another double standard as a weapon. It fights for rights for one class by denying rights to another. It is founded upon the social injustice it seeks to destroy—and thereby effects the preservation of injustice rather than its destruction.

When women advocate abortion as a solution to unplanned pregnancy, they are succumbing to the ever-present danger of the oppressed: as they become liberated from their oppressors, they become like their oppressors and thereby abdicate their hard-won liberty from systems of injustice. When the oppressed appropriate the ways of thinking by which their oppressors justify oppressive actions, surely the effect will boomerang; those who seek liberation will wind up reinstituting their own enslavement.

The Social Dynamics of the Abortion Debate

The abortion debate ranges amidst a complexity of confusion. Feminists advocate abortion on demand as a "right" essential to woman's liberation, failing to perceive that it is not anyone's right to kill unborn humans nor is it likely to liberate any women to do so. Traditionalists, on the other hand, speak out against abortion from the basis of their conviction that motherhood is every woman's highest calling and abortion is a denial of this calling—missing not only the point but also the audience.

Whatever the value of motherhood—whether it be woman's highest calling or woman's greatest nuisance—no pregnant woman has a carte blanche right to kill the innocent human life within her body. Even if the "right to abortion" were a necessary prerequisite for woman's liberation, no woman would be justified in purchasing her freedom at the cost of innocent human life. The traditionalist insistence on the joys of motherhood and the feminist insistence on women's rights both sidestep the central question, which is whether or not the fetus, as a developing human, has an inalienable right to life, which it is the duty of the mother—and the rest of society—to protect.

Unfortunately, pro-life arguments ring hollow to feminists when they issue from people who *are* against the idea of women's equality—and not just in the area of reproductive function (where women really are not equal) but also in areas such as vocational opportunity and intellectual aptitude (where women ought to be considered on an equal basis with men). It is easy for traditionalists to oppose abortion. This stance poses no threat to their agenda; they have nothing to lose. In their perception of feminism as adamantly opposed to motherhood, and in their consequent failure to show any sympathy for the cause of women's rights, traditionalists virtually invite pro-choice feminists to deflect the argument from the real issue and argue instead about women's rights.

So the strident cries of both camps drown out the central question, and the debate focuses instead on the perceived consequences of the two possible answers to the question, namely, traditional motherhood versus liberated womanhood. To compound the irony and confusion, it seems to escape everyone's notice that traditional motherhood is not a necessary consequence of prohibiting abortion, nor is it likely that legalized abortion will result in women's liberation.

A much more effective pro-life strategy would be to point out clearly and insistently that legalized abortion never has liberated women and never will liberate them—that, in fact, the practice of abortion perpetuates women's oppression and precludes true gender equality. Pro-choice people must be made to see that abortion is wrong—not because it is a means to women's liberation, but because it is a hindrance to women's liberation. They must be made to see that abortion is unjustifiable even as a "woman's right," that fighting for the right to abortion is like fighting for the right to shoot oneself in the foot.

In basing the pro-life argument primarily on antifeminist objections to abortion, pro-lifers have not only missed their audience, they have provided ample opportunity for pro-choicers to caricature them as narrow-minded bigots. Pro-life activists ought instead to find some common ground with their opponents—a concern for the legitimate exercise of women's rights, for example—and to make their case from this premise. Then the pro-choice contingent would be forced to confront its flawed rationale for "abortion rights" and to engage in productive debate rather than slogan-saturated name-calling. The pro-life movement needs to develop a convincing *public* voice—a rhetoric appropriate for the marketplace of ideas.[26]

It would be to the advantage of both pro-lifers and feminists to initiate and develop social reforms and services—such as crisis pregnancy centers—that would encourage and enable women to choose life for their unborn children. This was the goal successfully pursued by American pro-life advocates and feminists in the nineteenth century.[27] Modern feminists need to realize—as did their nineteenth-century foremothers—that promoting the quick fix of abortion does not advance the cause of women's equality. They would better serve the needs of women by working to create a society that not only respects women as persons—who, like men, have a variety of vocational abilities to offer the world—but also respects women's unique gift of bearing new life. Such a society would accommodate women in their role as mothers rather than punish them vocationally, economically, and socially when pregnancy occurs.

Abortion is not a solution to women's social inequality. The fact that it is perceived as a solution is itself an indication or symptom of women's inequality, the perpetuation of which abortion encourages rather than eliminates.

Varieties of Feminist Thought

The critique of feminism in the preceding chapter focused on secular radical feminism because it is the dominant type of feminism at present—or at least is what everyone tends to think of upon hearing the word *feminism*. But all secular feminism is not radical; there are other feminist theories about the reason and the remedy for women's long history of subjugation by men. And all radical feminism is not precisely secular; there is a religious wing to radical feminism which proposes a spiritual solution to patriarchy.

The distinctions between the various types of feminism can be seen in terms of the metaphor presented in the last chapter, whereby feminism is a physician and society the patient. The patient's set of symptoms is observed and deplored by all feminist physicians. All models of feminism take unhappy notice of unjust and inequitable attitudes and behavior toward women as compared with men. But the feminist diagnoses differ. The liberal feminist, in the tradition of nineteenth-century classical liberalism, diagnoses the problem as legal inequity that favors men and denies women equal rights and opportunities. The psychoanalytic feminist locates the cause of woman's subjugation in the development of the female psyche that occurs during early childhood. Both the diagnosis and the cure prescribed by psychoanalytic feminists involve a reinterpretation or revision of Freudian psychoanalytic theory. The Marxist feminist ascribes all societal ills—including the subjugation of women—to economic inequity and oppression occasioned by capitalism. And the radical feminist diagnoses society's primary ailment as patriarchy, wherein male behavior that takes advantage of the biological (reproductive) differences between men and women has become culturally institutionalized. Patriarchy, according to radical feminism, is not simply women's problem; it is the fundamental flaw of society, the most basic form of oppression from which derive all other oppressions (racism, classism, and so forth).

A Selection of Feminist Remedies

The prescribed feminist cures differ also, following as they do from the differing diagnoses. Adding to the variety is the fact that many feminists employ an eclectic approach and combine aspects from different diagnoses and cures. It should also be remembered that the remedies prescribed by different types of feminism do not *necessarily* follow from the diagnoses. There are, for example, better cures for the "disease" of patriarchy than those offered by radical feminists.[1]

The liberal feminist seeks to ensure that the law provides equal rights and opportunities for both men and women, in order that gender not be a basis for legal discrimination. The emphasis is on achieving equal rights and legal parity between the sexes. "Gender justice, insist liberal feminists, requires us, first, to make the rules of the game fair and, second, to make certain that none of the runners in the race for society's goods and services is systematically disadvantaged; gender justice does not also require us to give the losers as well as the winners a prize."[2] As was mentioned in chapter 3, this was the primary approach of the early feminists in the nineteenth and early twentieth centuries. Liberal feminism seeks to work within the existing social/political system in order to secure legal equality for women. It does not aim to overthrow the social systems of patriarchy or capitalism, nor does it succumb to the utopian and conspiratorial tendencies of woman-centered radical feminism. It does not point to the "class" of white males as the source of all social oppression, nor does it base its policies on a view of women as an oppressed class. Liberal feminism focuses more on the rights of people as individuals than on the rights of people as members of a class or group.

Liberal feminism essentially consists of an application of the precepts of liberalism to the cause of women's rights. But liberalism has changed a great deal in the last century. Whereas classical liberalism strove to achieve civil liberty for all individuals, modern liberalism attempts to achieve economic justice for society. Thus, in modern liberalism the role of the government is expanded to include the responsibility for ensuring not only legal equity but economic equity for its citizens. Most liberal feminists today espouse a modern view of liberalism; this naturally affects the type of laws that they seek to implement. It also creates an overlap between the political activism of modern liberal feminists and that of less-radical, radical feminists, both of which seek to create a political system that will break up the stranglehold on positions of power that culture has bequeathed to men. The goal is to distribute social power equally between men and women. These two categories of feminism together compose what I refer to as mainstream feminism, the influence of which has been conspicuous and considerable in American society over the past three decades.

Betty Friedan is probably the best contemporary representative of liberal feminism. The progress of her feminist thought—as of liberal feminism in general—has moved from an initial classical liberal orientation toward a more modern liberal approach. The National Organization for Women, which Friedan helped found, could also be identified with modern liberal feminism.

Many who today would be called conservative or neo-conservative are, for the most part, in line with the classical liberal thought of a century ago. There are traces today of a type of feminist thought which, like its nineteenth- and early twentieth-century predecessor, is emphatically pro-family in its goals and ideals. As a reviewer of two recent "conservative feminist" or "neo-feminist" books noted, the debate over the women issue is "now being joined by conservative women, and suggests a new phase of feminism, one that conducted properly could end by strengthening the family."[3]

The psychoanalytic feminist prescription seeks to remediate the psychological consequences that various traditional social customs tend to have on women's sense of self and/or social status. The emphasis can go in a number of different directions, but in general the remedies recommended include shared parenting and equal participation with men in the work force. Carol Gilligan's work in women's morality has made her one of the more popular proponents of a psychoanalytic approach to feminism.[4]

The Marxist cure for society awaits the revolution, which will result in the abolition of capitalism, the governmentally-sponsored redistribution of wealth through socialism, and eventually—theoretically—the utopian state of communism.[5] As for women, the prescription is employment, through which economic power is gained. The economically dependent homemaker is definitely not an option. As in all types of secular feminism, Marxist feminism fails to acknowledge the primary causative factor behind the oppression of women, namely, human sin. Gender inequity is not a product of capitalism, but is in part due to the self-centered, power-hungry men who make use of the capitalist system in order to keep most women—and as many men as possible—in a place of servitude. Because it misdiagnoses the cause of sexism, the Marxist remedy does not offer women liberation from oppression. Women in the Soviet Union, for example, were no more liberated than women in capitalist countries—especially since Soviet women were obliged to work full time *and* take full responsibility for the household. (Governmentally-imposed redistribution of wealth is not usually accompanied by the redistribution of housework among family members.)

Marxist feminism as a pure breed of feminism is less popular than it used to be. However, Marxist ideas have been combined with radical feminist ideas—and, to some extent, with the concepts of psychoanalytic feminism—to create a "hybrid" feminism referred to as socialist feminism. In fact, there is a fair amount of hybrid thought among feminists. Feminism is a protean and multifaceted movement, and classification systems can only paint a picture of the conceptual landscape with very broad strokes. The divisions between different types of feminism are permeable, and there are no hard-and-fast categories by which feminist theories can be easily and exhaustively identified.[6]

Radical feminism offers a variety of cures for the systemic disease of patriarchy. The cure most commonly associated with this branch of the movement is political. Unlike classical liberal feminism, which also prescribes a political cure for gender inequality, radical feminism—along with modern liberal feminism—insists on equality not merely of opportunity, but of result. Merely having the laws on the books is not enough. Therefore, the court system is utilized to ensure that equality for women is not just an opportunity but a reality. Practices such as preferential hiring and reverse discrimination are upheld as means of enforcing equality in the workplace.

Because the radical feminist diagnosis points to the biological differences between men and women, which men have used to subjugate women, many of the legal provisions sought by radical feminists attempt to remove the physical limitations inherent in women's biological (reproductive) differences. Thus, issues such as legalized abortion, governmentally-sponsored day care, and maternity work leave are paramount on the radical feminist political agenda. The latter two items are moving toward the forefront as mainstream feminists seem to be backing away from the 1970s' feminist focus on competing for economic parity with men in the workplace, and are turning toward motherhood as part of the package of fulfilled womanhood.

This emphasis on governmentally-ensured equality is consistent with the policy of the political left to rely on the government to solve all social problems. It is also consistent with radical feminism's diagnosis, which is that the reason for women's subordination goes beyond inequitable laws to the patriarchal social system. Therefore, more radical measures are called for than the simple legal equality of opportunity prescribed by classical liberal feminism. In a sense, radical feminism demands that the losers as well as the winners receive a prize.

More recently, some of the more radical feminists have been spearheading changes in laws concerning rape, sexual harassment, and pornography. These legal efforts are premised on a radical feminist analysis of sexuality, which holds that patriarchal values have conspired to associate male sexuality with violence and dominance and female sexuality with gentleness and submission. For many radical feminists, the power imbalance in sexuality is perceived as foundational to the power imbalance in society. This inequity is seen to require radical legal redress at the most basic level. Radical feminist efforts at legal reform can include setting up different standards of judgment for women (which are more favorable to women than the earlier, "male" standard), as well as re-making laws more in the image of woman than of man (i.e., conciliatory and relational rather than aggressive and competitive).[7]

Although some would classify any feminist effort toward political change as an element of liberal feminism, there do seem to be different premises behind the political endeavors of liberal feminism and radical feminism. Liberal feminism—whether classical or modern—seeks simple legal reform within the existing legal system. Radical feminism seeks radical change of the legal system in an effort to extirpate what is perceived as inherent androcentrism in the law. One way to generalize and simplify the difference would be to say that liberal feminism attempts to implement laws that ensure socioeconomic parity between women and men, while radical feminism aims to create a legal theory that grants special rights and/or consideration to women as a class.

Radical feminists, however, believe that "it is not just patriarchy's legal and political structures that must be overturned; its social and cultural institutions (especially the family, the church, and the academy) must also go."[8] This emphasis on abolishing the foundational institutions of society finds expression more in radical feminist scholarship than in political activism. Radical feminist theories concerning the root causes of women's oppression, and the way of their liberation from that oppression, vary widely and range across all academic disciplines.

Woman-Centered Feminism

A more extreme remedy for the disease of patriarchy, which has been prescribed by many radical feminists within the last decade, discards the mainstream feminist prescription for creating a society of gender equality through governmental intervention. Its proponents despair of ever attaining such a goal. They believe Western society cannot be cured of patriarchy; its condition is terminal. The solution is to hasten its demise and, in the place of androcentric society, to build a gynocentric, or woman-centered, society.

Initially, the focus of radical feminist scholarship was on the biological origins of women's oppression, but it is now moving toward an analysis of the gender system—the patriarchal system of socially constructed gender roles which restricts women's freedom and for which, it seems, there is but one remedy. The entire system must be uprooted and overturned. Women's reproductive capacities are being viewed less as a source of oppression and more as a means of liberation—provided women's reproduction is controlled by women and not by men, as in the patriarchal past. This recent emphasis on and advocacy of women's "motherly" nature reflects the radical feminist move away from androgyny as a solution to gender inequality, and toward a revaluation and/or redefinition of femininity or femaleness.

Clearly, the focus here is not on working within the system to reform it, but on working outside the system to destroy it. The goal is to replace male (androcentric) culture with female (gynocentric) culture. Gynocentric feminism is premised on the idea that human behavior, knowledge, and consciousness are determined primarily by gender. Effort is therefore made to structure society according to the basis of women's experience, which is perceived as radically different from the male consciousness which forms the present basis of society.

The traditional, patriarchal perspective consigned woman to the category of the "Other"; she was objectified by and separated from the male perspective.[9] Woman-centered ideology has taken this view and turned its implications upside down. Let woman be other than and outside of the male perspective. Who wants to be like men anyway? Women will structure society along the lines of the female perspective. Or so the reasoning goes. The traditional womanly traits of gentleness, cooperativeness, and motherliness are superior to the male traits of violence and competitiveness. Women ought therefore to develop and to emphasize their distinctive and superior womanly traits. (Note that the positive aspects of the female stereotype are contrasted with the negative aspects of the male stereotype.) Woman-centered feminism is expressed in various areas of feminist theory, including sexuality, academia, and spirituality.

Lesbianism has become for many woman-centered feminists a self-consciously public, political statement of a thoroughgoing rejection of men and the patriarchal society they have created. "But lesbianism is not merely a defiance towards male domination, the 'rage of all women condensed to the point of explosion.' It is also a belief that only women can give to each other a real sense of self, of personal identity."[10] This belief is premised on the idea that heterosexual relationships invariably tend to serve men and subjugate women. As one lesbian feminist theorist explains, "To survive in a misogynist environment, a woman must learn how to protect innate female power from a society designed to destroy it," and lesbian relationships are more likely to protect and less likely to destroy this "innate female power." But for heterosexual women, "the predicament is this: what kind of intimate, individual relationship is possible between the oppressor and the oppressed?"[11] Most woman-centered lesbian feminists, however, do not insist that all feminists become lesbians, but that heterosexual women accept and affirm lesbianism as a legitimate, or perhaps preferred, avenue of self-expression, especially for women who have been so emotionally wounded by men that no other option for close personal relationship seems possible.

Woman-centered feminism as expressed in lesbianism—and other denials of maleness or perceived maleness—is feminism without forgiveness. Since forgiveness is a central operating principle in biblical faith, this kind of feminism is antithetical to Christianity. The Christian response to such extreme, radical feminism should be neither to jeer at nor to join up with these women, but to do some hard thinking about the patriarchal premise—present in both church and secular society—that has caused these women to feel it necessary to take such a stance.

Academic Feminism

In the university setting, the radical feminist critique is directed against the traditional academic curriculum because it is based on Western civilization, which is considered incorrigibly male-biased, androcentric, and logocentric. Woman-centered feminist scholars (or, academic feminists) are not content merely to balance out the male-oriented curriculum with the female perspective. These feminists "call not only for a radical re-ordering of society but an epistemological revolution, i.e., a revolution in knowledge itself, which would extirpate masculine bias, replacing the 'male-centered curriculum' with a new curriculum inspired by a radical feminist perspective."[12] Academic feminist Alison Jaggar declares, "We are developing a whole reconstruction of the world from the perspective of women with the key word being 'women-centeredness.'"[13] In most universities, this gynocentric agenda dominates the Women's Studies departments and is influential in the humanities and sciences as well.

The central premise of woman-centered feminist scholarship is that gender itself is a force of cosmic proportions that fundamentally and profoundly affects every area of life, including the theoretical and scientific concerns of Western scholarship. Men and women think differently, it is supposed, and these differences fall along the traditional lines: men are objective and logical; women are subjective, relational, and intuitive. What is non-traditional here is that subjectivity and intuitive thought are valued more highly than objectivity and logical thought. Feminist sociologist Cynthia Epstein disputes this view:

> Many of the new feminist scholars have brought vision and criticism to their disciplines, resulting in corrections and additions to the work in their fields. But it would be difficult to note anything particularly "female" about the techniques women have been said to offer, such as affiliative, qualitative, and intuitive approaches. . . . [N]o evidence indicates any differences between men and women in styles of thought. . . . These theories and proposals for a particular women's methodology have the same flaws as many of the perspectives feminists have deplored. They imply that all women are essentially similar in psyche and behavior and that all men essentially think and behave alike, regardless of race, historical period, class, education, occupation, or marital status.[14]

It is not clear from academic feminist theory how these totally opposite, gender-specific ways of thinking have come about. The traditional, patriarchal view, of course, is that these alleged differences are innate, and that the male way of thinking is superior when it comes to scholarship. But academic feminists seem to lean toward the idea that these differences are an outgrowth of cultural gender roles; different experiences have shaped different thought styles in men and women. If this be the case, however, it would seem not to require that the male way of thinking give way in academia to the female way of thinking. Women's experience, after all, is rooted in cultural oppression and inequality. Once women are given an equal status in society with equal educational and vocational opportunity, shouldn't the gender differences in ways of thinking equalize as well?

It is also not clear how academic feminists can blame the discrimination against women in Western scholarship on male "objectivity." As Cynthia Epstein comments, "I must admit I am not altogether clear about this reasoning, but I certainly do not believe it was 'objectivity' that impaired the work of male scientists studying women" in the past. "Rather, I believe the work suffered from the subjectivity of biased, largely male, scientists."[15]

Having asserted that women think differently and find the male way of thinking alienating, academic feminists go on to say that the "male perspective" of the androcentric gender system distorts all Western scholarship. Patriarchy is deemed not only fundamentally wrong, but fundamentally determinative of *all* values and knowledge in a culture so characterized. Academic feminists therefore reject the traditional, Western approach to knowledge, which is grounded in the belief that reality is objective and available for anyone to study and know through the usual means of human perception and cognition. Such "cognitive rationality, both epistemologically and methodologically, is now declared to be part and parcel of an androcentric ideology of science."[16] In the academic feminist criticism of Western scholarship, there is more than a trace of the postmodern disdain for "logocentrism" (the valuing of logic as an objective tool for discerning truth and the nature of reality).

The idea that knowledge is determined by the sex of the knower rather than the object of knowledge leads to the idea that reality is not known purely and objectively, that there is no real object of knowledge. Reality comes to be seen as nothing more than a social construct—which feminist scholars seek to deconstruct and reconstruct according to the standard of women's experience. The purview of this reality reconstruction encompasses not only the university curriculum but all of Western society as well.

Such a goal is a far cry from that of classical liberal feminism, which sought merely to give women a voice of significance in society and had no thought of destroying Western civilization in order to do so. But apparently, woman-centered feminists believe that, since gender is the single most important factor determining human experience, woman's voice can be significant only in a society that she herself has created.

Pagan Feminist Spirituality

Radical feminists who seek a spiritual cure for the culturally instituted oppression of women look to the ideals of woman-centered feminism for their salvation, rather than to orthodox Christianity. In this revolutionary feminist spirituality, all ties with Christianity are severed and the Bible is condemned as without redeeming value. Because this is the most extreme and obviously anti-Christian variety of feminism, it is this to which antifeminist Christians frequently point when they wish to discredit the entire idea of women's rights. But radical feminist spirituality is as different from the women's rights propounded by classical liberal feminism as it is from biblical Christianity. Using such feminism as a "straw woman" to shoot down any and all brands of feminism is fallacious and unfounded.

Theologian Mary Daly is representative of this branch of feminism, in which the only sin is sexism, the only sinners are men, and the only means of salvation is gynocentric feminist spirituality. According to Daly's post-Christian feminist theology, the Bible and its God are hopelessly patriarchal. Pagan feminist spirituality calls for women to engage in a spiritual revolution and, from the perspective of their own woman-centered religious experience, to rename God, themselves, and the world. In this radical redefinition of religious reality, men (who are inferior) have no significant part to play.[17]

Keying in to the resurgent paganism and pantheism of the New Age movement, feminist spirituality asserts a gynocentric cosmology of the goddess, who is the personification of the "divine feminine" immanent in all women and in nature. Some outspoken proponents of goddess religion, such as the author Starhawk, define this divine woman-power as the power of witchcraft. Belief in the cosmic goddess is frequently bolstered by speculation that in prehistoric times women ruled in a peace-loving, equalitarian society and people worshiped the earth goddess instead of the distant, patriarchal "sky-god" of Christianity.[18] It may seem contradictory to assert equalitarianism in a society in which one sex is dominant over the other, but apparently the idea is that because women are cooperative, peaceful, and relational in their leadership style, whereas men are competitive, warlike, and power-hungry, a society can be fair and equitable only if men are kept out of power.

Radical feminist theories concerning prehistoric societies cast feminist witchcraft and goddess worship as a return to the true beginnings of human history. Patriarchy is deemed merely a long and tiresome chapter in the history of a cosmos which is intrinsically and originally feminine in essence. Female authority has been usurped by men due to Judeo-Christian meddling with the ancient order of the universe. Men are cruel, violent creatures undeserving of power; the same goes for the "male" God of Judeo-Christian religious belief. Woman's claim to rulership, then, is rooted in the radical feminist belief in the "divine feminine" within every woman, even as man's claim to rulership in patriarchal society is rooted in the traditional belief in man's resemblance to the "masculine" God of the Bible.

This modified pantheistic faith in the goddess within all women is clearly seen as subverting and overturning biblical Christianity, as is evident in the following statements by neo-pagan feminists. "We women are going to bring an end to God. . . . It is likely that as we watch Christ and Yahweh tumble to the ground, we will completely outgrow the need for an external God."[19] Particularly chilling is the assertion that "there is power in the blood of the woman."[20] Herein is truly the spirit of antichrist (see 1 John 4:1–6).

Errors in Feminist Spirituality

The world view of pagan feminist spirituality offers a spiritual outlet for the deep rage of women who have reached the limit of their tolerance for patriarchy and all its cultural, personal, and interpersonal effects. But it is premised on at least five major errors. First, the oppressive social system of patriarchy did not originate with the Judeo-Christian tradition, nor can blame for patriarchy be attributed to the God of the Bible. Feminists assert that men have derived their chauvinism from the ultimate male chauvinist, the patriarchal God of the patriarchal Judeo-Christian religion. But the reverse is the case. Male supremacy took hold independently of biblical revelation, and then men interpreted biblical revelation in light of male supremacy. As Faith Martin explains:

> The patriarchal structure was established throughout the Near East long before Abraham. . . . Although each society [at that time] had its own peculiarities and customs, they were all organized around one single universal rule: male ownership of property and male ownership of the female. . . . God did not direct the establishment of the Hebrew patriarchy—he qualified, reduced, and would eventually eliminate that society.[21]

Patriarchy was so pervasive that the Israelites would have been incapable of even conceiving of a society that was not ordered along patriarchal lines; certainly they could not have handled a command to construct a society that would be fundamentally at odds with all they had ever known to be true about social interaction. H. R. Rookmaaker points out that in regard to women's roles, God's method of progressive revelation utilizes the principle of "evolution, as opposed to revolution." Freedom and justice for women could not be enforced "at one stroke. Real change takes time, for it involves not only outward obedience to a law, but a change of mentality and attitude. Without an altered mentality, sinful men will only find ways to circumvent the laws and make the situation even worse."[22] Because of this, God's law for ancient Israel was adapted to the patriarchal cultures of that time. God did not invent nor did he sanction patriarchy. Rather, he allowed for and accommodated to it, even as his law made allowances for the hardness of the human heart (Matt. 19:8)—from which patriarchy derives in the first place.

The Old Testament narratives of women being treated more as property than as persons, even to the point of being brutalized and dehumanized, do not indicate that God approves of these events, but merely that they happened. As Gretchen Gaebelein Hull puts it, the biblical account of a patriarchal society is "a true record of a false idea."[23] We do not see God's mind concerning women's worth in those places in the Bible which merely record "normal" patriarchal social interaction. Rather, we see God's mind in those places where God clearly deviates from the patriarchal norm, such as when he authorizes the woman to have equal authority with her husband over their children (Lev. 19:3; Deut. 5:16; 21:18)—a practice that runs contrary to the absolute rule which the patriarchal father normally exercised over both his wife (or wives) and children. (Incidentally, this also runs contrary to the popular evangelical teaching on the "chain of command" which grants the man ultimate and final authority over the children.) We also see God's mind concerning women when he raises up a woman named Deborah to be the chief executive (judge and prophet) over Israel. She was both the spiritual and military leader of the nation. This occurrence was not an exception that proved the rule; it was an event that abrogated the patriarchal rule. Clearly, Deborah was put in her position of authority by God himself, and God does not make exceptions to his own law.

But the clearest indication of God's mind on the matter of women is evident in the incarnate Word, the Son of God, Jesus Christ. His compassionate, iconoclastic treatment of women was nothing short of astonishing, even to his disciples. At a time when women were not taught theology or even addressed by men in public, Jesus discussed theology with a woman at a public well—and then authorized her to preach his word to others (John 4:7–26). At a time when a woman's sole purpose in life was to be a mother, Jesus declared that hearing, learning, and obeying the Word of God was more important for women to do (Luke 11:27–28). When Jesus had dinner at the home of Mary and Martha (Luke 10:38–42), he again broke patriarchal custom by declaring that it is better for women to do what culture *prohibited* them to do (learn about God and the Scriptures) than to do what culture *required* them to do (serve the men who lived in and visited their homes).

Jesus Christ as God Incarnate also demonstrates that the God of the Bible is no distant and haughty patriarch in the sky. Far from holding himself aloof from humanity, God showed his compassion and loving identification with humanity by becoming a human, living with humans, and dying on behalf of humanity. "Greater love has no one than this, that he lay down his life for his friends" (John 15:13). God (in Christ) made us his friends and then laid down his life for us. The idea that the Christian God is an aloof and pompous patriarch who is totally transcendent over and separate from his creation is a diabolical distortion of clear biblical truth.

God *is* transcendent in that he is distinct from, other than, and sovereign over his creation. He is infinite; the created world is finite. However, God is not *wholly* other, nor is he completely removed from us. God is also immanent in that he has committed himself to a covenant relationship with his people, the terms of which he has himself communicated to us. God speaks, acts, helps, and heals on a moment-by-moment basis; he is deeply and lovingly involved in human life. As Paul pointed out to the Athenians, "God . . . is not far from each of us. For in him we live and move and have our being" (Acts 17:27–28).

Radical feminists tend to think of the biblical God in human terms and to assume that, since he claims to have all power, he is power-hungry and tyrannical—as he surely would be if he were merely human. To the feminist, God's claim to ultimate power coupled with his claim to be Father adds up to a God who is just like any human father whose patriarchal power has made him a domineering autocrat.

God *is* a patriarch in that he has all power and his authority is absolute. But God the Father is not like human patriarchal fathers: being righteous, he not only deserves his authority, he uses his power lovingly and wisely. His will is for our good. He has no "male ego," and his power is not grounded in maleness.

This brings us to the second erroneous assumption undergirding the radical feminist rejection of Christianity. Objections to Christianity on the grounds of its "male" God pervade the radical feminist project. But the biblical God is not male; he is not sexual. Whenever men have claimed supremacy on the basis of the belief that God is male, they have done so in profound and thorough error. Elaine Storkey points out that the problem feminists see with the fatherhood of God exists

> because of a flaw in the logic of the initial argument: the equation of God's Fatherhood with maleness. For although to be an earthly and human father is to be undoubtedly male, it does not follow at all that to be God the Father is

to be God the Male. God is neither male nor female. Sexuality is a characteristic of creaturehood. It is something which God has *put* into creation. It does not follow either that because God *created* sexuality he must be sexual, any more than because he created time he must be temporal.[24]

Why, then, is God revealed through the biblical writings more often in terms descriptive of fatherhood and masculinity than of motherhood and femininity? In order for God to reveal himself to people in a patriarchal culture as a being who is not only personal but absolutely powerful, the image of father was more appropriate than that of mother.

Moreover, a Mother-God would have tended to imply a sexual nature to God and would have evoked associations with the pagan goddess worship of surrounding cultures. It should be noted that these ancient cultures, while involving goddess worship, were nonetheless patriarchal. The image of a fertility goddess derived from the patriarchal view of woman as primarily sex object and procreator. W. A. Visser't Hooft points out that the modern feminist search for "feminine spirituality" in a revival of ancient goddess worship is misdirected:

> In the nature religions, women were not respected as persons, but regarded as the source of mysterious sexual power. . . . The battle fought in biblical times between faith in a personal and holy God and the worship of the goddesses of fertility is not just past history, but has validity for us today. . . . [W]e need the dimension of transcendence with its criticism of the closed world of the fertility religions, for it is precisely this transcendence that brings liberation.[25]

It was essential that Israel's understanding of *their* God be distinct from their understanding of the fertility goddesses of the neighboring nations.

Yet, despite the logic behind God's revelation as Father rather than as Mother, it should be remembered that the Bible does depict God in motherly, feminine imagery. God is portrayed as a mother who gives birth and who nurses and comforts her children (Deut. 32:18; Isa. 42:14; 46:3–4; 49:15; 66:13). Jesus likens himself to a mother hen (Matt. 23:37).

Third, the historical evidence for a primordial, universal goddess religion is dubious at best. Prehistory, after all, is just that; it concerns a time prior to known history. It is difficult enough to reconstruct events of the past even with the help of written records. Without such records, knowledge of history is bound to be more conjecture than fact.[26]

Fourth, the spiritual power that radical feminists draw upon—having rejected the true and holy God as a patriarchal myth—derives from unholy spiritual beings. Some feminists do acknowledge their religion as witchcraft, but they see it as a force that is creative and life-giving, rather than evil and destructive as witchcraft has traditionally been perceived to be. But such radical feminists are radically deceived. There is only one kind of witchcraft and spiritual power apart from the God of the Bible—that which derives from and serves the great deceiver, Satan. The Bible warns against the spiritualism of pagan practices and beliefs in Deuteronomy 18:9–13 and reminds us in 1 John 4:1–6 that we ought not believe every spirit, because not all spirits are from God.

Fifth, women are not superior to men any more than men are superior to women. Most brands of woman-centered feminism are based on the assumption of women's superiority to men, from whence derives women's right to put men in their place (although just where that place is has not been clearly elucidated). Here again—as in the modern feminist advocacy of sexual and abortion "rights"—is the tendency of the oppressed to become like their oppressors. But male chauvinism is no justification for an equal and opposite error on the part of women. Matriarchy is no solution to patriarchy. Both retain the root of the problem, which is the usurping of power by one sex over the other.

Feminism in Liberal Theology

Pagan feminist spirituality, or revolutionary feminist theology, is exotic and attention-getting, but it is a minority element within radical feminist theology. Far more representative is reformist feminist theology within the liberal theological tradition. With its understanding of the Bible as essentially advocating human liberation, theologically liberal feminism seeks to interpret Scripture according to the experience of women as an oppressed group. In this sense it is a form of liberation theology, which began out of concern for the poor in Latin America and has also been extended to blacks and other oppressed groups. Theologian Donald McKim notes, "Like other forms of liberation theology, feminist theology is a protest against traditional forms and methods of doing theology."[27] Unlike Mary Daly's revolutionary feminist theology, its protest does not entail a wholesale rejection of the Christian tradition; certain elements are retained, and the Bible is considered authoritative in a qualified sense.

In keeping with the radical feminist diagnosis of patriarchy as the cause of women's subjugation, liberal feminist theology rejects the biblical passages that are deemed patriarchal and retains as authoritative those which are considered representative of the overall biblical message of human liberation. Both revolutionary and reformist feminist theology share with traditionalist theology the belief that the Bible in places teaches patriarchy; the difference, of course, is that the traditionalists like it that way and therefore deem those texts normative, while the feminists dismiss the alleged patriarchal texts as culturally anachronistic.

Theologically liberal feminism dates back to nineteenth-century feminist Elizabeth Cady Stanton, who edited and contributed to *The Woman's Bible*. This two-volume work (published in 1895 and 1898) compiled comments from feminist women on passages of the Bible that were deemed of particular interest to women. The hermeneutic behind this work differed at several key points from that of the more standard evangelical feminist approach of that time. Most importantly, the contributors to *The Woman's Bible* held that the message of the Bible itself was tainted with the sexist views of the men who wrote it. Contrary to the more commonly-held evangelical feminist view, these women believed that the problem went beyond male-centered translation and interpretation. Misogyny was seen to be inherent in the text itself.

It would follow from this perspective that the Bible cannot be viewed as wholly authoritative and an infallible standard of truth. Like any other book, the Bible falls short of the truth in places, due to the cultural limitations of its authors. It contains some good and true insights, as well as some false and harmful ideas. It is up to the feminist critic to determine which is which.

But if the Bible is just like any other book in this respect, then why exert so much effort dissecting and discussing it? Simply because, Stanton explains, "the Bible has a numinous authority" for many men and women. "If feminists think they can neglect the revision of the Bible . . . then they do not recognize the political impact of Scripture upon the churches and society, and also upon the lives of women."[28] In other words, because so many benighted souls view the male-centered message of the Bible as authoritative, the Bible's message must be critically assessed and revised so as to correct for its intrinsic misogyny. Feminist theologians in the liberal tradition reason along similar lines today. The editors of *The Women's Bible Commentary*—the title of which "pays tribute to Elizabeth Cady Stanton's pioneering work"—state in the introduction that "the Bible has been one of the most important means by which woman's place in society has been defined," and that this is one reason why the meaning of biblical texts must be assessed "from a self-consciously feminist perspective."[29]

The crucial distinction between conservative (evangelical) and liberal biblical interpretation is likewise the crucial distinction between evangelical feminism and liberal feminist theology. The keystone is the view of Scripture. Evangelical biblical scholars—feminist or otherwise—view the biblical message as both objective and authoritative. The true meaning of any biblical text is grounded in the intent of the biblical author and exists independently of the reader's perception of it. The goal of biblical interpretation is to approximate as closely as possible the true meaning of the text, because it is this meaning that is God's authoritative word to every believer. While the practical application of the meaning of a particular biblical text may change over time, the basic meaning of the text—rooted in authorial intent—is not altered by the circumstances of the interpreter. Evangelicals differ in their interpretations, due to differences in their preunderstandings and particular methods of interpretation. But evangelicals will never be found arguing for the relativistic view that one interpretation is as good as another.

By contrast, the hermeneutic of liberal theology, including liberation theology, is grounded in a person's or group's experience or consciousness. Preunderstandings are regarded not as a hindrance but as a legitimate element of the exegetical task. The meaning of any given text is subjective—determined in "conversation" between text and reader. It is thus likely to vary depending on the time, place, and persons involved in the interpretive process. Because interpretive results are different for each interpreter, and because there is no right or wrong way to approach the Bible according to liberal theology, the sense in which any biblical text is deemed true and authoritative depends on the view that each reader or group of readers takes of it. Authority is thus vested more in the world view or preunderstanding of the interpreter(s) than in the biblical text itself. In liberal feminist theology, the interpretive process is guided and determined by the concerns and experiences of women.

As Sharon H. Ringe explains in *The Women's Bible Commentary*, "There is no single 'correct' or 'acceptable' way to work, but what should be kept in mind is that the various approaches [to biblical interpretation] yield different results or conclusions."[30] The purpose of feminist biblical studies, then, is to reach an interpretation that reflects "the voices of poor women and rich women, white women and women of color, single women and married women, women from one's own country and from other parts of the world, lesbians and heterosexual women."[31] The goal is not to ascertain the objective sense of the text, but to attain a subjective sense of the text which resonates with the views and experiences of its female readership. The modern hermeneutic of liberal theology lends itself well to the agenda of feminist theologians who frankly seek to use the Bible to support their feminist beliefs.

Keying in to the subjective, person-relative approach to biblical interpretation is the belief of liberal feminist theologians that there is a thoroughgoing difference between women's and men's approaches to Scripture and to spirituality. If men's understanding of spirituality is fundamentally different from women's, then a book about spirituality written entirely by men—such as the Bible—necessarily will present only a "male" version of spiritual reality. In order to be compatible with women's spirituality, such a document must be revised and reconceptualized from a woman's point of view.

The idea that men and women understand Scripture and spirituality differently can be held in various degrees of extremity. In moderation, this notion is harmless and can even be helpful. Certainly, women bring to their understanding of the Bible some life experiences that are quite different from men's experiences, and this can create some variations in the ways men and women tend to approach biblical material. But these gender differences are not so radical as to render men's ideas about spirituality irrelevant to women, or vice versa. The human commonality between women and men, especially in the spiritual dimension, is far greater and far more fundamental than the sum of their differences, and it is to this basic human spiritual dimension that the Bible speaks.

It is true that both women and men need to be involved in biblical interpretation and exposition, in order that the church not be unbalanced in its approach and favor one sex over the other. Women as well as men should have opportunity to teach and to be taught the Word of God. But the main problem with biblical interpretation having historically been the exclusive domain of men is not simply that the Bible has been understood from a male perspective, but that it has been understood from a male-*centered* perspective. The two are not the same. Women can (and often do) have a male-centered view of things, while there are men who manage to avoid adopting this perspective. The male-centered view—held by most theologians throughout church history—is grounded in the belief that men are central and normative, and women are secondary and different. Such a premise, when applied to biblical interpretation, naturally results in a view of God as "male" or "masculine" and a doctrine of the church that esteems men more highly than women and views women as existing primarily to serve men.

The solution, however, is not to replace this male-centered view of the Bible with a woman-centered feminist perspective, but to replace it with a gender-neutral, human-inclusive perspective. But if—as liberal feminist theologians maintain—gender bias has been written into the Bible, gender neutrality is not an option when interpreting the Bible. One must either adopt the male bias of the biblical writers, they say, or hold a feminist perspective which necessitates revising or rejecting the sections of Scripture deemed intrinsically sexist.

There are two assumptions behind the idea of liberal feminist theologians that when women read the Bible "self-consciously as women" they will arrive at interpretations significantly different from those of men. The first assumption (shared, interestingly, by traditionalists) is that gender differences are profound and pervasive, splitting humanity into two virtually separate spheres of knowledge and existence. The second is the liberal hermeneutical premise (rejected by evangelicals, including evangelical feminists) that the Bible's meaning is found not simply in the text itself, but in a fluid interaction of biblical text with biblical reader. From these two assumptions, it follows that the Bible will mean something different for women than it does for men. It therefore becomes the work of feminist theologians to ascertain the meaning (or meanings) of the Bible for women.

Liberal feminist theology is not woman-centered in the sense of advocating the separation and superiority of women with regard to men, as is the case with revolutionary feminist theology. But it is woman-centered in that biblical interpretation is grounded in women's experience, and theology is restructured along "feminine" lines. Equalitarian relationships replace authoritarian hierarchy, and the emphasis is placed on knowing and serving rather than on leading and succeeding. Interestingly, these supposedly "feminine" traits were all advocated and practiced by Jesus Christ, although he did not label them feminine, but simply good and God-pleasing.

Feminist theologians in the liberal tradition differ somewhat in their approaches to the Bible. On the most conservative end of the spectrum of liberal theology, Phyllis Trible seeks to reclaim woman's story from the Bible by emphasizing the texts that are supportive of women's equality and significance, as well as the biblical stories about women that have been either ignored or misunderstood. The more liberal approach of Rosemary Radford Ruether and Letty Russell calls on the overall theological principle of liberation in the Bible to critique as fallible texts alleged to be sexist and patriarchal. Ruether refers to the biblical perspective of human liberation as the "prophetic tradition"; the Bible thus contains the resources to critique itself.

On the most liberal end of the spectrum, Elisabeth Schüssler Fiorenza sees Scripture as prototypical rather than normative. Failing to find any liberating, prophetic tradition in the Bible, she approaches Scripture with a "hermeneutic of suspicion." She sees the early Christian church as the proto-typical "women-church," for which the Bible serves as an obscure record and resource. Schüssler Fiorenza describes women-church as "a movement of self-identified women and women-identified men in biblical religion."[32] Because it acknowledges women-church rather than the Bible as the normative authority, this brand of feminist theology is sometimes classified with revolutionary feminist theology. However, it does not reject the Christian tradition entirely, but theologically and historically reconstructs it so as to support the concept of women-church.

It should be clear from this review of the many varieties of feminist thought that very few generalizations about feminism can justifiably be made. Not only do different types of modern secular feminism diverge sharply from one another at various key points, but—as the next chapter will show—evangelical feminism is fundamentally different from them all.[33]

Evangelical Feminism Compared with Other Views

The terms *biblical* and *evangelical* are used interchangeably to describe a feminism rooted in the Christian world view, which looks to the Bible—not "women's experience"—as its final authority. The biblical diagnosis for the "disease" of sexism recognizes that legal and economic inequity and the cultural institution of patriarchy are some of the factors that perpetuate gender injustice. But human sin is identified as the root cause of sexism as well as of the factors that perpetuate it. Genesis 3:16 spells out God's commentary on sin's consequences in the area of male/female relationships. Sin has resulted in women being ruled by men in every context—legal, economic, cultural, and personal.

The cure for this universal malaise is the same biblical cure prescribed for every ill effect of human sin: repentance, forgiveness, and reconciliation. Men must repent of their tendency to use women simply to facilitate their own agenda; women must repent of their tendency to circumvent this male domination through sexual manipulation, as well as their tendency to give in to passivity and an unfaithful stewardship of the gifts with which God has entrusted them. As they accept God's forgiveness for their sins, men and women must forgive and be reconciled to one another. This will result in women and men dropping sexist prejudice and no longer regarding each other as typecast by gender (i.e., not seeing men as self-centered and emotionally stunted or women as irrational and superficial, and so on). Instead, each man or woman will be regarded as an equal, an individual, a fellow believer in Christ whom God calls us to love and to serve in ministry.

Unlike mainstream feminists who often seem only to be trying to imitate men, and woman-centered feminists who seem bent on being separate from and superior to men, biblical feminists aim for both women and men to become more balanced people who are more harmoniously related to one another. The goal of evangelical feminism is that men and women be allowed to serve God as individuals, according to their own unique gifts rather than according to a culturally predetermined personality slot called "Christian manhood" or "Christian womanhood."

Also unlike many secular feminists, women who identify with evangelical feminism are not motivated by a greed for power or a self-centered desire to prove themselves equal or superior to men. Rather, they are motivated by a sense of justice and the conviction that the traditional order which has been imposed on women and men is not in keeping with God's will for his people. They desire to see women liberated from the stultifying effects of exclusively male leadership, and they are impelled to seek the opportunity to serve God and minister to others to the full extent of their abilities in obedience to the call of God.

Elaine Storkey concludes her discussion of feminism by noting the other-centeredness of evangelical feminism. Faithfulness to the tradition of evangelical feminism does not consist in working and praying for equality simply for one's own benefit, but for the benefit of those who are most in need of liberation from inequity and injustice.[1] Traditionally, evangelical feminism derives more from a spirit of "preaching the gospel to the poor" than an attitude of self-assertion and self-fulfillment. Speaking of the nineteenth-century women's missionary movement, Ruth Tucker echoes similar sentiments: "Women missionaries generally were motivated by the needs of others rather than their own. They may have looked and acted very much like feminists when they launched the women's missionary movement in 1861, and when they individually fought for ministry opportunities equal to men's, but beneath the surface the issues were very different."[2]

Far from being a struggle to gain power and dominance, the goal of biblical feminism is that men and women in the church might be liberated from the preoccupation with power and authority that characterizes the traditionalist agenda, so that everyone may serve God freely and wholeheartedly without the anxiety that one might be stepping out of one's place in the "chain of command." Evangelical feminists believe that when male authority is billed as biblically mandated, this is not an inconsequential error. Such teaching entails the unavoidable implication of the male's unique relationship to God—that he is more representative of God and closer to God in the "chain of command"—and it is therefore harmful to both men and women spiritually, socially, and emotionally.

Biblical Feminists and the Bible

Biblical feminists are distinguished from other feminists in their diagnosis and prescribed cure for the problem of sexism, and in their motivation for attempting to solve the problem. They also differ in their use of the Bible. Other feminists either reject the Bible entirely or seek to interpret it from the perspective of "women's experience." Evangelical feminists regard the Bible as authoritative in its entirety and maintain that sexism in the church derives from the traditional practice of interpreting the Bible in the patriarchal light of "men's experience." The corrective to this androcentric hermeneutic is not a gynocentric hermeneutic, but one which is free of any hidden gender agendas. A biblical feminist hermeneutic is no more woman-centered than it is man-centered; it simply seeks to correct a historic imbalance in traditional biblical interpretation as regarding the role of women. It does not attempt to rewrite the Bible or to usurp biblical authority.

From Sarah Grimké in the 1830s to the early evangelical feminist biblical scholars in the first decades of the twentieth century, evangelical Christian women leaders in early American feminism maintained that the Bible had been mistranslated and misinterpreted so as to appear to teach the subordination of women as a universal norm. This twisting of the true message of Scripture, they believed, occurred at the hands of men who approached Scripture from the premise that men are primary and women secondary. Naturally, male translators and interpreters with such a preunderstanding tended to find in Scripture what they expected to find—a central role for men and an ancillary, subordinate role for women. But evangelical feminists believed that, although the Bible was written in the context of male-dominated cultures, it does not teach male domination as a universal, God-ordained norm. Although evangelical feminism today has gleaned some truths from modern secular feminism, it is not a product of the women's liberation movement of the 1960s or 1970s, nor does it find inspiration in the pagan feminist spirituality which has emerged since the late 1970s. Rather, biblical feminism is simply continuing along the lines of a tradition begun nearly two hundred years ago.

For evangelical feminists, the Bible is more than a cultural and religious force with which to be reckoned. It is God's infallible and authoritative word—every believer's source of truth. It is for this reason that evangelical feminists for the past two centuries have sought the accurate translation and interpretation of Scripture. Respect for the veracity and authority of God's Word is central to the evangelical feminist enterprise, and this is primarily what distinguishes it from the theologically liberal feminist approach to Scripture that has developed in the last century.

The biblical feminist hermeneutic includes the following eight strategies. The first and most fundamental principle of biblical interpretation is to endeavor to be faithful to the biblical author's intent in writing the specific passage in question. We must try to determine why the biblical author wrote what he wrote, and in determining the "why" we determine the basic biblical principle or message of the text. That principle can then be applied to our own situation. All other strategies of biblical interpretation follow from this basic objective.

In order to know *why* the biblical author wrote a particular text, it is essential to know exactly *what* he wrote. Therefore, a second hermeneutical principle is the accurate translation of the passages traditionally used to silence and subjugate women. Biblical feminists have found that many texts which are in fact less than clear in their original language have been translated so as to appear unequivocally to support the idea of male authority. One example is found in 1 Timothy 2:12, which is translated in the New International Version, "I do not permit a woman to teach or to have authority over a man; she must be silent." The traditionalist prohibition of women occupying positions of church leadership hinges on the translation of the Greek word *authentein* in the usual way of "have (or usurp) authority over." But because *authentein* is not used anywhere else in the New Testament, and because *authentein* seems to have a wide variety of meanings in ancient Greek usage, the traditional translation of this verse appears to be open to legitimate debate.[3]

Another example of the traditional tactic of making an ambiguous text appear to be unequivocal in its support of male authority is found in 1 Corinthians 11:3–16, which serves as the biblical backbone for the traditionalist "chain of command" teaching. Yet this passage is "full of notorious exegetical difficulties. . . . The ['head'] metaphor itself is often understood to be hierarchical, setting up structures of authority. But nothing in the passage suggests as much; in fact, the only appearance of the word *exousia* ('authority') refers to the woman's own authority (v. 10)."[4] But because it would contradict the "chain of command" teaching for verse 10 to be speaking of the woman's own authority, the literal translation of "authority over (or on) her head" is augmented to read "a sign of authority on her head" (NIV). This leads conveniently to the idea that the veil or covering that the woman is to wear serves as a symbol or sign of her submission to the authority her husband has over her. Such an understanding of the verse is far from obvious when one considers only the literal translation of the text. But when the text is augmented and the meaning adjusted so that the authority to which the verse refers becomes that of the man under whom the woman is placed in the chain of command, then it seems to support the traditional interpretation of the passage. The Living Bible even goes so far as to say: "So a woman should wear a covering on her head as a sign that she is under man's authority."

Third, it is important to maintain interpretive consistency with the rest of a biblical author's writings as well as the whole of Scripture. Toward this end, unclear and/or isolated passages are not to be used as doctrinal cornerstones, but are to be interpreted in light of clear passages which reflect overall biblical themes. This hermeneutical principle prohibits building a doctrine of female subordination on 1 Corinthians 11:3–16 and 14:34–35 and 1 Timothy 2:11–15, for these texts are rife with exegetical difficulties. Principles clearly expressed elsewhere in the Bible must inform one's interpretation of such "proof text" passages.[5]

Fourth, texts couched in a context of culturally-specific instructions are not to be taken a priori as normative for the present day. Biblical texts that have a universal, doctrinal orientation are more likely to be considered directly transferable to the present day than those texts that were intended for immediate practical application in a particular cultural situation. Millard Erickson points to water baptism and footwashing as illustrative of the difference between a biblical command that is put into a universal setting (the Great Commission, Matt. 28:18–20) and a command given in a culturally specific situation (John 13:14–16). The biblical principle behind the footwashing incident is that we always ought to maintain a humble attitude of servanthood, rather than that we ought to institute a permanent sacrament of footwashing. "In that culture, washing the feet of others would symbolize such an attitude [of humility]. But in another culture, some other act might more appropriately convey the same truth."[6]

This leads to a fifth hermeneutical principle, which is that culturally-specific instructions are to be interpreted not only in light of biblical doctrine and principle, but also in light of the culture to which they were written and the author's reason for writing them. For example, when Peter instructs wives to be submissive to their husbands (1 Pet. 3:1), it must be remembered that in Roman society civil law granted husbands absolute authority over their wives and that Peter's instruction is couched in the context of similar exhortations for believers to submit to the civil authorities. The biblical message, then, would seem to be that Christians are to be respectable, law-abiding members of society by behaving appropriately in the society in which they live, rather than that God has commanded all husbands for all time to be in authority over their wives.

Sixth, events recorded in the Bible should also be understood in light of the culture of that time. For example, a woman leader in a highly patriarchal culture would have more significance than a woman in leadership today. While both instances indicate that women are capable of leadership, chances are that the presence of a woman leader in a patriarchal culture— unless she is the wife, mother, or daughter of a male leader—indicates that something other than cultural forces propelled her to that position. We can therefore surmise that women in ancient Israel or the New Testament church who were in positions of leadership were quite likely in those positions by virtue of God's design.

Seventh, because of the progressive nature of God's revelation in the Bible, New Testament texts concerning women should be considered more accurate indicators of God's intent for women than those provided in the Old Testament. The familiar traditionalist idea that a man is the priest of his home, for example, fails to consider progressive revelation. The Old Testament arrangement whereby priests were always male Levites (or, in pre-Mosaic times, the patriarchs of households) was superseded by the new covenant, wherein Jesus serves as the permanent high priest (Heb. 7:21–24) and the one mediator between God and humanity (1 Tim. 2:5), and *all* believers serve as priests unto God (1 Pet. 2:5–9; Rev. 5:10; 20:6). Concerning the priesthood of all believers, F. F. Bruce comments, "If, as evangelical Christians generally believe, Christian priesthood is a privilege in which all believers share, there can be no reason that a Christian woman should not exercise her priesthood on the same terms as a Christian man."[7] In discussing progressive revelation, Millard Erickson notes,

> In some cases, the essence of a doctrine was not explicitly realized within biblical times. For example, the status of women in society was elevated dramatically by Jesus. Similarly, Paul granted an unusual status to slaves. Yet the lot of each of these groups did not improve as much as it should have. So to find the essence of how such persons should be treated, we must look to principles laid down or implied regarding their status, not to accounts of how they actually were treated in biblical times.[8]

Eighth, the propensity for male translators and interpreters to read their bias into the biblical text exemplifies the ever-present need to guard against interpreting the Bible in conformity with one's own cultural preunderstanding or personal expectations. In addition to safeguarding biblical interpretation from emotional interference, it is important to rely on the direction of the Holy Spirit as well as one's God-given reasoning abilities in the interpretive process.[9]

The net effect of the evangelical feminist hermeneutic is the discovery that—contrary to what both traditionalists and radical feminists believe—the Bible does not teach male supremacy as a transcultural norm but teaches instead mutuality and equality between women and men. The biblical principle of the essential equality of man and woman—each made in the image of God—is set forth in Genesis 1 and 2. In Genesis 3:16 God delineates some of the consequences of human sin; he does not issue a command for men to rule women, as some have believed. The entrance of sin into God's created order destroyed the equality and mutuality of the relationship between woman and man; cultural patriarchy was the result. God revealed himself and his plan for his people by means of patriarchal cultures, but progressively made known his redemptive plan whereby the essential equality of all people would be restored and the practice of sexual hierarchy brought to an end. This ethic of male/female equality was put into practice by Jesus Christ, who countered the prevailing patriarchal norm by treating women as persons in their own right. It was summarized by Paul in Galatians 3:28 and was put into operation by Paul and the early Christians as they sanctioned the service of those women who had been called by God to leadership in ministry.

In view of the existing customs of the surrounding cultures, however, the principle of biblical equality was exercised with restraint and moderation in New Testament times. It was important, for the sake of the testimony of the gospel, that Christians appear to the onlooking world as respectable, law-abiding members of society. Clearly, the highest priority of the early church was spreading the gospel of Jesus Christ. The principle of human equality and liberation which was entailed by the gospel message could not be implemented on a widespread basis, at the risk of alienating non-Christians from that gospel message. "Thus the early church, even while tolerating slavery for the sake of the missionary principle, pointed to a vision of Christian justice and community which would eventually leave slavery behind. So too, Christian feminists argue, does the Bible point beyond the patriarchy tolerated, yet progressively modulated, throughout salvation history to a vision of mutuality between brothers and sisters in Christ in marriage, church and society."[10] Today, when non-Christians are offended, not by an equalitarian gospel, but by a hierarchical gospel, there is no reason to continue in the cultural practices that were initially intended for Christians living in a patriarchal society.

As already noted, evangelical feminism differs from liberal feminist theology in that it views the entire Bible as authoritative, and it does not interpret any biblical text to be teaching male supremacy. But there is another difference. Liberal feminist theologians understand the principle of social equality and liberation to be the central, controlling theme of the biblical message; they therefore deem normative and authoritative only those biblical texts that clearly bespeak this principle. But evangelical feminists understand the principle of social equality and liberation to be an implication of the gospel message, not the primary content of the gospel message. The heart of the gospel is repentance and forgiveness of sin through the grace of God in Christ, which secures our eternal and abundant life and serves to glorify God. This message has priority over the social reform that grows out of it. The main point of the gospel is not the destruction of patriarchy, but the destruction of the stronghold of sin in the human heart which impels not only patriarchy but a host of other evil deviations from God's intended order.

Traditionalists, for their part, maintain that, while extreme patriarchy is not God's intent for society, a benevolent exercise of male authority is. They accordingly accuse feminists of violating God's order in refusing to agree that God has ordained men to have authority over women in the church and at home. Feminists respond that any manifestation of male supremacy can only be unjust. But at this point neither side has clarified the issue. The conflict of opinion does not consist simply of justice versus God's order. Traditionalists do not think God's order is unjust any more than evangelical feminists believe that to seek justice is to disobey God's order. The difference is one of emphasis, and the different emphases arise from different presuppositions. Traditionalists emphasize the hierarchy and order of rigid gender roles because they believe this is the key to understanding the meaning of maleness and femaleness. Evangelical feminists emphasize the idea of justice because they believe that a hierarchical understanding of the meaning of human sexuality is incorrect and therefore results in unjust treatment of women by men. Justice can only be had as women and men are liberated from the artificial restraints of strictly-prescribed gender roles.

Mark Noll clarifies the presuppositional differences between the traditionalist and the evangelical feminist approach to biblical interpretation:

> Evangelicals who believe that the Bible in general teaches the progressive manifestation of a New Creation, who hold that the Bible's central purpose is to communicate new life in the Spirit, or who feel that developments in

modern western society are at least potentially instructive to Christians, more easily find convincing those scholarly explanations [of biblical teaching] that allow fuller scope for women's activities. On the other hand, those who believe that the Bible in general teaches a divinely ordained chain of command, who hold that the Bible offers a detailed blueprint of God's will for everyday life, or who feel that western society has entered into an apocalyptic decline, more easily find convincing those technical explanations that reinforce traditional male-female roles.[11]

If traditionalists believe "that the Bible offers a detailed blueprint of God's will for everyday life," but evangelical feminists believe "that the Bible's central purpose is to communicate new life in the Spirit," then the traditionalist tendency will be to confer a much greater importance to rules and regulations governing male/female relationships. This emphasis on the "blueprint" approach to biblical interpretation can easily lead to an overemphasis on secondary issues and an underemphasis on the primary message of Scripture. As Elaine Storkey points out,

We can be greatly in danger of getting some themes way out of perspective. Even those who take (wrongly in my view) an authoritarian view of the relation between men and women need also to recognize that in the light of other biblical truths this is insignificant anyway. Far deeper issues about the relationship between men and women are at stake than that of who makes the (somewhat mythical) 'final decision'. Far more crucial is the teaching on love: self-giving and self-denying love which should characterize all relationships. . . . The way others will know that we are Christ's disciples is in the way we love one another, and not in the way we exercise authority over one another.[12]

In short, both traditionalism and liberal feminist theology deem the issue of gender roles and status to be of the utmost importance in the Bible. Evangelical feminists, however, do not view the gender issue per se as central to the biblical message, but rather emphasize mutuality and equality as elements of the relationship all believers—male and female—should have one to another, within the community of the new covenant in Christ.

Misunderstanding Evangelical Feminism

The foregoing description of biblical/evangelical feminism should probably be appended by the disclaimer that not all those who call themselves biblical or evangelical feminists are in line with the tradition outlined here. Some may well be insincere in their claim to respect biblical authority, and instead desire simply to agree with Scripture where it can be made to appear to agree with their preconceived ideas. Antifeminists ought not characterize all of evangelical feminism by these individuals.

Efforts have been made by some Christian feminists to argue for homosexuality as part and parcel of evangelical feminism. But this is a departure from historic evangelical feminism and is rooted primarily in a mix of modern feminism and modern sexual ethics. Like the pro-abortion stance of modern secular feminists, a pro-homosexual position attempts to create equality between men and women where equality does not exist. The equality that evangelical feminists have sought for the past two centuries is simply the equality of opportunity for women to make full use of their gifts and abilities in church, home, and society, even if that entails sharing authority with or exercising authority over men. But where sexual behavior is directly involved, men and women cannot legitimately qualify for equal treatment. One cannot assert on the basis of "women's equality" that a woman has as much right as a man to have sexual relations with a woman. Evangelical feminists believe simply that sexuality does not determine role prescriptions for women and men in *every* area of life; they do not maintain that sexuality makes no difference at all. It is, after all, in their sexuality that men and women differ. But it is in their common humanity that women and men are equally deserving of the opportunity to express their humanness.

Moreover, for at least three reasons, a biblical defense of homosexuality cannot be derived from an application of the hermeneutical principles followed by evangelical feminists. First, there are no positive biblical examples of homosexual behavior, as there are of women in leadership (despite the fact that in biblical times female leadership was far less common than homosexuality). Second, most biblical texts condemning homosexuality are direct and incontrovertible; they are uncluttered with translational ambiguities and are written as general mandates or observations. Third, homosexuality is at variance with the clear biblical principle of marital faithfulness between a man and a woman, as unequivocally demonstrated in the creation account of the first man and woman. The sexual/marital ideal as presented in Genesis 1 and 2 (especially 2:24) is clearly heterosexual. Here the traditional position has undeniable biblical support—unlike the highly debatable traditionalist view that attempts to ground male authority in Genesis 2.[13]

These observations should be balanced, however, with the awareness that the attitudes of many evangelicals toward homosexuals are less than

Christ-like.[14] When those in the church allow their rejection of homosexual behavior to lead to a rejection of homosexual persons, they are not evidencing the love of Christ toward all people; nor are they remembering that homosexual behavior is simply sin—no more, no less—and sin is something with which we are all well acquainted in our own lives.

The organization that best represents the evangelical feminist position on this and other issues is Christians for Biblical Equality. Biblical scholars and theologians who hold to evangelical feminist beliefs include Catherine Clark Kroeger (president of C.B.E.), Aida Besançon Spencer, Gilbert Bilezikian, W. Ward Gasque, Ruth Tucker, Walter Liefeld, Roberta Hestenes, Roger Nicole, David Scholer, Millard Erickson, Gordon Fee, Kenneth Kantzer, Richard Mouw, and Vernon Grounds.

It should also be noted that, because evangelicals are understandably alarmed at the approach of liberal theologians to Scripture and because feminist theology tends to be largely identified with this type of hermeneutic, great confusion often ensues concerning the nature of evangelical feminist biblical interpretation. When feminist biblical interpretation is an effort to revise the Bible to serve the feminist cause, it must be rejected. But when an unprejudiced look at Scripture yields *from Scripture* a new and different perspective that points toward equality rather than hierarchy between the sexes, then it should be heeded. But often it is not heeded. It is simply assumed that the Bible *couldn't* be teaching anything other than what tradition has declared it to be teaching.

Traditionalists usually acknowledge that, unlike theologically liberal feminists, evangelical feminists claim to view the Bible as authoritative. But the implication is that despite evangelical feminists' claims to do so, they simply do not respect biblical authority any more than non-evangelical feminists do. Evangelical feminists are therefore condemned—along with liberal feminist theologians—for using Scripture merely to support feminist ideas imported from secular culture.

This accusation serves as a quick and convenient way of dismissing a significant body of careful evangelical scholarship. It is premised on two dubious assumptions: 1) that any belief in equality for women could only come from secular culture and not from the Bible, and 2) that contemporary secular culture is false and church tradition is true, in toto. These two assumptions are grounded in an even more fundamental assumption, namely, that male supremacy is an integral element of God's created order. Contemporary culture, therefore, is categorically rejected because it claims to favor equality for women. But centuries—or even decades—ago, when secular culture was more patriarchal, church leaders dipped freely into the secular well of ideas and customs in building and maintaining the church tradition of male supremacy—which is now billed as biblical and not cultural. So it is not simply that feminism is deemed wrong because it is cultural; it is also that contemporary culture is deemed wrong because it is feminist. The reasoning is ultimately circular.

To say that evangelical feminists are intent on twisting Scripture to suit their own preferences, and that their claim to respect biblical authority is simply cosmetic, is to disregard the facts and to impugn the integrity of evangelical feminists. After making some false generalizations about the nineteenth-century feminists' disrespect for the Bible, Susan Foh asserts that biblical feminists today "have abandoned the biblical and historic position of the God-breathed, inerrant Scriptures. . . . They maintain that the Bible is defective when it says, 'The husband is the head of the wife as Christ is the head of the church . . .' (Eph. 5:23) and 'I permit no woman to teach or to have authority over men; she is to keep silent' (1 Tim. 2:12)."[15] As Ruth Tucker states in response, "Foh's charges are simply untrue. I do not know of anyone identified as a 'biblical' or 'evangelical' feminist who would claim that Paul's admonitions regarding women are in actuality errors in the Bible. Biblical feminists deal with these passages straightforwardly, exegeting the Greek language with as much respect for the text as traditionalists do."[16]

Many evangelicals—including evangelical feminists—believe things they understand the Bible to be teaching even though they do not personally *like* those doctrines. (Belief in hell, for instance, is usually not maintained out of personal preference.) Many who are evangelical feminists today, myself included, used to believe in the "chain of command" for no reason other than that they believed the Bible taught it—even though they did not like the idea and even though they found the secular case for women's equality appealing. Many such people were not persuaded that equality between women and men was biblical until they began to research the matter themselves and to read the works of evangelical scholars who argued the case. The arguments that ultimately convinced these evangelicals were not from secular culture, but were from biblical teaching, the biblical languages, and an understanding of the cultures of biblical times.

Not a few of today's evangelical feminists first encountered compelling biblical arguments for women's equality in books written in the early twentieth century, decades prior to modern secular feminism.[17] One such early evangelical feminist work, *God's Word to Women,* was written by Dr. Katharine Bushnell, who agreed to obey God's call to preach only after years of research in the biblical languages had convinced her that God had not consigned women to a permanent place of silence and subservience.[18]

An example of the traditionalist tactic of attributing guilt to evangelical feminism by identifying it with theological liberalism may be found in the third article of a three-part series on liberation theology in the *Christian Research Journal*. This article on "feminist theology" did not address mainstream, liberal feminist theology, as would have been expected; rather, it presented evangelical feminism as "a variety of liberation theology" and, primarily on this basis, rejected it.[19] Although this publication's analyses are usually incisive, accurate, and helpful, in this case it joined its voice with the other traditional evangelicals who fail to recognize that, because the evangelical feminist hermeneutic differs fundamentally from that of liberation theology and liberal feminist theology, it rightly belongs in another category altogether.

The temptation to categorize—and dismiss—evangelical feminists along with the liberals, humanists, and/or pagans has proven irresistible to many evangelical antifeminists. This traditionalist strategy deserves a closer look and will be addressed in more depth in chapters which follow. But before concluding the discussion of different types of feminism, I want to set these differing schools of thought in the context of a continuum of views on gender roles, in order to highlight the similarities and dissimilarities between them.

Positioning the Polarities

The various views of gender roles can be positioned on a spectrum of opinion, with traditional patriarchy on the far right and woman-centered radical feminism on the far left. At the far right, traditional patriarchy considers men to possess superior leadership skills and therefore to be well deserving of their power; women, by virtue of their inferior rational ability and their weaker, dependent nature, are assigned to be the men's subservient assistants.

Moving from the right toward the center, various ameliorations of this hard-core patriarchy may be found, including what is currently referred to in the evangelical church as traditionalism. These modified positions include assorted combinations of the following views: the husband is the leader in the home, but is a "servant-leader" who must be sensitive to his wife's needs; the husband is not in authority over his wife so much as he is responsible for taking care of her; men and women have innate mental/emotional differences which suit them to occupy "complementary" roles within a hierarchy (the man is "over" the woman), but they are nonetheless "equal" somehow, usually only in a "spiritual" sense; men and women are to share authority but are "complementary" in their innate mental/emotional differences; men and women are both capable of leadership, but nonetheless occupy different places on the chain of command, with the woman becoming "fulfilled" in her femininity as she submits to male authority.

All current traditionalist models are attempted modifications of stark patriarchalism, but in most such attempts, mutually exclusive features become incorporated into the same model. It is, for example, logically inconsistent to maintain—as traditionalists do—that the husband is to be in authority over his wife (as in traditional patriarchy) and at the same time to be emotionally intimate with her and to regard her as his equal (as in feminist thought). Traditional patriarchy was at least logically consistent; the patriarch of the household was—as all those with absolute authority must be—stern and emotionally distant from those over whom he held power.[20]

Moving to the left of center, we find the mainstream feminists (modern liberal feminists and less-radical radical feminists), who are most obviously identified as the activists for legalized abortion. Interestingly, this position holds in common with traditional patriarchy an androcentric analysis of women's childbearing function: it is viewed as a disempowering experience that renders women socially weak and dependent. In fact, much of the efforts of modern secular feminism attempt to compensate for the social limitations that are perceived by traditionalists as well as many feminists to be inherent in women's reproductive biology. Traditionalists also make an effort to compensate for women's weaker social status, but they do so by speaking of "the awesome significance of motherhood" and of "making a home as a full-time wife."[21] (Apparently a married woman who doesn't consider motherhood awesome enough to make a full-time career of it—even as few men consider fatherhood their career—must be considered only a part-time wife.)

Women's reproductive biology looms large in the gender role models of both traditionalism and mainstream feminism. The fact that a pregnant or nursing woman has special needs and limitations that hamper her freedom is seen by both camps as necessarily contributing to her dependent, secondary status. *Freedom* is defined androcentrically by both camps; a woman's loss of freedom occurs when she is unable to do everything a man can do. The difference, of course, is that traditionalists want women to be in a dependent role, and feminists do not. So traditionalists proceed to build upon women's physical differences all manner of exaggerated and extrapolated "feminine" traits, which include social, intellectual, and even spiritual limitations. But mainstream feminists seek to avoid any limitations entailed by the physical differences—indeed, to deny that these differences need to make any difference at all. They do this primarily through asserting for women the "right" to total "reproductive control," which translates into abortion on demand. Women are thereby relieved from ever having to bear the freedom-hampering responsibility of motherhood if it doesn't fit with their plans in a world which still defines success in male terms.

Moving further toward the left, we find feminists who *emphasize* gender differences, particularly the "maternal" characteristics of women, and usually with a view to the superiority of such traits over male aggression and rationalism. The trend here is toward acknowledging gender differences and advocating social reform that takes these differences into account.

At the far left, gynocentric or woman-centered feminists attempt to use female "superiority" as a weapon against a masculine culture. Such feminists are less interested in competing with men as equals than they are in ignoring them altogether in their effort to remake society in women's image. While mainstream feminists in general want both women and men to develop personalities that incorporate the best of traits stereotypically associated with masculinity and femininity, gynocentric feminists are eager to assign all masculine traits and manifestations of male consciousness (such as Western civilization and its Judeo-Christian religious heritage) to the scrap heap. After all, they figure, if androcentric masculinity is responsible for all the problems of Western society (this being a central premise of their thought), then why try to redeem the ruthless and power-hungry male? Woman-centered feminists follow the traditionalist typology of male/female differences, but value the traditional female virtues and devalue the traditional male traits, declaring that these gender differences equip women for and disqualify men from positions of social power and prerogative. Ironically, when these feminists declare that all rational, linear thought is "male" and ought therefore to be done away with, they are lending credence to the traditionalist contention that women can't think straight and that logic is rightfully a male domain.

Here at the far left, feminism shares with the right-of-center views a sexocentric approach to the issue. A premise foundational to both gynocentric feminism and (androcentric) traditionalism is that gender is the single most important factor determining the definition, identity, value, role, and experience of a person's life. As traditionalist James Dobson puts it, "everything we do is influenced by our gender assignment."[22] This justifies the strong emphasis in both camps on what are perceived to be pro-

found differences between the sexes, and the superiority which those differences inevitably accord one sex over the other. Whether androcentric or
gynocentric, both views tend toward prejudice and chauvinism, according
superiority to the "central" sex and marginalizing the other sex. A person's
value and prerogatives (or lack thereof) therefore depend on that person's
sex rather than on that person's individual attributes.

In short, both views are characterized by a "group think" determinism;
that is, a person's rights or lack of rights derive, not from that person's humanity or individuality, but from that person's membership in a particular
gender group. Sociologist Cynthia Epstein notes, "Today, as we have seen,
scholars who are feminists join with scholars who are traditionalists in declaring that basic differences between the sexes guide their responses to
the world, that men and women live in two cultures, two domains, that they
are, in effect, two species."[23]

Both traditionalists and woman-centered feminists deem women and
men to be totally opposite from one another and therefore unequal. Both
assert that women don't think rationally in linear, logical terms, but are
emotionally expressive and relationally oriented. The two camps differ,
however, in their valuation of and explanation for these alleged male/
female differences. The feminist camp claims these differences render
women superior, while the traditionalist camp maintains that male rationality equips men to assume authority—by any reasonable standard, a position of superiority—over women.

Traditionalists believe that these gender differences are innate, natural, and God-ordained and that they render men best suited for the decision-
making "male" roles, and women better equipped for the nurturing, subservient helper role at home. Most woman-centered feminists, however,
seem to believe that these differences are largely a result of the socializa-
tion process in patriarchal society that teaches men and women to behave
according to the traditional gender stereotypes. Thus, they refer frequently to women's consciousness and women's experience which, they point
out, has been largely repressed and ignored and is the result of women being historically assigned to a very different position from men in society.
These feminists, however, are less concerned with explaining the reason
for gender differences than they are with reassessing the supposed female
nature as superior to the male.

It is interesting that woman-centered feminists for whom lesbianism
is a political statement are presuppositionally akin to those philosophical
"fathers" of Western patriarchy—the men of ancient Greece who despised
women and focused their sexual and romantic interest on boys.[24] Homo-

sexuality is not always—perhaps not even usually—a result of hostility toward the other sex; but it certainly can be seen as a logical outcome of it.

Finally, it should be noted that one of the most fundamental premises of traditionalism is also fundamental to the radical feminist critique of Western tradition. The views both to the right and to the left of center maintain that the Bible advocates male dominance, that the biblical God is in some sense male (or at least "masculine"), and that male dominance is part and parcel of Christianity. Traditionalists, therefore, agree with all nonevangelical feminists that to advocate women's equality is to reject biblical authority.

The extreme right and the extreme left then, though mortal enemies of one another, hold much presuppositional ground in common. Both sides hold that men and women are unequal, that one sex is superior to the other, that the God of the Bible is male or masculine, and that a person's sex is fundamentally determinative of far more than the marital and reproductive roles entailed by physical sexuality. Woman-centered radical feminists have gone so far to the left that they have nearly come full circle. The matriarchy machine uses the same fuels of competition, distrust, and oppression that run the patriarchy machine; the main difference is that men and women have changed places. Of course, the patriarchy machine has been running full steam for millennia, but aside from some talk of prehistoric feminism, the matriarchy machine has not yet emerged from ideology into reality (except, perhaps, in some isolated sectors of society).

The View from the Center

Positioned at the center of the spectrum is a gender role model that holds premises diametrically opposed to those which the two poles hold in common. It does not prescribe or predict male or female behavior according to stereotyped gender differences; it views men and women primarily as individuals, rather than as members of two different groups. Women and men are judged on the basis of their unique individuality as persons rather than prejudged according to generalizations about the "typical" man or woman. One sex is not accorded license to rule over the other sex. Authority is shared equally in marriage, and in society it is assigned on the basis of individual qualification rather than gender.

This centrist, equalitarian position is, in most respects, typical of evangelical feminism and classical liberal feminism. Although this position is also termed *feminist*—in the sense that any view that deviates in any way from traditionalism is feminist—the label is misleading. *Feminism* calls up images of man-hating, power-hungry women who are out for revenge; but such left-of-center feminism is at least as unlike centrist equalitarianism as it is unlike traditionalism—in some respects even more so.

At the center of the spectrum, men and women are viewed as essentially equal psychologically and spiritually, in that both sexes possess basically the same human needs, desires, and aptitudes. What differences do exist in these areas are considered less significant than the similarities. The biological differences between men and women are not exaggerated to entail non-biological ramifications which predetermine differentiated gender roles in every sphere of life, but neither are the very real implications of biological differences disallowed.

Reproductive function *is* different for women than it is for men and is calmly accepted as such by centrists without going on to say—as traditionalists do—that because women *can* have babies, they ought to make motherhood their life's vocation. On the other hand, the obligation entailed by women's reproductive role is not denied, as it is when women claim for themselves a "right" to abortion. The parental position—whether it is acquired by "accident" or intention—always consists of a responsibility to protect the life of the offspring and never entails a right to terminate the life of the offspring. Motherhood becomes a liability or a limitation to women—and "abortion rights" a perceived prerequisite to women's freedom—only when men make use of pregnancy to push women to the periphery of their "man's world."

Unlike traditionalism and woman-centered feminism, equalitarianism does not sexualize the entire person. Gender is not viewed as the primary determinative factor in a person's life; spiritual, intellectual, experiential, relational, and personality factors are likewise important. A person's sex does not deterministically and indelibly color all of a person's character, being, and life experience. Sexual identity is not conflated with personal identity.

Also in disagreement with both traditionalism and radical feminism, evangelical feminism does not believe the Bible advocates male authority, but rather equality and mutual submission. Nor does it hold that God is "masculine" or that male supremacy is inherent to Christianity, but rather that these beliefs have been derived more from cultural prejudice and patriarchy than from biblical teaching.

The position at the center holds in common with those to the right a respect for the family and an adherence to traditional morality. With those to the left it shares the conviction that a male-dominated and male-centered culture has in many ways dealt with women unjustly. The objective of the center position is to achieve a just and tempered equality; it therefore finds unacceptable any social system (of either the right or the left) that grants prerogatives to one sex and withholds them from the other.

8

The Feminist Bogeywoman

In *The Way Home,* traditionalist Mary Pride fires on feminism with both barrels blasting. Using a cutting tone, she declares that anything remotely related to feminist thought (including contraception and careers for women) is part and parcel of the radical feminist spirituality that endorses homosexuality, sexual promiscuity, abortion, witchcraft, and pagan goddess worship. In Pride's mind, budging so much as a step from the traditional woman's role will inevitably cause women to be "duped into becoming devotees of a false religion which bills itself as the 'primordial, always present, and future Antichrist.'"[1]

Pride, furthermore, informs her readers that biblical "inerrancy and a 'modern' role for women are at odds, and that in fact every advocate of Liberation within the church has abandoned inerrancy."[2] She maintains that it is impossible for a Christian to divide the wheat from the chaff in feminist thought, because feminism itself is a religion based on the modified humanist notion that "woman is the measure of all things." Therefore, Pride says, "the burning question becomes, 'What will fulfill me as a woman? Anything that interferes with my sovereign "fulfillment" is to be destroyed—and I mean *anything.'* Let's take a look at what our nice, tame, evangelical feminists are willing to destroy," she continues. "First, they endorse abortion."[3] And on she goes.

If I knew nothing else about feminism, Mary Pride would certainly induce me to sound a vigorous call for a return to traditional gender roles in the church—as she surely has done for many of her readers. The approach to this issue that is adopted by many evangelical traditionalists, and is typified here by Mary Pride, is the product of what I consider to be crucial errors in cultural analysis as well as biblical interpretation (and no, I have not "abandoned inerrancy"). Because the traditionalists' view of the role

129

of culture in this debate is foundational to their view of evangelical feminism, this will be the main focus of the remaining chapters.

One-Size-Fits-All Feminism

Evangelical treatments of feminism such as Mary Pride's exemplify stereotypical thinking. Feminist ideas are stereotyped; a one-size-fits-all definition of feminism—descriptive of the most radical secular feminism, of course—is used to characterize any idea that deviates from the traditional woman's role at any point. This approach suits the traditionalist cause well, because traditionalism today, by definition and objective, equals antifeminism; it is wholly opposed to anything "feminist." It is therefore easy (although incorrect) for traditionalists to view any and all feminist thought—whether secular or biblical—as being in turn wholly opposed to every view held by traditionalists.

Evidence of this view of evangelical feminism may be found in an advertising blurb for the antifeminist manifesto, *Recovering Biblical Manhood and Womanhood:* "In the past decade, evangelical feminists have questioned almost *all* of the traditional Christian ideas about men and women."[4] In actuality, evangelical feminists have questioned relatively few of the "traditional Christian ideas about men and women," leaving quite intact the fundamental biblical doctrines concerning the sanctity of marriage as a permanent and exclusive covenant between a man and a woman, and the primary obligation of both father and mother to protect and provide for their children (whether born or unborn). It is modern *secular* feminism, not evangelical feminism, that has questioned and rejected "almost all of the traditional Christian ideas about men and women." But the inaccuracy of the one-size-fits-all definition tends to escape the minds of traditionalists who refuse to recognize any significant conceptual distinctions between modern secular feminism and evangelical feminism.

British sociologist Elaine Storkey comments concerning such traditionalist assessments of feminism:

> Many books and articles written by Christian authors have something detrimental to say about the women's movement. The most vehement are probably American. In those, even a mild veneer of courtesy to feminists is uncomfortably absent. What is frighteningly similar about all these writings however is (unavoidable) evidence that they start from a position of ignorance. Caricatures and stereotypes of feminists are curtly offered; accusations are hurled and indictments are made. . . . All feminism is the same: radical or extremely radical.[5]

Traditionalists' prejudice against evangelical feminism is evident in their prejudgment of evangelical feminism as essentially identical with radical feminism.

The Fortress of Tradition

Many evangelicals have lately been concerned that the wall of demarcation between the church and the world has been breached by assorted evils, including feminism. So the traditionalist troops have been adopting a position of retrenchment (i.e., a wall of defense behind the main fortification to which troops retreat when the outer line is penetrated). In this retrenchment effort, feminism is deemed wholly evil and traditionalism wholly biblical. A wholesale retreat to tradition is advocated as the only defense against the encroaching evil of feminism—which seems to be perceived as equally menacing whether it is secular or evangelical.

All the cultural assumptions about male/female roles and differences which were taken for granted fifty to one hundred fifty years ago, and which have lately been assailed by feminism, are being dusted off, shaken out, bolstered by biblical proof texts, and put on prominent display. Faith Martin notes, "Reactionary forces are redefining the position of women in conservative churches. There is a growing consciousness about being male or female. It is too early to predict the outcome, but if the present trend continues, women will find their role even more restricted and more at odds with Scripture."[6] Ruth Tucker and Walter Liefeld observe in *Daughters of the Church* that the "reaction to the feminist movement" has "manifested itself in many ways—one notable example being the introduction of a bachelor's degree in marriage and motherhood by the fundamentalist Hyles-Anderson College"; there have also been "stricter controls on women's ministries."[7] In a more recent book, Ruth Tucker states that "today the traditionalist movement is probably stronger in the church than it has been at any other time in this century. There has been a backlash against the feminist movement, and traditionalists have begun to organize."[8]

Falling back on tradition in order to circumvent the confusion and uncertainty of social change is not warranted, for the simple reason that that which traditionally has been understood to be biblical is not necessarily biblical at all.[9] Jesus himself made this clear when he upbraided the Pharisees, saying, "You have let go of the commands of God and are holding on to the traditions of men" (Mark 7:8). Tradition should be examined with suspicion for evidence of its tendency to take sinful patterns of human behavior and enshrine them as normative. As Blaise Pascal sagaciously observed, "Whatever the weight of antiquity, truth should always have the advantage, even when newly discovered, since it is always older than every opinion men have held about it."[10]

The Council on Biblical Manhood and Womanhood

A notable indication of the retrenchment effort has been the formation of the Council on Biblical Manhood and Womanhood, which published its "Danvers Statement" in numerous Christian periodicals in early 1989, detailing the standard traditionalist doctrine on gender roles. The council has since published a 566-page book propounding a view of gender differences so extreme that not even all traditionalists agree with it. Susan Foh, for example, questions whether the book's "definitions or any definitions of manhood or womanhood [are] found in Scripture."[11]

Although editors John Piper and Wayne Grudem write in more measured tones than are usually found in antifeminist literature, they nonetheless include in the volume some rather strident essays. For example, David Ayers asserts that "all the elements of censorship, intolerance of opposing viewpoints, fallacious reasoning, and argument-by-assertion that I have seen in contemporary feminism are evident in the 'new' feminist evangelicalism." An endnote explains that "new" is in quotation marks because evangelical feminism is really nothing newer than Gnosticism, an ancient heresy.[12] In one fell swoop, evangelical feminism is pronounced to be both secular and heretical. Harold O. J. Brown's less-than-irenic endorsement on the back cover of the book echoes these sentiments.[13] The one-size-fits-all definition of feminism appears to be a convenient weapon in the hands of many evangelical antifeminists.

Realizing that what is traditional is not necessarily biblical, Piper and Grudem disavow the label *traditionalist* to characterize their position, although they readily identify themselves as antifeminists. Yet the beliefs that the council holds on gender roles do not differ substantially from the beliefs of other evangelicals who call themselves traditionalists. Moreover, the chapter on women in church history upholds tradition as authoritative. The fact that women have not usually held leadership positions in the history of the church, the author says, "testifies" that the church throughout its history has been faithful to what the Bible teaches concerning woman's role.[14] This statement is a logical sleight of hand. It begs the question, which is, has the church traditionally understood the Bible correctly in this regard? Women's relative lack of involvement in leadership throughout church history proves nothing except that women have traditionally been subordinate to men. The statement that church tradition "confirms" the church's faithfulness to biblical teaching does not prove that the church has traditionally understood the Bible's teaching accurately; it assumes it. It is therefore an argument from tradition: this is the traditional way, this is the correct way.

Piper and Grudem also say they "prefer the term *complementarian,* since it suggests both equality and beneficial differences between men and women," and they "certainly reject the term 'hierarchicalist' because it overemphasizes structured authority."[15] Yet, they state, the thesis of the book is "that men alone are called by God to bear the primary teaching authority in the church," and they speak of their "vision of marriage that calls the husband . . . to bear the responsibility of primary leadership in the home."[16] To devote 566 pages to a defense of the thesis that men are to have authority over women in the church and the home, and then to "prefer" the term *complementarian* over *hierarchicalist* to describe that thesis, is not appropriate. The male-over-female authority structure at the heart of the council's understanding of gender roles is nothing if not hierarchical. The term *hierarchicalist* may not sound as friendly as the euphemism *complementarian,* but it is accurate.

The confusion that can result when tradition collides with social change is exemplified by the effort to retain the tradition of male authority (hierarchy) by couching it in terms compatible with contemporary psychological and theological ideas about the equality of men and women (complementarity).

Moral Breakdown of Society

The fervor with which the council holds the ten affirmations listed in the Danvers Statement is evident in the final affirmation: "We are convinced that a denial or neglect of these principles will lead to increasingly destructive consequences in our families, our churches, and the culture at large."[17] Wayne Grudem gave voice to his consternation on a "Focus on the Family" broadcast:

> We are alarmed at what is happening in the evangelical world. This feminist agenda to reinterpret Scripture and to say that Scripture doesn't apply today as it applied in the first century . . . is gaining such inroads that we need to . . . try to put a halt to this. . . . If the evangelical feminists have their way, and if their interpretations of Scripture prevail in the church, I think there will be exceptionally destructive consequences on the family itself.[18]

This sense of moral urgency is a recurring theme in antifeminist writings. It reflects an alarmist mentality, an all-or-nothing view of the situation: either we will reinstitute the traditional model of male authority, or the family, church, and society will be destroyed. Traditional gender roles are deemed God-given or God-ordained, and any deviation from these roles constitutes capitulation to radical feminism. Adherence to traditional gender roles is therefore considered a moral issue of the utmost import. (For traditionalists, the God-ordained gender roles include not only marriages that are heterosexual, monogamous, and permanent—this is undoubtedly God-ordained—but other concerns, such as who cares for the children, who earns the family income, who keeps the house, and who makes the "final decisions" in the home.)

In short, traditional gender roles (as traditionalists now define them) are seen to constitute God's established order for society. Feminism seeks to change this God-ordained social order; it is therefore deemed an evil, secular influence that the church must vigorously resist at every point.

Traditionalists emphasize the moral urgency of the feminist threat in repeated allusions to a causative link between feminism and the moral decline of society, particularly in the areas of family breakdown and sexual promiscuity. The equation of feminism with sexual sin often assumes a "slippery slope." After the order of Mary Pride's argumentative strategy, traditionalists contend that to deviate from the traditionalist agenda at any point (such as gender role flexibility in the home) is to step out onto a slippery slope that will have us sliding swiftly into sexual promiscuity, abortion, homosexuality, paganism, witchcraft, and the destruction of civilization. For traditionalists, the blasphemous excesses of radical feminism taint all feminism.

The ethic of "sexual liberation" espoused by modern secular feminism and other modern *isms* has produced a society that is overridden with divorce, unwed mothers, mistreated (and aborted) children, AIDS, and other diseases. The result of the traditionalist tactic of laying all these broken homes, broken children, and broken bodies at the door of feminism is that anything that smacks of feminism—that is, anything that questions any traditional gender role—is roundly condemned as a social evil. This blanket condemnation sweeps into its path even the efforts of biblical feminists to allow greater opportunity for women to grow in their giftedness in service to God and the church.

Although it may sometimes appear that spokesmen for traditionalism are driven primarily by the desire to have authority over women, I do not think this is their controlling motive. Rather, it seems, traditionalists believe that if such social ills as marital instability, unwed mothers, aborted babies, sexually transmitted diseases, and a general moral breakdown in society are the price we must pay for women's liberation, then the price is too high. If that really were the price, then perhaps it would be better to return to the benevolent form of patriarchy the traditionalists recommend. Perhaps the trade-off would be worth it, if by it we could preserve the moral fiber of society. The problem is that it is both historically and logically untenable to maintain that the liberation of women from male rule necessarily results in a complete disintegration of social morality. That did not happen with early feminist efforts originating in the nineteenth century, nor would it happen if the beliefs of today's evangelical feminists were implemented in church and society.

Neither evangelical feminism nor today's social ills are direct consequences of modern secular feminism. Rather—as mentioned earlier—modern secular feminism and the moral malaise of society were both occasioned by widespread, aggressive, radical individualism. Modern evangelical feminism, on the other hand, came about through women in the church wanting to use all their gifts for God's glory. Perhaps secular feminism did play a part in convincing women in the church that they had untapped resources needing to be utilized. But the social model and the theological justification for this use of female talent in ministry is not found in modern secular feminism; rather, it is rooted in the efforts of the nineteenth-century evangelical feminists to understand and implement the biblical principles of Christian equality.

Another difficulty with the traditionalist custom of blaming feminism for social and family breakdown has to do with how children were treated before and after feminism. Traditionalists frequently complain that feminism has resulted in children being mistreated. But, as noted in chapter 1, children actually fare much better today, even with feminist/career mothers, than they did for centuries under the traditional, pre-industrial social system. The emergence of feminism in the nineteenth century coincided with a cultural concern for the upbringing of children and the sanctity of the home—values shared by the feminists of that period. The early feminists believed that giving women more legal rights and social power would improve the lot of home and children by giving women opportunity to see that such were legally protected.

History offers little evidence to support the contention that feminism is responsible for the mistreatment of children. Neither does sociology support this view. As discussed in chapter 2, the likelihood of abuse in the home—other things being equal—is higher when the family is structured along hierarchical lines than when the husband and wife hold "feminist" equalitarian values. This is not to say that feminists never err in their parenting styles; putting career success ahead of children's needs is always wrong for either mother or father. But, historically and sociologically, the abusive treatment of children cannot be considered a consequence of feminism.

When traditionalists define as "feminist" any belief that deviates at any point from the traditionalist agenda, and when they advance their agenda as the only means of preserving biblical family values, then any questioning of "traditional family values" is "feminist" and anything feminist is destructive of family, church, and society. Moreover, it is assumed that all feminism is alike and that any feminist position has more in common with extreme, radical feminism than it has with traditionalism. Feminism thus becomes the all-purpose enemy, the bogeywoman that is abhorred with grave loathing and resisted with great diligence.

Antifeminist reasoning can be summarized in the form of a logical syllogism: (1) All feminism is alike. (2) Feminism destroys the God-ordained social order. (3) Therefore, any kind of feminism—including evangelical feminism—necessarily destroys the God-ordained social order. The conclusion is logically valid, given the premises. But the premise that all feminism is alike is quite false, which I hope I have made clear in the preceding seven chapters. Although the idea that modern secular feminism destroys the God-ordained social order is not too far off the mark, it would be claiming too much to say that every contribution modern secular feminism has made to society has constituted a rebellion against God's order, or that it is the chief cause of social and moral breakdown.

Sliding into Apostasy

Radical feminist Naomi Goldenberg stated in 1979 that "the feminist movement in Western culture is engaged in the slow execution of Christ and Yahweh. Yet very few of the women and men now working for sexual equality within Christianity and Judaism realize the extent of their heresy."[19] Christian antifeminists such as Mary Kassian and Mary Pride take these words—uttered by a virulently anti-Christian proponent of radical feminist spirituality—to be absolutely true.[20] Although they are at opposite ends of the "gender spectrum," radical feminists and traditionalists share Goldenberg's premise that a masculine God and a male-dominant social order are intrinsic elements of biblical Christianity, which to disavow is to disavow both the authority of the Bible and the fundamental tenets of the historic church. In other words, to embrace women's equality is to move ultimately and inexorably toward apostasy.

With careful scholarship grounded in conservative theology, evangelical feminists have challenged the assumption that male authority is integral to biblical Christianity. Yet the evidence that has been summoned in support of biblical equality is often dismissed as merely a culturally-induced rebellion against the sexual hierarchy traditionally believed to be mandated by the Bible. Evangelical feminists are simply and summarily consigned to the same corrupt category as the most radical of radical feminists. Mary Kassian, for example, maintains that all feminists—including evangelical feminists—have grounded their thinking in the "faulty presupposition" or

> precept of feminism which exalts the importance of personal experience in defining one's worldview. In doing so, they have stepped over the watershed onto a slope that will certainly lead to total acceptance of radical feminism. The only difference between the conservatives and the radicals is that conservative Biblical feminists have not yet followed their presuppositions through to their logical end.[21]

But this type of antifeminist argument rests on the questionable notion that evangelical feminists—heedlessly and unwittingly—have absorbed antibiblical motives and assumptions from secular feminist ideology and have grounded their views in these motives and assumptions. But how feasible is this notion? Certainly no evangelical feminist would actually claim women's personal experience as an authority higher than or equal to biblical revelation. In fact, it is precisely their refusal to do so that distinguishes evangelical feminists from all other feminists.

Nonetheless, traditionalists insist, the same idolatrous and heretical premise of other varieties of feminism lurks behind evangelical feminism as well. Why? Simply because, according to traditionalists, all feminism is alike. It is all, at root, a rebellion against God's order. It cannot possibly be true. Because evangelical feminism is presumed to be false, its premise is presumed to be unbiblical. Its "unbiblical" premise is then invoked as evidence of its error. Rather than taking evangelical feminists at their word, antifeminist apologists seek recourse in hidden motives and insidious agendas of creeping apostasy. An issue that evangelical feminists insist is a matter of exegetical debate comes to be regarded instead as a watershed dispute concerning the acceptance or rejection of biblical authority.

In casting the conflict in such stark terms, traditionalists view evangelical feminists as at once inside the fold and outside the fold. They *are* evangelicals in that they overtly affirm a conservative theology and a respect for biblical authority. But they are not evangelicals in that they teach a theology of gender that is deemed so blatantly erroneous that it can be arrived at only by replacing biblical authority with the authority of "feminist ideology." They are not evangelicals in that, if they continue in their feminist beliefs, they themselves will eventually acknowledge their inevitable renunciation of conservative Christian theology. Evangelical feminists are—unbeknownst even to themselves—wolves in sheep's clothing.

Not only does the traditionalist assessment put evangelical feminists in a peculiar and contradictory position, but it claims a virtual infallibility for the traditionalist interpretation of biblical teaching on gender. The traditionalist critique of evangelical feminism as a misbegotten offshoot of antibiblical modern feminism would crumble to the ground if any admission were made as to the *debatability* of the traditionalist and evangelical feminist interpretations of Scripture. The rejection of evangelical feminism as a product of modern secular feminism entails a view of evangelical feminists as headed toward heresy, and of traditionalists as undebatably correct in their interpretation of biblical teaching on gender.

A disagreement that is in reality a matter of legitimate debate over biblical interpretation *within* the bounds of orthodoxy is thereby construed to be an epic conflict between heresy and orthodoxy itself. On these terms, the conflict is unresolvable. Healthy debate is ruled out, because the matter has been ruled undebatable a priori. One does not, after all, entertain the tenets of heresy as a plausible interpretation of Scripture.

Because the unity and integrity of the church is at stake, we need seriously to assess the traditionalist construal of evangelical feminism as a new gospel—a heresy, in fact—that has been imported to the church directly from modern culture. This sweeping claim should be questioned carefully, rather than accepted automatically as an easy resolution to a controversial issue. On what grounds is an affirmation of biblical equality deemed ultimately heretical?

In a "Focus on the Family" interview, Mary Kassian stated that once women rebelled against being viewed as merely housewives and servants of men (which is how she correctly described the initial stage of modern feminism in the 1960s), secular feminist thought followed a "very logical progression" by which feminist women came eventually to deify themselves and to make God female.[22] If extremely radical, woman-centered feminism is the logical conclusion of even the moderate feminist idea that women's vocational options should consist of more than homemaking, then evangelical feminism, which also seeks to expand women's vocational and ministerial options, is bound for the same blasphemous end as radical feminist spirituality. Consequently, any non-traditional view of gender roles in the evangelical church is judged to be simply a product of the incursion of modern secular feminism into the church, which will lead logically and inexorably to the deification of woman and the feminization of God. This is also Mary Pride's position.

In a sense, the progression in feminist thought in modern secular feminism *was* inevitable, because modern secular feminism is premised on modern individualism, which absolutizes the will of the individual. This leads logically not only to a rebellion against women always being only housewives and servants of men, but also to a denial that women are accountable to anyone or any standard of moral authority outside of themselves. This denial of responsibility is expressed in such practices as sexual promiscuity, abortion, and no-fault divorce. It is also expressed in a rejection of the biblical God and in the worship of a goddess made in woman's own female image.

Having noted the false premise of modern secular feminism, have we disallowed biblical validity for *any* view that maintains that women ought not restrict their vocations to being housewives and servants of men? Hardly. In its initial stage, modern secular feminism asserted some of the right things for the wrong reason; but because of the faulty premise, the ultimate conclusion was faulty as well. It happened, though, that in its early years modern secular feminism hit upon a true idea: that women ought not always be governed by men, and that they ought to have the freedom to be persons in their own right, even as men have this freedom. Modern secular feminism, however, bases this idea on modern individualism; therefore it does not balance it with a recognition of the responsibilities that both women and men have toward each other and toward their families, church, communities, and God.

In contrast to modern secular feminism, evangelical feminism bases the idea of woman's equality on the premise of biblical equality: that man and woman are created equally in God's image (Gen. 1:26–27) and that in Christ there is no distinction in privilege or prerogative between male and female (Gal. 3:28). This premise leads to the rejection of the idea of underclasses consisting of such people as women, slaves, and Gentiles (or, translated to present-day categories, women and minorities). But it does not lead to granting the formerly oppressed *special* rights by which they are favored over their oppressors. Nor does it lead to rejecting such moral imperatives as marital fidelity and parental responsibility—which were commanded by the God in whose image all people are made. It certainly does not lead to a quasi-pantheistic religion that worships the goddess within.

A rejection of the ideology of modern individualism does not logically entail a categorical rejection of all the beliefs modern secular feminists have derived from it. We have no grounds to reject those beliefs that can also be derived from biblical principles. All feminism is not alike. Secular feminism and evangelical feminism may share some similar beliefs, but the premises and the ultimate conclusions of each are worlds apart.

The Androgyny Alarm

Repeatedly in antifeminist efforts, the specter of androgyny is invoked as the primary aim of all feminist ideology. The inevitable result of this androgyny agenda is seen to be the complete obliteration of any meaningful distinction between male and female, which will lead inexorably to homosexuality and the breakdown of the family and society. With such an understanding of androgyny, and of feminism as the relentless purveyor of this perversity, it is no wonder that feminism is feared. The traditionalist fear of feminism appears in large measure to be the fear of the social legitimization of homosexuality. In defense against this threat, antifeminists resort to traditional ideas about women and men which entail very different psychological natures and vocational callings. This they see as their only safeguard against the evil intrusion of androgyny.

This common traditionalist perception of the feminist agenda is misguided in three ways. First, apparently unbeknownst to many traditionalists, very few feminists advocate androgyny as traditionalists understand it—which is as a refusal to acknowledge any differences between men and women other than reproductive function. The remarks during James Dobson's interview with Wayne Grudem and Mary Kassian[23] illustrate the traditionalist confusion on this score. Please note that the following criticism of their discussion is intended only to point out what I believe to be a significant misunderstanding of the evangelical feminist position on gender differences; it should not be taken as a denouncement of the ministry of "Focus on the Family" in encouraging and strengthening the family and its place in society today.

In speaking of the "Christian feminism" advocated by Mary Stewart Van Leeuwen in *Gender and Grace,* Mary Kassian "explains" that Van Leeuwen teaches that "the reason we have [gender] differences is because of sin, so we should try and overcome differences to become the same." James Dobson quickly adds to this misreading of Van Leeuwen by saying that in "the section" he read, "she is obviously attempting to say we are virtually identical except for the ability to bear children. And that is feminist ideology. . . ." He then states what he believes to be the result of this "feminist ideology": "You undermine the basis for that one-flesh . . . interaction with one another, and you destroy the family." Traditional gender differences, and the gender roles based upon these differences, seem to be viewed by traditionalists as the foundation on which marriage and the family depend. Any alteration of this view of gender differences is apparently seen as a denial of *all* gender differences and a certain step toward the destruction of the home.

Since, it would seem, Dobson had read only a section of *Gender and Grace* before speaking out against the "feminist ideology" of Van Leeuwen's Christian feminism, he must have missed the book's definition of Christian feminism (listed in the index under "Feminism, Christian (defined)"). A Christian feminist, states Van Leeuwen, is "a person of either sex who sees women and men as *equally* saved, *equally* Spirit-filled and *equally* sent." Although there is nothing in this definition that entails the notion that men and women are the same in every respect except the ability to bear children, Van Leeuwen proceeds to guard against just such a misinterpretation. She goes on: "Please note this does not imply that there are no differences between men and women. The notion of justice between the sexes does not have to mean that men and women must always do exactly the same things in exactly the same way."[24] I do not know what led James Dobson and Mary Kassian to believe that Van Leeuwen was trying to obliterate all differences between men and women, but after carefully reading the entire book, I have concluded that the moderate but flexible approach to gender differences stipulated in Van Leeuwen's definition of Christian feminism is maintained throughout the book.

Mary Stewart Van Leeuwen's perspective on gender differences is shared by other evangelicals who believe in women's equality in the church. Ruth Tucker states,

> It is difficult to argue that there are no differences between men and women—be it innate or socially acquired. The very fact that women are usually the primary caregivers in the home and in the extended family gives them a different perspective on life from the one men would normally have. . . . Women are typically more outwardly emotional than are men, and they often have a perceptiveness akin to a sixth sense—call it women's intuition, if you will. All this adds up to a potential difference in how a woman would handle decision making and problem solving. For these and other reasons, there are

distinct advantages in having both women and men in leadership roles in the church and in Christian organizations.[25]

Nicholas Wolterstorff's comments follow a similar line:

> We've been created and re-created differently. We must not try to obliterate that and become some Christian in general; rather, we must prize our particularities. What the church has lacked over the years are the particularities that women can typically bring—and bring at the highest levels of leadership to the presence and action and voice of the church. What we've had is men speaking with the voice of their particularity. And what we need now is women speaking with the voice of theirs. What we don't need is everyone trying to sing bass. We need each voice to find its place in the chorus, and for that we've got to listen to each other—especially we men to the women.[26]

Evangelical feminists do affirm that women and men are different. But the differences for which evangelical feminists see evidence do not justify exclusively male authority, whereas the gender differences propounded by traditionalists serve precisely this function. Elaine Storkey clarifies the distinction between a denial of gender differences and a desire for gender justice: "God created people as male and female, and this difference will always be there. What need not be there are the penalties women pay for their sex in so many areas of life."[27]

Not only is the ideal of androgyny uncharacteristic of evangelical feminism, it is uncharacteristic even of radical feminism. As mentioned in chapters 6 and 7, a fairly recent trend in radical feminist circles has been to reverse androcentrism and, by highlighting femininity, to demonstrate its superiority over masculinity. "Female power" is the battle cry of the gynocentric, extremely radical feminists. Rather than incorporating the "masculine" into the "feminine" to form an "androgynous" whole, these women reject masculinity entirely.

Androgyny, as traditionalists understand it, is not espoused by evangelical feminists, and it is not popular in radical feminist circles. Moreover, androgyny is nowhere to be seen in the popular culture's perception of women and men. Whatever the problems may be with the popular, media-promoted attitudes about sexuality (and problems there are, to be sure), they do not entail a denial of gender differences. On a recent television special, "The Search for the New Ideal Man," television personalities could be seen pontificating along these lines: "Men are creatures of logic, whereas women are creatures of emotion. So it makes it difficult . . . to understand what the other person is talking about" (Will Smith). "I don't think men and women speak the same language at all. In fact, I don't even think we're the same race" (Roseanne Arnold).[28] These people may be quite "modern" in their ideas about "sexual liberation," but they haven't ventured very far from traditional folklore when it comes to gender stereotypes.

Second, the traditionalist fear of androgyny is misguided not only in its exaggerated concept of the extremity and pervasiveness of androgyny, but also in its understanding of the implications of *some* feminists' denial of *some* of the traditional gender differences. In order for sexuality to be meaningful, men and women do not have to be viewed as the functional equivalent of two different species who are opposites in virtually every respect (as the traditionalist view would seem to have it). Rather, the potential for meaning in marriage is far greater if allowance is made for individuality, role flexibility, and the possibility of common ground between a man and a woman. It does not promote homosexuality to acknowledge that both men and women have basically the same human needs, desires, and range of abilities and vocational callings, and that those differences which exist in these areas are less significant than the commonalities. Such a view of men and women will not change heterosexuals to homosexuals; if anything, it should increase the staying power of male-female romantic relationships by offering the possibility of real friendships with common interests.

Third, traditionalists are misguided in their apparent belief that to argue against androgyny is also to argue against feminism and for traditionalism. For one thing, as already mentioned, the denial of differences between men and women is *not* the central premise of all types of feminism.[29] For another, the fact that many feminists reject the idea of androgyny—focusing instead on the differences between women and men—shows that merely to affirm gender differences is not to affirm the tenets of traditionalism.

In order to justify male authority and traditional gender roles on the basis of gender differences, traditionalists must do more than simply demonstrate the existence of gender differences. They must also show four things to be true about these differences. First, men and women must be shown to be different *innately,* as opposed to merely culturally. There must be gender differences that derive from biology rather than social conditioning. Most people on both sides of the feminist divide are willing to acknowledge this much. There *are* some biologically-based gender differences which influence functions other than reproduction. Second, these innate gender differences must be shown to be significant and substantive and relatively impervious to cultural conditioning. Their effects on human behavior must be more than incidental, minor proclivities. These differences must have a direct bearing on behavior, such that different roles and statuses follow logically from them. Third, these innate and significant differences must somehow be shown to be part of God's original design for men and women, and not a sinful distortion of that design. To demonstrate that men, for example, "naturally" tend more toward crime and violence is not to demonstrate an aspect of God's ordained plan for the male nature. Fourth, having ascertained the existence of innate, significant, and God-ordained gender differences, traditionalists must show that these differences unequivocally indicate that men are better suited to lead and women are more in need of being led. They must clearly show men to be better equipped intellectually for serious scholarly and creative endeavors and women to be better equipped for domestic duties. Gender differences must justify traditional gender roles. Men and women must be shown to be inherently fitted for unequal status.

Frequently, antifeminists will first assert that androgyny is the premise of all feminism, then will set about giving evidence for the existence of innate gender differences, and then will assume that feminism has thereby been discredited and traditionalism vindicated.[30] This simply doesn't work.

Jumping to Conclusions and onto Bandwagons

The bandwagon mentality is at the heart of much of the consternation over feminism in the church. It is an outlook that dispenses with rational discourse and careful examination of evidence and ideas, and instead classifies every idea about gender roles as either feminist and wholly opposed to tradition, or traditionalist and wholly opposed to feminism. This, in part, is why any effort to modify the traditional view of gender differences is simply viewed as the obliteration of all gender differences.

Such a way of thinking not only promotes prejudice, it precludes accurate assessment of the options available. It asserts that anyone who speaks of equal rights for women advocates equality in the same sense as the radical feminists. This is not a new tactic for traditionalists to use against feminists; it was employed by the opponents of women's suffrage. Comments historian Andrew Sinclair: "As was usual in anti-suffrage propaganda, the few feminists who advocated complete equality with men in all areas of life were wrongly equated with the mass of the suffragists."[31] Those who opposed women's suffrage fought the movement by caricaturing *all* suffragists as radical extremists.

Probably for many traditionalists, some early encounter with feminists of the strident, angry, Bible-despising variety engendered in them a lasting conviction that this is what feminism is all about. A person so persuaded is unlikely to be open-minded about a feminism which claims to be biblical and which, in reality, has more in common with traditionalism than it has with left-wing radical feminism. People who reject evangelical feminism for this reason are not unlike those who reject Christianity on the basis of some chance meeting with an unappealing Christian—an uneducated, bigoted, Bible-thumping preacher, for example—who is not a representative of Christianity but a caricature of it. As Mary Stewart Van Leeuwen points out, "We need to think of the feminist movement the same way we would like nonbelievers to think of us as Christians. That is, we don't like it when someone observes questionable activities in a sect or cult and jumps to the conclusion that all Christians must be like that. Yet Christians often look at some of the disturbing things coming out of . . . feminism and conclude that all feminism is bad."[32]

But instead of employing the Golden Rule and the principle of charity (that is, not immediately assuming the worst about someone before getting all the facts), it seems that traditionalists are sometimes too eager to employ emotionalized and even inflammatory rhetoric in denouncing the evils of feminism—which, to their mind, includes evangelical feminism. All too often, when someone in the church dares to offer a suggestion deemed "feminist," the guardians of "God's established order" quickly and quietly whip out the branding iron, and that person is stigmatized as an ungodly, anti-family feminist before she even has opportunity to define and defend her views on biblical grounds.

In *Decisive Issues Facing Christians Today,* John Stott exemplifies a more fair-minded traditionalism. After reviewing with appreciation Elaine Storkey's survey of feminist thought, he observes that "feminism cannot be dismissed as a secular bandwagon which trendy churches (in their worldliness) jump on board."[33] Unlike many traditionalist writers, Stott has taken the time and effort to hear what feminists have been saying, and he recognizes some legitimacy in their ideas. Unfortunately, his approach does not seem to characterize that of many traditionalists.

Making—and Missing—Important Distinctions

The fellowship breakdown between feminists and traditionalists in the church is exacerbated still further by the traditionalists' frequent failure to distinguish between two types of Christian feminists—those who share their respect for the authority of the Bible and those who do not believe in the full authority of Scripture. There is a world of difference between these two types of feminists, yet both are often referred to as Christian feminists.

Compounding the confusion are feminists who call themselves "biblical" and "evangelical," yet who espouse a theologically liberal view of Scripture and condone homosexuality and abortion. Roberta Hestenes pinpoints the distinction between the truly biblical feminists and all others: "There are some feminists who believe that if feminism and Christianity come into conflict, Christianity must change. That's wrong. I'm a feminist because I believe the Bible teaches the full partnership of women alongside men in the church."[34]

Because theologically liberal feminism has gained a greater influence in mainline denominations than has theologically conservative feminism in evangelical churches, a traditionalist is quite likely to think only of liberal feminist theology when he hears of something called Christian feminism. This would especially be true of a traditionalist whose impression of biblical feminism was formed in the 1970s, when nearly all feminist biblical interpretation was more liberal than evangelical feminism is today. In her critique of evangelical feminism, Mary Pride relies entirely on the early efforts of Christian feminists; from thence she concludes that evangelical feminism endorses abortion and homosexuality and is not substantially different from secular feminism.[35]

Even current traditionalist works tend to assume that the 1970s writings of so-called biblical feminists are representative of evangelical feminism today. Mary Kassian states:

> Whereas Christians have traditionally believed that the *whole* Bible is inspired by God, Biblical feminists maintained that only *some* Scripture is so inspired. The rest is so male-biased, so influenced by the writers' own culture and prejudices, that it is inapplicable to the contemporary Church.[36]

In support of this judgment, Kassian harks back to a statement of Virginia Mollenkott in 1977 that some of the apostle Paul's writings on women reflected his own male bias and cultural conditioning.[37] Mollenkott's views, of course, are not representative of an evangelical feminist approach to Scripture, but rather are much more closely aligned with liberal feminist theology. (Evangelical feminists maintain that there has been a male bias in traditional biblical interpretation; liberal feminist theologians assert that male bias is inherent in the actual text of some portions of Scripture.) Such remarks as Kassian's do violence to the fundamental distinction between the evangelical feminist historic commitment to the authority and inspiration of the *whole* of Scripture, and the relativistic approach to the Bible which has been adopted by liberal theologians in the last century.[38]

It is probably due in large part to the traditionalists' sweeping con-

Cultural Discernment:
The Contemporary versus
the Conservative

Because it is so easy to respond emotionally and jump to accusatory conclusions concerning those whose view of gender differs from our own, it is
important that we disentangle visceral reaction from rational reflection and
develop a sound, principled approach to evaluating cultural ideas from a
Christian perspective. A standard ploy of both traditionalists and feminists
is to fling at one another the indictment, "Your viewpoint is just cultural."
In a sense, they are both right. Both traditionalism and feminism are cre-
ations of culture; they are systems of human behavior that have developed
in interaction with the world views of certain members of a particular society at a particular time in history. But in another sense, evangelical feminists and traditionalists are both wrong if they think they have proved the
opposition's viewpoint unbiblical simply by labeling it "cultural." As
Christian sociologist Alvin Schmidt points out, "The question is not which
theology of women is shaped by culture, but which theology is most consistent with the teaching, practices, and mind of Christ, whom the church
considers its lord."[1]

Culture is not a dirty word; it is not in itself either good or bad. It is an
outgrowth of our humanness, a consequence of our createdness and our cre-
ativity. It is, in fact, exactly what God intended humans to produce. Cultural pursuits are indicated in God's "cultural mandate" given to the first
man and woman to fill, subdue, and rule the earth (Gen. 1:28).

Cultural Conditioning

People not only create culture, we are, in a sense, created by culture, as it in turn influences the ideas and actions of humans in society. As such, culture is a potent, pervasive, yet largely hidden force in everyone's life. The person most influenced by a particular cultural perspective is the person most likely to be unaware of its influence. (Hence our tendency to see the cultural conditioning in our opponents' viewpoints while failing to see it in our own.) Alvin Schmidt remarks on this phenomenon: "If fish could think, the last thing they would likely discover is water. Moving from fish to people, who can think but frequently do not, the last thing they discover is culture. Fish are immersed in water. People are immersed in culture. Yet neither is conscious of how their environment influences and affects them."[2] Schmidt goes on to point out that the concept of culture did not even exist until relatively recently in human history. Just as it took humankind several millennia to become aware of the cultural water we all swim in, so it often takes individual humans a great deal of time before they grasp the concept and the influence of culture in their own view of the world.

Until we are able to discern which ideas about gender stem from folklore and which are rooted in fact, men and women will continue to have difficulty understanding this issue. We need to ask: What do people really *believe* about women and men? What are the unwritten, unspoken cultural "givens" behind and beneath our attitudes and value judgments concerning the sexes? Where do our ideas come from? Are they valid? Are they Christlike? Should they be changed?

The natural human tendency is not to ask these questions, but simply to assume that the way one's own society is ordered (or used to be ordered in the "good old days") is the "natural" way for all societies to be ordered. From this follows the conclusion that the "natural" way is the correct way, in fact, the God-ordained way, and that any social system which deviates from this way is in violation of God's plan for humanity. The descriptive (the way things are) becomes prescriptive (the way things ought to be).

Scott Bartchy remarks that for many people, what seems to be natural and right is what they were brought up to believe. The ideas concerning gender roles that are currently circulating in society do have an impact on our understanding of biblical teaching. But a far more potent influence on what we perceive to be God-ordained is "the whole set of circumstances and ideas from which each of us learned in a particular way what it means to be male or female in our society. . . . It is very difficult not to hope that we will find confirmation of these deep childhood impressions in the words of Scripture."[3]

"Restorationist" Thinking

The antifeminist animus is impelled by the twin convictions that: 1) the traditionalist agenda consists of divine standards received directly from above, and 2) evangelical feminist beliefs derive entirely from the cultural contamination of the church.

This sort of mindset is characteristic of religious movements purporting to restore "God's original pattern" (however that may be articulated) in the face of perceived apostasy and moral degeneracy. Such thinking can lead to a simplistic view of good and evil and a formulaic, rigid, and dogmatic view of the biblical rules and requirements for the implementation of that "original pattern."

Different kinds of restorationist movements have cropped up in the history of the church. In one form or another, they arise for the purpose of overcoming some cultural corruption that is believed to have crept into and defiled the church. Usually these movements entail a breaking away from the established church in an effort to recover and re-establish what is understood to be the original order of things. Illustrative of such efforts are the Protestant Reformation, Puritanism, the Churches of Christ, and the Pentecostal/charismatic movement.[4]

Today's traditionalism differs from these other restorationist movements in that the traditionalists' campaign to counter corruption in the church has not led them to flee church traditions but to return to them. The traditionalist perception of the problem is not that the church needs to break away from the culture of its own religious traditions, but that the church needs to escape from the influence of secular culture. Despite this twist on the restorationist pattern, the intellectual impetus is the same. There is a strong drive to delineate right from wrong—to define the "right" in terms of how things were done in biblical times and the "wrong" in terms of the specific cultural conventions being shunned.

Mark Noll describes the "conceptual landscape" of restorationist thought as marked by "intellectual overconfidence, sectarian delusion, and stunningly naive confidence in the power of humans to extract themselves from the influences of history."[5] In noting the "problem with balance when it comes to biblical interpretation" in the charismatic movement, Garry Nation comments: "It is one thing to interpret the Bible literally as the supreme authority; it is quite another to use the Bible dogmatically and in a way that insists that congregational life today must replicate that of the first-century church. Restorationists often seem not to know the difference between rules and principles."[6] With the substitution of "family life" for "congregational life," both descriptions of restorationist thought would appear applicable to the conceptual landscape of traditionalism.

Traditionalism—like restorationist thinking in general—seems to be highly vulnerable to committing two major errors. First, there is a tendency to overestimate the ease of freeing one's own ideas and assumptions from the pull of culture and history. Second, having underrated the force of history and the difference it makes, the tendency is to understand all biblical directives as literally binding for the present time—without alteration or modification. There is a failure to apprehend correctly the role of culture in shaping theology, and consequently a failure to distinguish principles (which do not change) from rules (which can change from one cultural setting to another).

It should be pointed out, however, that despite the pitfalls of restoration-type thinking, such movements generally do accomplish a great deal of good, especially in the early stages. Certainly the traditionalist movement—with its campaign against such social evils as abortion, pornography, inadequate childcare, divorce, and sexual promiscuity—has been a force for the good in many ways.

The Church and Secular Culture

In its efforts to relate to secular culture, the approach of the church has been similar to the attitudes held by modern secular feminists toward men. Just as feminists usually try either to be separate from men or to be like men (in their wholesale appropriation of traditionally "male" behavior), so the church historically has chosen either to be separate from secular culture or to follow the lead of secular culture. A paucity of perceived options concerning the church's relationship to the world and a naivete as to the coercive force of culture has haunted the church's understanding of how to be "in the world but not of the world." But *separating* from what is evil in culture, *conserving* what is good in culture, and *transforming* what can be changed are all essential in order for the church to maintain a biblical stance in regard to secular culture.[7]

Those who are theologically liberal readily recognize the influence of contemporary culture on their ideas—if only because they welcome it. The liberal emphasis is primarily on conserving what is perceived to be good in culture. Theologically conservative Christians, on the other hand, make an effort to reject contemporary culture. Because of this, conservatives often conclude that they are rejecting all cultural influence and are devoting themselves instead to the "pure" biblical revelation. They are unaware of how easy it is, in rejecting modern culture, simply to endorse the secular culture of the past. When culture is denied entirely and separation is stressed to the exclusion of transformation and conservation, culture sneaks in through the back door. Human society—even religious society—is impossible without human culture.

Again we see the similarity of traditionalism to restorationism; in both, culture and human tradition tend to creep in unawares. Restorationist "groups regularly proceed to establish the particular forms of their restoration . . . as 'traditionless traditions' that become every bit as inflexible as the supposedly corrupt traditions that the movements came into existence to overcome."[8]

Biblical feminists believe that the doctrine of male authority taught in conservative churches today has slipped into church doctrine from the traditional patriarchal culture of the past, not from the faithful application of biblical principles. They point to many things to substantiate this belief, not the least of which is the clear, incontrovertible presence of patriarchy (in varying degrees) in all cultures throughout all of recorded history. This is in contrast to the fact that the Bible, although adapting the form of its message to the form of patriarchal culture, does not make a clear advocacy of male supremacy but rather teaches principles of mutuality and equality which actually subvert cultural patriarchy.[9]

Faith Martin perceptively comments, "The church must drop its defensive attitude on the question of women and come to terms with the culture into which Christianity was born. To what extent did the church conquer pagan culture? In the determining of the role of women, which has had the greatest influence—the teaching of Scripture or a male-dominated culture?"[10] Conservative Christians routinely underrate the degree to which the theological formulations of the church were shaped through the centuries by the sexist attitudes and beliefs of secular culture. "They believe that culture only recently has begun to influence theology, which, of course, makes it 'liberal.'"[11] In their concern to remain separate from theological liberalism, conservatives tend to equate being culturally aware with being liberal, and so they steer away from efforts to understand culture and its effects. The result of this line of thinking is a denial of the pervasive influence which culture has on the ideas and actions of *every* person, including conservative theologians.

In their reaction against the liberals' culture-consciousness, conservatives also underrate the importance of understanding the cultural settings of the biblical writings in order to understand the basic message and intent of the biblical writers. Because liberals have been known to invoke the irrelevance of ancient culture in justifying a rejection of certain portions of Scripture as uninspired or merely cultural, conservatives often conclude that any talk of understanding the culture of ancient times can lead only to an irreverence for the Bible. Since conservatives are (understandably) determined to avoid such irreverence at all costs, they do so, often at the cost of a clear understanding of biblical principles and how they were applied in biblical times and ought to be applied in our own.

The error toward which conservatives tend is to regard the Bible as something akin to a magic book: open it at any point and apply the instructions directly to your own life. The error in liberalism is to regard the Bible as a wax nose: mold it into whatever shape is compatible with current cultural trends. Whether liberal or conservative, until we are aware and duly suspicious of our culturally preconceived ideas and expectations, we will not realize how significantly they are likely to distort our understanding of what the Bible teaches.

Culture and Biblical Interpretation

Knowing what the Bible says is not the same as knowing what it means. The effort to determine the biblical meaning or message and to apply that message to people today is the work of biblical interpretation. There are a number of ways in which culture can influence biblical interpretation. Some are negative, some are positive.

Culture can surreptitiously and insidiously shape our sense of what is right and fitting. We tend to *expect* Scripture to say what we think is right and fitting, and then we are inclined to see in its words the meaning that we expect to see. Culture of any time period can have such an influence. Contemporary culture, the cultural lessons learned in childhood, or even the traditional biblical interpretations which were themselves a product of cultural influence in the past, can mold our expectations and hence our understandings of the biblical message. Culture is most likely to affect biblical interpretation in this negative way when those interpreting Scripture are not aware of their susceptibility to cultural preunderstandings.

People who *are* aware of the danger of cultural influence—but only that of *contemporary* culture—may interpret the Bible according to their reaction against culture. Thus, they will presume that whatever the Bible means, its meaning will *not* be in agreement at any point with contemporary culture. This too is a way of allowing culture to shape biblical interpretation.

Another way in which culture can have a negative effect on biblical interpretation occurs when contemporary culture is consciously taken as an authoritative source of truth higher than or equivalent to biblical authority. The Bible's meaning is therefore molded to fit the priorities and premises of modern cultural thought. Those texts which disagree with this revised biblical message are deemed unauthoritative. This is the liberal error and, as discussed in chapter 6, is the hermeneutic of liberal feminist theologians.

In a positive sense, culture can inform us concerning aspects of truth which are not elements of the Bible's core message (the message of who God is and how we are to relate to him), but which are implications of that message and/or are compatible with that message. Cultural concerns, such as civil rights, abolition of slavery, or women's equality, are not central to the Bible's core message of salvation. In other words, biblical salvation does not hinge on the liberation of slaves and women; this is why the New Testament writers were willing to make some accommodations to ancient patriarchal culture in this regard. But the biblical truth of the equality of all persons under God is entailed by the biblical message of salvation. This truth is grounded in creation, as indicated in Genesis 1:26–27 (all humans are created in God's image). It is a basis of God's offer of salvation to all, as indicated in Acts 10:34 (God shows no favoritism for one group of people over another). And it is a consequence of God's act of salvation, as indicated in Galatians 3:26–28 (all are "sons" in Christ; there is no distinction between slave or free, male or female). Christians who have sought the liberation of slaves and women have generally done so believing that their liberation is clearly implied by this principle of biblical equality. Viewing such social movements as *implications* of the gospel, however, should be distinguished from the approach of liberation theology, which maintains that the liberation of oppressed peoples *is* the gospel message.

Until society begins to mobilize on a cause of liberation and social justice, the church will often be blinded to the social implications of the biblical message. Sometimes—as happened most notably in abolitionism and early evangelical feminism—a social movement will be impelled in part by the cultural influence of Christians who see the biblical truth of the cause before the rest of the church realizes it. So there can be a mutually reinforcing interaction between truth discovered in the Bible and truth discovered in culture. But how could so many people in the church remain blind to a truth until it comes up in culture? It is because of the strong tendency (as discussed above) for culture to shape theology subtly and surreptitiously. The cultural acceptance of slavery and social inequality in the nineteenth century was so complete that the Bible was interpreted in light of it. Biblical proof texts were cited in support of slavery and other forms of social injustice.

Culture can also contribute to our knowledge of truth in areas such as the sciences, for which the Bible does not serve as a comprehensive text-book. When truth discovered about God's creation is compatible with biblical teaching, it can enrich our understanding of God, ourselves, and the Bible's message to us. Robert Bowman explains:

> There are many truths—mathematical, scientific, historical, psychological, and other sorts of truths—that are not found specifically in the Bible. All such truths, if indeed they are truths and not mistaken notions, must cohere with the Bible. Sometimes our knowledge of the Bible will lead us to correct our mistaken notions about history or science or psychology. On the other hand, sometimes advances in our knowledge in these fields will force us to reexamine and refine, even correct, our understanding of the Bible. This happened, for example, when Galileo proved that the earth revolves around the sun and therefore that the earth moves, contrary to the standard interpretations of the Bible at that time.[12]

Certainly, the Bible is the highest authority and the final arbiter of truth. But truth that does not contradict biblical truth—and is either implicit in the Bible or simply not addressed in the Bible—can still be learned from culture. Just because an idea has its source in culture doesn't mean it is false. As has often been observed, all truth is God's truth. Truth is true, wherever it may be found.[13]

Poisoning the Well

"There is a principle which is a bar against all information, which is proof against all arguments and cannot fail to keep a man in everlasting ignorance—that principle is contempt prior to investigation."[14] People have a marked propensity for confusing the source of an idea with the reason to believe the idea. If the source is despised, the idea is automatically despised also. This error in thinking is often referred to as "poisoning the well." Many Christians have poisoned the well in the evangelical feminist/traditionalist debate; they have formed the a priori opinion that any idea of gender roles that deviates from traditionalism is "feminist," that anything feminist can only derive from secular culture, and that anything that comes from today's secular culture can only be opposed to biblical truth. Such thinking entails not only poisoning the well—or the source—of feminist thought, but misidentifying that source as well. But even assuming for the sake of argument that evangelical feminism is derived *entirely* from secular culture (which it is not, as we have seen in chapters 3 and 4), it would still be logically unfounded to presume that there is no truth in secular culture, and so to conclude that there is no truth in any feminist thought. Rather than prejudicing the issue thus, a wiser move would be to investigate the actual claims of feminist thought and then decide.

Nicholas Wolterstorff explains the understanding John Calvin held in regard to the relationship of culture and truth.

> Calvin's own idea, which he states officially in his *Institutes,* is this: that the Spirit of God rules over humanity and produces culture. . . . But Calvin recognized a fallenness in human beings. What emerges in culture is always an ambiguous mixture. One has to say a yes and a no. One needs to appropriate, but to appropriate critically, with discernment. The [Calvinist, or Reformed] tradition never says that any movement, including feminism, is wrong through and through. It says that what is called for is a critical appropriation, a discerning critique of what is good and what is bad.[15]

The idea of civil rights was not derived merely from within the church through biblical exegesis, but arose primarily from historical developments in secular culture. The evangelical church today does not repudiate the idea of civil rights because its source lay in secular culture (although there was a strong tendency at the beginning of the civil rights movement for the church to do so).[16] Rather, the evangelical church has come to see—after the fact—that the idea of legally guaranteed equal rights for all citizens is a consistent outworking of the principles of biblical truth. The analogy, Gilbert Bilezikian claims, holds for the issue of gender roles.

> It is a documented fact that some evangelicals were already advocating an egalitarian interpretation of Scripture prior to the emergence of the feminist movement. However, other egalitarians may well acknowledge their indebtedness to secular feminism for their new awareness of Scripture. This indebtedness does not make them *ipso facto* secular, feminist, or heretical. Nor does adherence to civil rights make others secular, radical, or heretical. Throughout history, God has demonstrated that he may use a wide variety of resources to shock his people out of their complacencies.[17]

Chronological Snobbery

Just as we must avoid the snobbery that despises any idea which appears to be "cultural," so we must beware of the chronological snobbery that selectively despises cultural ideas, depending on the point in history at which an idea surfaced in culture. The primary distinctive of the two polit-

ical (and theological) bandwagons in America—liberal and conservative—
is their differing valuation of historical chronology. The liberal position values the contemporary, regards change as progress, and decries the traditional. The conservative bandwagon values the traditional, resists change,
and clings to the customs of the recent past. The bottom-line judgment of
each of these positions concerning any given idea will depend on the point
in history at which the idea was culturally prevalent. Thus the method of
cultural critique is fairly straightforward for those who take refuge in the
cultural fortress of either conservatism or liberalism. They simply peer
through the windows of their fortress at everything that is happening outside and roundly condemn it all.

Such a method of truth determination is severely flawed, due to the fact
that at any point in history, culture will be a mixture of both truth and error.
Yet, because truth and error coexist and interrelate in any cultural system
of thought, they appear to be all of a piece and therefore inseparable; so the
customary approach is for the entire system of thought to be either rejected as false or accepted as true. But truth and error in culture are not inseparable if judgment is made according to biblical standards rather than according to historical chronology.

The trend in modern society is to accept all that is new, regardless of its
value. On the other hand, many Christians are reacting to today's rapidly
changing society by clinging for security to "traditional values," failing to
discern the actual merit of those traditions. The assumption is that if something is old and familiar, it must be good. But a love for security untempered
by a love for justice and truth blocks needed reform. When tradition is examined and found to be unjust and false, then "conservatives" must not hes-
itate to offer a corrective. Yet we need to be careful not to fall off the other
edge into the liberal mentality and come to value all change as progress, and
in the process to throw out more than one baby with the bath water.

Chronological snobbery—whether in the form of preference for the new
or preference for the old—is a huge barrier to the development of a sound,
biblical position concerning gender roles.[18] In evaluating today's social customs and attitudes about the roles of men and women, we must ask of both
traditionalism and modernity: at what points are these world views in line
with biblical principles, and at what points do they deviate from the truth?

Historical Myopia

The liberal inclination toward the contemporary and the conservative
penchant for the recent past afflicts both groups with a case of historical

myopia; they tend to be unaware of and unconcerned with historical developments prior to their preferred point in history. Traditionalists, for example, routinely complain that the idea of equal opportunity for women is rooted in modern (post-1960s) feminism rather than in biblical principles and ought, therefore, to be uprooted directly. But history shows that evangelical feminism is not simply a spin-off from contemporary radical feminism. Its roots go back much farther—not to a purely secular movement, but to the evangelical revivals of the nineteenth century.[19]

In its emphasis on equal rights for women—particularly in the area of public ministry—today's evangelical feminism should be seen as a continuation of the emphasis of nineteenth-century evangelical feminism. This continuity is not interrupted by the fact that *secular* feminism of the late twentieth century has based its understanding of equal rights for women on some very unbiblical ideas not shared by evangelical feminists of either the nineteenth or the twentieth centuries.

Another insight from the past, which is often obscured by historical myopia, is that the conservatives of the late nineteenth century were also guilty of chronological snobbery. The early feminist campaign for equitable legal rights for women (primarily the right to vote, own property, and receive a college education) was met with horror by the traditionalists both within and without the church, who predicted widespread social disaster were these feminist ideas to be implemented. Fortunately, not all within the church were of such convictions.[20] One nineteenth-century objection to allowing women to receive a college education was that it "would make women dissatisfied with their divinely-appointed roles in society, and disrupt the complementarity that is at the heart of the marriage relationship."[21] This rings a familiar note. Traditionalists today declare that allowing more equality and mutuality between the sexes will destroy the God-ordained roles for men and women and, as a result, destroy marriage, family, and society.

The traditionalist complaint concerning evangelical feminism's supposed source in modern culture founders on the illogical shoals of chronological snobbery, historical myopia, and poisoning of the well. Any cultural idea—whether traditional or contemporary—should be evaluated in the light of logic and biblical truth rather than prejudice and preconceptions.

Emotional Resistance
to Evangelical Feminism

In addition to the conceptual confusion surrounding the issue of gender roles, there appears to be a deeply felt need among many people to hang on to the traditional roles as if for dear life. This fervent resolve to retain the roles learned in the past can cause some people to evade careful questioning of their assumptions and can also rouse in them a volatile emotional response whenever their beliefs are challenged. There is a lot at stake here—not simply theologically, but psychologically as well.

Nicholas Wolterstorff provides some food for thought concerning the emotional reasons behind the evangelical resistance to equality for women:

> The oddity in my own [Christian Reformed] denomination, though (and I daresay the situation is comparable in some other settings), has been that committee after committee appointed by Synod has always said in its majorities that the conservative interpretation of the passages was not compelling. But that didn't lead people to give up. . . . Why the resistance? In good measure it has been a struggle for males to hang on to power, a struggle partly generated by fear. And just not wanting women there! . . . In the face of a three-century-long process of reinterpreting the Bible under the influence of historical criticism, people have been afraid that if they changed their mind at any point on what this or that passage meant, everything was going to slip and slide away. Never again would they find a place to dig in their heels. . . . Once upon a time men said, "They're too emotional, they can't think as well." And so forth. But conservatives writing synodical reports have usually not said that. In fact, they have said just the opposite, oddly, that women are just as good at it as men, but God said women shouldn't preach.

. . . I've noticed in some of these people a deep irrational revulsion at the very prospect of women preaching.[1]

The earlier justification for women's subordination to male leadership—that women are not competent to lead—is now seen by many not to be viable; yet the emotional appeal of gender role stratification remains strong. As Wolterstorff points out, fear of the imagined slippery slope and the desire to continue to exclude women from the activities of the menfolk are two reasons that account for the emotional resistance to women's equality in the church.

Nostalgia and Fear of Change

Other emotional factors clearly at work in the antifeminist response are nostalgia for the security of 1950s'-style American suburban home life and a fear of social change of any sort. This attitude fuels the traditionalist bandwagon.

More than at any other time or place in history, people today have ample cause for consternation over rampant social change. Modernity has brought pluralism, relativism, skepticism, subjectivism, individualism, and a host of other *isms* which have cut away many of the traditional underpinnings of society. Regardless of whether these changes are good or bad—and they can be both good and bad—they are stressful. The rules have changed. People who came of age in the 1950s before the social upheaval of the 1960s are especially likely to be distressed that the old rules they were taught no longer seem to apply. There is a natural human tendency to hang on to the old, familiar ways learned in childhood. If they can be enshrined as "God's order for society," so much the better. As Scott Bartchy observes, "The ideas and actions we have learned and seen as little children . . . have shaped our feelings about which activities, ambitions, and attitudes are appropriate for males and which are appropriate for females."[2] The emotional equanimity of many adults appears to hinge on their ability to continue in these convictions of childhood.

Easy answers and "scriptural" formulas are a comfort to those who are homesick for simpler times and overwhelmed by the modern plethora of choice. Traditional gender roles—and the burgeoning market of Christian books, tapes, videos, seminars, and radio and television programs that promote them—fill the bill for security in a time of change.

Nostalgia for the good old days is evident in many of the articles in James Dobson's *Focus on the Family* publication. In one article, the moral degradation of the current television "family" sitcoms is rightly deplored.[3] But the television family shows of the 1950s and early 1960s are nostalgically referred to as "idyllic." (Photos of scenes from these shows framed the article.) The traditionalist tendency is to view the pre-1965 "traditional" family as virtually perfect and any deviation from it as, therefore, morally wrong. The nostalgia mentality overlooks the possibility that perhaps we don't have to choose for our family ideal *either* "Roseanne" *or* "Leave It to Beaver." Perhaps the reactionary social swing to "Married . . . with Children" was in some part due to the deficiencies of the "Father Knows Best" model.

Submission versus Selfishness

The disruption of the security and comfort of the 1950s social order was due in part to a generalized rebellion in post-1960s society against all authority. Feminism in its most radical form seems to share this modern contempt for authority. While biblical feminism does not reject authority per se, it does reject certain aspects of the traditional authority structure that has governed a woman's "place" in society. Along with most forms of feminism, evangelical feminism maintains that authority should not be abolished, but should be granted to those who have earned it rather than to those who have been born into it. But many people seem to confuse this revaluation of the proper criteria for authority with the abolishing of all authority. They then react emotionally against any questioning of traditional authority, fearing that feminism—of any variety—will inevitably result in a chaotic and anarchic society. The possibility that God might want to liberate women from a false, human-imposed authority structure—but not from the overarching structure of God's moral authority—seems not to be entertained.

Related to the fear that all feminism is out to abolish authority is the conviction that feminism encourages women to be self-centered and unsubmissive, which results in the destruction of their families and marriages. Jill Briscoe comments perceptively on this fear:

> I think we need to be wary of the emotionalism that's involved in this entire issue. Frankly, the most hostile reactions against women in leadership come from women, not men. The average Christian woman isn't really interested in what we're talking about; she's more worried about the possibility of her marriage and family breaking down. And many think that the feminist movement has caused marriages to fail. So they really aren't interested in becom-

ing feminists. They're holding on to their marriages by their fingernails, and the feminist movement scares them. As Christians, we need to provide an alternative to the secular view. We need to affirm an honorable tradition of families as well as an enlightened view of women. That will take an education of the mind rather than dealing with this issue so emotionally.[4]

Evidence of this emotional reaction against feminism may be found in the letters women have written to the editor of *Focus on the Family* magazine. For instance, "Feminism has nothing to do with serving God. It has to do with serving self." And, "I've never met a feminist or a 'women's libber' who cared about anything except what they can get for themselves."[5] Feminism, for these women, is another word for selfishness—not a godly virtue by any means.

Why do people believe that a feminist wife is a selfish wife and that feminism destroys marriages? Is a wife who has a career in addition to her homemaking duties self-centered? Married men have careers outside the home. Does this make them selfish too? The traditionalist perspective seems to be that married career women are selfish because they are working for their own fulfillment; married career men are not selfish because they are working to provide for their family. This double standard arises from the traditionalist belief that it is the duty of a wife to serve and submit to her husband, to organize her life around assisting him in his career. Any deviation from this duty, such as having a career of her own, is considered a violation of her God-ordained role; this, it is believed, will work toward the destruction of her marriage.

It is quite true that a marriage without submission is doomed to failure, and that secular feminism does not stress submission or selflessness. Marriage—whether it is self-consciously "liberated" or not—all too often amounts to a series of self-centered wranglings over the spouses' respective "rights." But it is not true that wifely submission as traditionally defined is the only alternative to a marriage without submission. We need not choose between either hierarchy or anarchy in marriage. We may choose the biblical option of mutual submission.

Rather than eliminating submission altogether, biblical feminism calls for more submission. It calls both husband and wife to an attitude of submissive love toward each other and toward the Lord. Unlike the established power of hierarchy or the grab-for-power of anarchy, mutual submission sets aside the power struggle and yields to the rule of love. Love and selfishness are mutually exclusive. Where there is love expressed in mutual submission, each partner will lay down his or her life for the other and take responsibility for the welfare of the other. No marriage fails for lack of authority and control; rather, marriages fail for lack of mutual love and submission.

A woman who converts from secular feminism to Christianity and throws herself into the traditionalist agenda for marriage may testify to the wondrous, peace-producing effects of wifely submission in marriage. It is no wonder. One-way submission is better than no submission. But would not two-way submission then be twice as good? If practiced, it certainly would not destroy a marriage, but rather nurture and preserve it.

Endangered Motherhood

Many people are firmly persuaded that feminism spells the end of motherhood and that, if feminists were to have their way, children would be born only to be ignored in institutional day care centers. This is a picture guaranteed to arouse emotional indignation in any person cognizant of the needs and rights of children. But it is not a particularly accurate picture, and it is certainly not representative of evangelical feminists—who are as pro-family as traditionalists. Many feminists do not despise but highly value both children and motherhood. They simply maintain that motherhood need not always be a full-time vocation, and that mothers are not necessarily the only people qualified to provide loving, competent care for their children. But traditionalists define motherhood as a full-time job, and any deviation from this definition is viewed as a rejection of motherhood itself.

"Motherhood went out of fashion when feminism came in," declares Connie Marshner. "In our postfeminist society, any task having to do with the care of children has been downgraded socially and robbed of all prestige."[6] It is a common conviction among traditionalists that modern feminism is entirely responsible for the devaluation of motherhood as an occupation. But the duties of motherhood were socially denigrated long before the rise of either modern feminism or today's traditionalism. Historically, societies everywhere have ascribed lower social value to women's work than to men's work.[7] Children have been depreciated as well. Because motherhood involves work done *by* women *for* children, it has been doubly denigrated. Any devaluing of motherhood by today's feminists has been preceded by a centuries-old tradition of socially downgrading anything deemed "women's work." Since motherhood is certainly "women's work"—and, in the nineteenth and early twentieth centuries, was considered to be women's *only* work—it has been viewed as less than the most prestigious occupation in society. The social devaluation of motherhood ought not be blamed on feminism when it is, in fact, rooted in tradition.[8] Those modern secular feminists who do regard the work of childcare as lacking in dignity are resting their assessment of motherhood on the traditional valuation of women's work. (Some secular feminists are at last beginning to realize this and are attempting to stand up for the dignity and value of work as a mother.)

When motherhood is viewed as the mandatory, full-time vocation for all married women, it comes to be seen as an occupation that requires no special talent, skill, or training; it is simply assigned automatically to all married women. If childcare is perceived as work that any woman can do, and that only women can do, then it will not be perceived as a very challenging or desirable occupation. It is significant that few if any men clamor for the right to occupy themselves with childcare; yet many women do clamor for the right to occupy themselves with work traditionally reserved for men. If childcare were a prestigious occupation, men would do it, and be well paid for it.

In other words, the male-centered bias of traditional, patriarchal culture—far more than feminism—has depreciated the work of women with childcare responsibilities. The denigration of motherhood is rooted in the traditional denigration of womanhood. Mothers will not be properly valued in society until women are properly valued.

The Hyper-Feminine Ideal

Another emotional pull to traditional gender roles is illustrated by the words of one traditionalist author, who speaks of being "overwhelmed by . . . longing for the beauty of the truly feminine, that allure that feminine women possess," and who recalls with yearning and nostalgia the "girls" from his college days "with their pretty dresses and long hair."[9] This man then irately blames feminism for destroying femininity—as he defines femininity. But it is hardly fair to expect all women to conform to his hyper-feminine ideal.

There is among men a tendency—to which all feminists vigorously object—to value women mainly for their physical appearance. The idea is ingrained in the minds of many men that a primary function of women is to be decorative. Such men prefer it this way and get annoyed at the idea of a woman acting like a human being ("like a man," they would call it) rather than like a china doll who exists primarily for the viewing pleasure of the male.

Certainly a woman should look like a woman and not try to conceal her feminine appearance. But I can only utter a hearty "amen" to the feminist conviction that women ought not have to "prove" their femininity by conforming to a standard set by men who regard them more as objects to view than as persons to know and respect.

Woman as Childlike and Mysterious

Some people want to hang on to traditional gender roles because they believe women *need* male leadership. Traditionally, women have been seen as somewhat childlike in character and therefore in need of the guiding hand of a man. Those who have an impression of females as irrational, weak, delicate, and childlike must surely shudder at the idea of giving women equal status with men. The notion that many men seem to have concerning the unworldly weirdness and "mystery" of women also demands that women be under male control. Like children, women are deemed emotional and unpredictable; there is no telling what they might do when left to themselves. A man who views his wife in this light would be understandably alarmed at the prospect of sharing his authority with her. So, because women are childlike and mysterious, they *must* be under male management.

This deep-rooted conviction is empowered by the force of tradition, and it resides—although often unacknowledged—in the minds of many people, both men and women. It serves several purposes. First, as already noted, it provides a justification for male authority (a central tenet of traditionalism). Second, it boosts men's self-image; a view of women as radically different from men and radically deficient without them makes men feel more manly by contrast. Manhood is thereby affirmed and vindicated.

Third, some women actually like thinking of their femininity in this way. Perhaps being dependent on a man makes them feel cherished and protected, and free from the demands and anxieties of adult responsibility. Or perhaps it simply resonates with what they have come to believe womanhood is all about. "Females in our society are taught by word and by powerful silent example that it is acceptable, if not desirable, to become polite manipulators of males, perhaps even seductive enticers, if they act slyly and in good taste. . . . Further, they are encouraged to find their personal identity through the ideas and actions of a male of the species rather than in their own interests and activities."[10] Women who follow the traditional rules for female behavior help perpetuate the male view of women as emotional, dependent, and unpredictable.

Woman as Sexual Temptress

The picture of woman as mysterious and emotional is often accompanied by a picture of woman as sexual temptress. This idea is rooted in ancient history and is a primary reason for the cultural requirement—still imposed in traditional Islamic cultures—that women be veiled in public. What appears to be behind the view of woman as sexual siren is the anxiety that many men have over their own lust. But the situation is not usually recognized in these terms. The traditional tendency is for a curious twist to take place, whereby male lust ends up being excused as a result of the male "nature" (the way God made them) and the alleged female practice of "asking for it." This maneuver relieves men of responsibility for dealing with their "weakness" and justifies the assertion of male authority over female temptresses. Alvin Schmidt describes this process as "psychosocial projection," whereby man's "weaknesses have been (and still are) unconsciously projected onto woman."[11] The view of woman as evil seductress is no longer promoted overtly, as it was in ancient times; but it lingers nonetheless and influences the assumptions and prejudices of both women and men.

Especially in conservative churches, women are sometimes restricted from certain ministry positions simply because men are afraid of what it might "do to them." Elaine Storkey reports that a bishop in England explained his objection to the ordination of women by stating that, if he were to see a woman administering the sacraments or preaching in a pulpit, his instinct as a man would be to take her in his arms.[12] The humorous book *Growing Up Born Again* offers a typical pastoral answer to the question of why women can't be ushers: "Women ushers would simply be too distracting to the male parishioners. . . . Trying to hide a blush, [the pastor] goes on to explain that men are different from women in that they are tempted by what they *see*. He doesn't say the word *lust* but you know that's what he's talking about. . . ."[13]

The problem here is simply the fear that some men have of female sexuality, and their resultant reductionistic view of women as primarily sexual beings rather than human beings. Men who habitually regard women more as sex objects than as persons will have a strong emotional resistance to sharing leadership with women or—worse yet—serving under the leadership of women.

Man's "Helpmate"

A man may want to retain traditional gender roles in his own home because of the benefits he obtains through his role as leader and his wife's role as his helpful assistant. With the husband as leader in the home, the household—consisting of wife and children—tends to revolve as a unit around the life goals and interests of the husband. If the husband were to lose his status as chief executive of the home, his career—and hence, his reputation and status in the world—would suffer. If the husband and wife were to acknowledge each other as equals, the wife may (but would not necessarily) discover that her life goals and interests entail more than house, spouse, and children—even as the husband's interests involve more than house, spouse, and children. This would remove the man from the center of the household constellation.

Men who are happy with the wife-and-children satellite revolving about them would as soon claim biblical justification for continuing in this pattern. Losing the full-time services of a wife would not be merely an inconvenience. For many men, the degree of vocational success they have attained is directly dependent on these full-time services, and their sense of success as men (according to traditional ideology) is directly dependent on vocational success. Take away the wifely assistant, and it all comes tumbling down.

The Emotional Demands of the "Male Ego"

Much is made among feminists of how men have hurt women, and much is made among traditionalists of how women's anger over this situation serves as a motive for them to become feminists. But some men have also been hurt by women, and these wounded men may take refuge in the sense of male supremacy that traditional gender roles offer them. (Completing the circle of emotional pain, the angry, hurting, radical feminists provide a convenient target of ridicule for the wounded men who seek revenge on uppity women.)

But even without the emotional wounding wrought by the hands of heartless females, that creation of androcentric culture known as the "male ego" tends to be most comfortable in a situation of supremacy. This can provide a formidable deterrent to a realization of the ideal of biblical equality.

Equality, by definition, excludes the domination of one person by another. Therefore, equality between a man and a woman would not entail her dominating him any more than it would entail him dominating her. But many men have become accustomed to taking charge with women, and when they are obliged to treat women as equals, they can interpret the loss of their customary male control as *being* controlled. This will be quickly tied in with a feeling of a loss of manhood—because, traditionally defined, masculinity equals leadership. When a man begins to fear losing his manhood, he will feel threatened and will act aggressively and defensively in an instinctive effort to regain it. So it happens that when women seek equality, some men will see this as a bid for control and domination, and will resist it accordingly. This emotional response of male self-defense, of course, is an inappropriate response to women who simply desire equality and have neither interest in nor intention of being dominant themselves.

Whatever the cause, the emotional "need" of many men to be in control—especially where women are concerned—provides a powerful force in favor of traditional gender roles. Scott Bartchy comments,

> This socially approved connection between male self-esteem and dominative power lies at the basis of that fear of losing domination, which is the essence of both racism and male sexism. In order to feel good about himself, this type of male needs someone or some group to give him permission to dominate. Our culture encourages the anxieties of growing boys regarding potential loss of power over their own lives and gives them permission to expect that females will serve them.[14]

Traditional Manhood and the Christian Man

When a man defines manhood in the traditional terms of power and control, it becomes imperative that he not lose his grip on his male authority, lest he lose his grip on his own sense of manhood. This is especially a concern for the Christian man, because his manhood—as traditionally defined—is already threatened by his association with the church, which emphasizes the "feminine" values of sacrifice, nurture, and obedience more than the "masculine" values of power, financial success, and competition that prevail in secular society. Psychologist Mary Stewart Van Leeuwen hypothesizes, "one of the ways that men can soften the conflict between their cultural masculinity and their feminization as Christians is to turn churches and other Christian agencies into thoroughly hierarchical institutions, with women kept as low in the hierarchy as possible. . . .

Another way males can cope with the cultural view that Christians are 'effeminate' is to become quite authoritarian as husbands and fathers." But "because self-esteem is so closely tied to gender identity that any threats to the latter are often denied on the conscious level and dealt with only by unconscious defense mechanisms," such men are not likely to admit openly that they assert their Christian manhood by dominating women.[15]

It is probably true that men who feel this way are not likely to be aware of it themselves, much less admit it openly to others. They would have reason to keep such dubious motives to themselves. But I recently witnessed a well-known television evangelist explain it all quite clearly on one of his television programs. After profiling his godly mother who prayed him to faith in Christ, he commented on what he considered to be a hindrance to faith for many men who have believing mothers. "There are many men like I was who didn't want to be a little boy again," he said. "You grow up and you want to be a man and you don't want to be under your mother. It's the same with a man and his wife. Men want to be men. They don't want to be subservient to their wife. Somehow they feel that if they come to Jesus that this is going to mean that they've got to submit as a little boy again." He went on, exclaiming that "when you do come [to Jesus], you realize, hey, I'm really coming into manhood now. I'm really entering into my role as a high priest with God. I am accepting the responsibility as a true man." Then followed an admonition to wives not to "make this a deal where your husband is doing what you tell him to do. If you do you're going to turn him away from the Lord. You say, 'Husband, you be the high priest of the household. You hear from God, then you be our high priest.'" He then talked about some Christian heavyweight boxers he had recently interviewed and how they served as evidence that "Christian men can be *men,* not wimps."[16]

In this revelation of this man's "Christian" male ego, there is, first, the familiar false dilemma that, unless a man dominates his wife, he will be subservient to her. Equality between husband and wife is not even viewed as an option. Second, there is a wholesale acceptance of secular society's false definition of manhood as consisting essentially of physical strength and authority: authority over the wife at home and physical strength over the opponent in the boxing ring. Third, there is the unbiblical definition of the Christian man as "high priest" of the home (a grandiose variation of the more common man-as-priest-of-the-home teaching).[17] And fourth, most interestingly, there is the frank acknowledgment of the psychological comfort assured many men by the traditional headship doctrine. It seems that this man would not let go of his "headship"[18] for anything: his sense of manhood depends on it, and his sense of self-worth depends on his sense of manhood.

Having listed some of the emotional inducements of traditionalism, I want to make an important clarification. Simply because some people who hold to traditionalist beliefs may do so for reasons that are less than noble or compelling, this does not in itself mean that traditionalism is false. But it does mean that if it *is* false, its falsehood will not be made immediately apparent through rational analysis alone. There appears to be a significant psychological investment in the tradition system—for both men and women, but especially for men. And this investment is not likely to be abandoned lightly.

The Spiritual Dimension

As was discussed in chapter 4, women in the evangelical church around the turn of the century were afforded unprecedented opportunities to work alongside men in ministry. This movement toward equal rights for women in the church was encouraged by the pro-family, Christian-compatible feminist movement of the nineteenth century, which was in turn impelled in large part by the evangelical revivals of that period. But the openness of the evangelical church toward equality for women ended in the 1920s.

I believe that ever since that time of Holy Spirit-inspired liberty for women, Satan has employed two tactics extremely successfully to reinstate women in the state of silent subjection in which he had held them for many millennia. Both strategies have struck the church through secular culture. The first was an antifeminist uprising in American secular culture which occurred largely as a by-product of another evil, namely, back-to-back world wars. And the church, as usual, went along with the cultural trend in its view of woman's "place."

Then, when it became clear that women in society were again on the brink of revolt, Satan's second strategy was employed. Instead of simply resurrecting the beliefs and principles of the earlier women's movement, the new feminism moved briskly into a radical and reactionary departure from virtually every moral and family value traditionally held by Western society up until that time. This wild leap over all middle ground between the two extremes of traditionalism and radical feminism provoked another reaction in the evangelical camp.

The church decreed that feminism was to be rejected, at all costs, in all its aspects, lest it wreak the ruination of church, home, and society.

Feminism—in *any* form—was condemned as an unmitigated evil. Evangelicals who tried to explain that the idea of equality for women was not in itself wrong were summarily silenced and were denounced as evidence of the incursion of this evil movement into the church. In its instruction that women be silent and subservient, the contemporary evangelical church has been even more vocal, more thorough, and more insistent than it was before modern feminism took hold in secular society.

Those in the evangelical church who have responded to twentieth-century secular culture—first in compliance, then in reaction—to keep women subjugated to men, have not done so believing that they were working against the will of God, the work of the Holy Spirit, or the good of women and men in the church. They have sincerely believed their position to be the biblical one. And, in a sense, it is natural enough to look to tradition for guidance in the face of the rapid change and bewildering events that have occurred in this century. I am not saying that antifeminists in the evangelical church are maliciously in league with the devil. Their views simply fall short of the full truth in some crucial areas. And this shortfall Satan has been only too happy to use to hurt and oppress women in the church, as has been his wont for millennia.

In short, we must realize that in this arena, as in every dimension that affects and afflicts the church, spiritual forces are at work behind the scenes. The conflict is, at root, spiritual—not merely cultural, psychological, or theological.

"Culture Wars" and the Traditionalist Fear of Feminism

Having surveyed some of the evidence of and reasons for the traditionalist fear of feminism, I would like now to explore in more depth the nature of the evangelical feminist/traditionalist debate. What impels traditionalists to view evangelical feminism as such a grave threat to the preservation of the Christian family and the social order? What preconceptions are powering the traditionalist antagonism toward evangelical feminism? What do traditionalists fear will happen if evangelical feminism takes root in the church?

It should first be understood that this debate within evangelicalism is not occurring in isolation from contemporary culture; all of society appears to be in an uproar over the collision of tradition with social change. The traditionalist resistance to evangelical feminism, in fact, is premised on the conviction that this in-house evangelical conflict is a smaller-scale replica of the cultural conflict in progress in secular society. Because of this, *Culture Wars*—a recent work by noted sociologist James Davison Hunter that discusses the war of ideas in secular culture—is helpful in clarifying the traditionalist perception of evangelical feminism in the church.

Two World Views

In *Culture Wars,* Hunter defines "cultural conflict very simply as political and social hostility rooted in different systems of moral understanding. The end to which these hostilities tend is the domination of one cultural and moral ethos over all others."[1] In other words, both the genesis and the *telos*—the beginning and the end—of these cultural conflicts have to do with competing views of morality. The specific issues and squabbles are symptomatic of a deeper fundamental disagreement concerning the basis of moral authority. The real issue is that each side wants *its* understanding of morality to become the cultural norm. This is Hunter's construction of the conflict of ideas in secular culture, and it is, I believe, the same construct which is presupposed by traditionalists in their war against evangelical feminism.

Hunter describes the two competing belief systems as "orthodox" and "progressive." Orthodoxy is "the commitment on the part of adherents to an external, definable, and transcendent authority."[2] Surely this is an indispensable foundation to the Christian world view.[3] How could a person be an evangelical Christian—who, by definition, respects the ultimate, binding authority of Scripture—and also be a progressivist, who, by Hunter's definition, denies the "binding power" of "traditional sources of moral authority" in attempting "to resymbolize historic faiths according to the prevailing assumptions of contemporary life"?[4]

Each base of moral authority, according to Hunter, gives rise to a predictable position on any given social issue. The same constellation of political action groups finds itself on the same side of the fight in every social issue. Hunter believes that the alignment of these groups reflects the view of moral authority each group holds. One constellation of groups has an orthodox world view, and the other constellation of groups has a progressivist world view. The alignments are predictable because they follow from the different views of moral authority.

Hunter infers these different world views; the two sides do not generally articulate their moral philosophies, although most activists on either side would probably agree with Hunter's assessment of their viewpoints. This is true, however, only for those on the extreme ends of the spectrum of controversy. For those occupying the middle ground, the story is different.

According to Hunter, those people (the majority of Americans) who do not consistently line up on one side or the other are in the middle ground because, rather than embracing one moral vision wholeheartedly, they inconsistently and thoughtlessly vacillate between the two.[5] The middle ground—"a wide spectrum of values and perspectives"—is occupied by the many "ordinary Americans" with "ambivalent moral commitments."[6] Therefore, those in a middle-ground group such as Feminists for Life must be viewed as having failed to delineate a consistent and coherent presuppositional basis for their pro-woman, pro-life position. They occupy the middle ground between the two polar extremes because they are sometimes progressive (when it comes to women's equality) and sometimes orthodox (when it comes to the human right to life). Consequently, Feminists for Life—as well as all the nineteenth-century feminists—must be deemed morally confused and logically inconsistent.

According to Hunter's lay of the land, a person cannot be consistent with the Christian belief system (which entails an "orthodox" adherence to a transcendent source of authority) while taking a position on a particular issue which is also the position of the progressives (who base their stance on a relativistic view of morality). Such is impossible because the positions taken by those on the extreme ends of the spectrum of controversy result from and are based in their respective world views.

Taking Sides on Social Issues

Hunter's certainty about the ideological correlation between the orthodox view of moral authority and the orthodox position on issues is evident. "Based on this general [orthodox] understanding of moral authority are certain non-negotiable moral 'truths.'" The most relevant of these he proceeds to enumerate; one is the idea that "the human species is differentiated into male and female . . . according to role, psyche, and spiritual calling." From this follows the prohibition of homosexual relations.[7]

Here we have a common traditionalist assumption: those who believe that the ultimate source of moral authority is external and transcendent (as in biblical authority) must necessarily also believe that the male/female differentiation entails different spiritual callings, roles, and psychological natures. This is "non-negotiable." Conversely, those who disagree with the traditional position on gender differences are thereby denying not only the basis for it (which is the authority of God himself), but are also denying the basis for the biblical ban on homosexuality. By implication, they are left without a reason not to condone the homosexual lifestyle as a viable option.[8] Hunter's construction of the nature of the current cultural conflict will not accommodate any position that embraces orthodox principles but denies some of the applications or implications that have historically been associated with those principles.

As I read Hunter's description of the progressivist view of moral authority,[9] not only did I disagree on moral grounds with the view he described, but I was—as always—struck by the incoherence and inadequacy of relativism as a basis for morality. Yet, according to Hunter's cultural map, one must say that because some of my beliefs concerning gender differences are closer to those espoused by the progressives than by the orthodox, I am either quite confused morally and philosophically, or I am simply two-faced, claiming to believe in one source of moral authority when I really believe in another. This is, in fact, the opinion traditionalists tend to hold in regard to evangelical feminists.

Such a view is a direct consequence of the assumption that, just as Scripture authoritatively prohibits all sexual relations outside of heterosexual marriage, so it also clearly delineates traditional gender differences and prescribes traditional gender roles (as traditionalists currently define them, that is). The traditionalist understanding of the biblical teaching on sexuality is presumed to be God's law from above, which to reject is also to reject God's word, the Bible, as the source of moral authority. Therefore, the only consistent way to dispense with traditional, sex-typed roles is to dispense with *any* absolute basis for morality and to embrace instead a relativized view.

This assumption seems to be a result of a failure to distinguish between truth itself and the process by which we come to know the truth. To say that truth is revealed progressively in Scripture is not to say that truth (God's view of what is true) changes from one end of the Bible to another. To acknowledge that the church's knowledge of biblical truth grows and changes as it is brought to light by the Holy Spirit is not to claim allegiance to the progressivist vision wherein truth itself "tends to be viewed as a process, as a reality that is ever unfolding."[10] After all, it took nearly four hundred years after the birth of the church for theologians to come to a consensus on something as basic to orthodoxy as the doctrine of the Trinity. Truth is unchanging, but our understanding of what is true is not unchanging because it is not infallible.

When we affirm an orthodox view of truth and morality as timeless and absolute, then we must not only reject a relativized, subjectivized, progressivist view of truth, we must also reject an understanding of orthodoxy which appeals to tradition as the final arbiter of what is true. If, as in the orthodox vision, truth exists independently of human opinion, then human opinion— whether modern *or* traditional—cannot be considered an infallible indicator of what is true. The failure to make the distinction between truth (which is not progressive) and our knowledge of truth (which is progressive) results in consigning to the category of "moral relativist" anyone whose view of gender roles deviates at any point from the traditional view. Women's equality is not a "new" truth. Rather, it is a truth rooted in the first chapter of the Bible—a truth which was obscured as a result of the fall, but which has been and is being progressively made known by God to his people.

This basic confusion over what is and is not fundamental to an orthodox, absolute, unchanging, biblical view of sexuality is at the very root of the seemingly irreconcilable hostility between traditionalists and evangelical feminists. This is what is preventing evangelical feminism from getting a fair hearing. Hunter and those who agree with his ideological landscape have stacked the deck against a proper rational analysis of the debate. The only way this cultural conflict can be resolved is to let go of the idea that the political configuration of the conservative and radical bandwagons are the logically necessary outworkings of opposing world views. We must begin instead to question the "logic" of some of these "non-negotiable truths" held by either side—but especially those held by the Christian "orthodox" side.

The assumption on which Hunter bases his analysis of the culture war in secular society is precisely the assumption that fuels the culture war in the evangelical church. It is, as already discussed, the conviction that the positions taken by today's conservative and radical groups can only be based on the orthodox and progressivist views of moral authority, respectively, and that someone in the middle ground is therefore confused about what ought to be the basis of moral authority. It is this assumption which causes conservative Christians to reject *all* feminists on the grounds that feminist ideas can *only* be rooted in a rejection of the orthodox vision of moral authority and an acceptance of the inherently anti-Christian progressivist vision. The possibility that there may be more than one way to arrive at a particular position—that there might be more than one presuppositional basis for any given belief—is not even entertained. The neat and tidy package deal of the two world views—whereby a certain position is necessarily evaluated according to the political bandwagon with which it is commonly identified—precludes open evaluation of specific positions according to the reasons given for those positions. Instead, it encourages jumping to conclusions about what these people *really* believe and are *really* up to.

The line-up of opposing teams presented by Hunter represents the actual, current constellation of positions on social issues in secular culture. But I do not believe that it represents the logically necessary constellation of positions. By and large, the positions of each side do generally follow from the premises Hunter has assigned to them. But in some cases (such as the "orthodox" view of gender roles), I believe the position follows, not by virtue of ideological correlation, but by virtue of sociological correlation. For example, it happens that in contemporary American society, most people arguing for women's rights do so from a progressivist world view (as Hunter defines it). But in the nineteenth century, when an orthodox view of morality was the cultural consensus due to the general Christianization of American society, there were within this consensus those who argued for women's rights as well as those who argued for maintaining women's subordinate social status. Simply because most people who argue for women's rights in American society today are progressives is no reason to conclude that anyone who believes in women's rights must necessarily espouse a progressivist view of moral authority.

To put it in terms of formal logic, where P is the progressivist world view and Q is a belief in women's equality, the statement "if P then Q" may well be true—at least for American culture at this time. However, the statement "if Q then P" does not follow from "if P then Q." (This logical fallacy is referred to as affirming the consequent.) "If Q then P"—that is, if one supports women's equality in any sense, then one has a progressivist world view—may be sociologically probable at this time, but it is not necessarily entailed by the "if P then Q" statement that those with a progressive world view will support women's equality.

Principle and Application

Unlike modern secular feminism, evangelical feminism is premised on an orthodox view of morality as absolute and universally binding. But evangelical feminists question whether *every* matter concerning gender roles which has traditionally been viewed as a matter of moral obligation ought in fact to be viewed as such. Is there not a morally legitimate gender role flexibility in certain limited areas, such as in the division of responsibilities in the governance of church and family? Are we morally obligated to assign women to subordinate positions, while men are favored for the superior ones?[11] Evangelical feminists dispute the traditional understanding that male authority is a matter of moral obligation and propose that, instead, authority be assigned freely according to whomever is best qualified.

But by questioning the claim that traditional gender roles are biblically and morally mandated, evangelical feminists are not saying that *nothing* is morally mandated in relation to sexuality. Evangelical feminists are not throwing out all sense of moral obligation to absolute standards and replacing it with a relativistic advocacy of personal freedom. They have not, by virtue of their beliefs concerning gender roles, traversed from orthodoxy to progressivism. Likewise, neither does the evangelical transition from Prohibition in the 1930s to a personal-freedom approach to drinking alcohol today indicate an abdication of faith in biblical authority. In both instances, the implications and applications of biblical principles of morality have been reevaluated, while the orthodox vision of that moral authority has been maintained.

Someone who maintains that a traditional *principle* (such as an orthodox view of biblical authority) can reasonably give rise to a non-traditional *application* of that principle ought not be summarily dismissed as a deceitful character—a wolf in sheep's clothing—who has in reality abandoned the traditional principle but won't acknowledge it. Simply because a moral principle has been traditionally associated with a particular application of that principle is insufficient cause to conclude that that particular application is the correct or the only logically acceptable application of the moral principle. Yet this is what is happening in the evangelical church. Traditionalists are warning the church that evangelical feminists have essentially abandoned the orthodox principle of biblical authority. Orthodoxy is identified with tradition, and the traditions of the church are presumed to be non-negotiable applications or consequences of orthodoxy.

Just as most Christians now question the idea of a moral mandate to abstain from all forms of public entertainment and propose instead that individuals be free to decide on these matters in accordance with biblical moral principles, so evangelical feminists propose that men and women in the church and home be free to determine their roles according to their consciences (under God), rather than according to an incontrovertible rule book. In short, the disagreement concerns the definition and scope of what constitutes legalism (that is, pharisaical "traditions of men" which falsely appropriate for themselves the status of commandments of God). The conflict does not concern the foundations of morality itself. Some fundamentalists may still believe that to go to *any* secular movie is to break God's law, but most Christians recognize that God does not command an across-the-board avoidance of all forms of secular entertainment. So, too, evangelical feminists do not deny or reject the commandments of God, but merely disagree that God's decrees extend to the detailed regulations propounded by traditionalists concerning what each sex is required to be and to do in the home and the church.

The fundamentals of God's law for human sexuality remain intact in evangelical feminism: the marriage covenant must be between one man and one woman, must be a permanent commitment, and can be the only setting for sexual relations. If conception occurs, the mother and father are both morally obligated to protect and provide for their offspring at every stage of development. These fundamental moral parameters are received from God and are not a product merely of culture. To say that someone—such as an evangelical feminist—who adheres to these moral principles is nonetheless in some sense a secularized moral relativist, is without rational justification.

Even if the opposing sides in cultural battles hold their respective positions as "non-negotiable" consequences of their "competing moral visions," this does not mean that their positions *are* in fact non-negotiable on logical grounds. What people believe to be true and reasonable is not necessarily true and reasonable. Even if a majority of those who hold an orthodox view of morality believe that men and women are morally obligated to adhere to traditional gender roles,[12] this does not mean that the majority are thinking at all clearly or logically; they could simply be following along with the general ethos of a cause or crusade. Perhaps, due to complex cultural factors which have little to do with reason, a traditional view of gender roles follows sociologically, but does not follow logically, from an orthodox view of morality.

The fact that, during Prohibition, a majority of Christians believed that drinking alcohol should be forbidden on grounds of biblical morality does not mean that a philosophy of teetotalism follows necessarily from a view of morality based on biblical authority. It does mean, though, that sociologically a connection had been forged at that point in history between evangelicalism and teetotalism such that it had come to be perceived as a package deal.[13] Evangelicals now realize that the Bible does not legalistically mandate total abstinence from alcohol, but offers basic principles concerning self-control and responsibility which people have the freedom (under God) to apply as they deem best.[14]

Likewise, some evangelicals realize that the Bible does not mandate legalistic rules and roles for women and men, but rather sets forth such principles as marital fidelity, godly character, mutual submission, and the full equality of both men and women as "sons" (heirs) of God. People have the freedom under God to determine the roles to which each individual is best suited and "called" by God. Such an approach to gender roles is not "progressive" in Hunter's sense, does not deny biblical authority, and does not evidence moral confusion or logical inconsistency with respect to its premise of biblical authority.

Statistics: A Mixed Message

As discussed above, I do not believe that all the issues Hunter links with the two competing moral visions follow logically from those visions. A conservative feminism, as well as a principled understanding of human rights, can and should be derived from an orthodox view of moral authority, although Hunter categorizes these views as consequences of the progressivist vision. But not only do I question whether all the issues follow logically from the moral visions with which Hunter has identified them, I am unconvinced that these issues even follow sociologically.

If it were true that, for each issue, a majority of the orthodox supported the conservative position and a majority of the progressives supported the liberal position, then there would be a clear sociological connection. But according to Hunter's survey of religious leaders within Protestantism, Catholicism, and Judaism, that is not the case. The most that can be said is that for each issue the orthodox are more *likely* than the progressives to take a conservative position and the progressives are more likely than the orthodox to take a liberal position. But on an issue such as pre-marital sex, a majority of both orthodox and progressives tend to take the conservative position. On issues such as husbandly authority and employment for mothers, a majority of both orthodox and progressives tend to take a liberal position.[15]

According to Hunter, when the orthodox come to view some of the traditional rules for gender roles in a more flexible light, they thereby migrate toward the progressivist side of the cultural divide; they draw a little more from humanistic and a little less from biblical sources of moral authority.[16] This, according to Hunter, is how the orthodox, including evangelicals, will come—and are coming—gradually to endorse more progressivist views of gender roles: by further weakening their commitment to their orthodox moral underpinnings.

However, this "process of an accommodation to the spirit of the times"[17] should not, according to Hunter's scenario, discriminate between *which* progressivist positions the orthodox adopt and which they reject. That is, there should be no reason for a *selective* appropriation of progressivist positions. But the data—for which Hunter offers no explanation—indicate that evangelicals are refusing to endorse abortion or homosexuality, yet *are* beginning to accept other ideas, such as non-traditional roles for women.[18] I do not believe this shows that evangelicals have been swept into an unprincipled drift toward the unbiblical and relativistic ideas of contemporary culture. Rather, it seems that many evangelicals have reevaluated the supposed biblical basis for the traditional orthodox positions and have found some of these positions to be grounded more in tradition and prejudice than in biblical moral principles. It is these positions that are changing. Positions that *are* grounded in biblical morality—such as a disapproval of abortion and homosexuality—are being retained. This explanation accounts for the selective drift on issues; Hunter's does not.

War in the Church

While making many helpful observations and explanations concerning the *dynamics* of the culture war, Hunter seems, at least in part, to misunderstand its *nature*. This misunderstanding, which is itself an element of the culture war, serves only to heighten the hostilities.

More than anything else, what precludes a fair assessment of evangelical feminism by evangelicals are the entrenched convictions that: 1) feminism—of any stripe—is part of a package deal which includes sexual immorality and irresponsibility of every kind; 2) an orthodox view of morality can *only* lead to a traditional, antifeminist view of gender roles; and 3) any view which accords women more equality than they are allowed by today's traditionalists can *only* follow from a loose or progressivist view of morality which denies the binding authority of the Bible. These convictions, exemplified so clearly by Hunter, are the basis for the traditionalist fear of feminism.

This underlying view of evangelical feminism as a package deal explains why antifeminists are persuaded that its certain outcome would be the destruction of the family and society. I have often wondered how practicing mutual submission and shared authority in the home could destroy the family and society. But the imaginations of traditionalists don't stop with shared authority in the home (although, given their view of gender differences, that in itself probably seems bad enough). When traditionalists look at a married couple who love, respect, and submit to one another and make decisions together as equal partners, they see a slippery slope at the foot of which is the breakdown of all moral authority and social order. Why? Because traditionalists believe that an equalitarian marriage can derive *only* from a humanistic, relativistic, thoroughly unbiblical view of morality. And once the door to moral relativism has been opened wide enough to let in equalitarian marriage, then it is only a matter of time before all the other evils come bursting through and consume us all.

Hunter states that, in the conflicts between the orthodox (conservatives) and the progressives (liberals), "what is ultimately at issue are deeply rooted and fundamentally different understandings of being and purpose."[19] The battlefield offers no "common moral ground from which to build and resolve differences."[20] This is why, in secular culture, "each side of the cultural divide can only talk past the other."[21] The lack of common ground for logical discourse results in a cranking up of the emotional volume; it becomes a war fought with the weapons of slogans, accusations, and caricatures.

This may well be a factor in perpetuating the overcharged emotional climate of conflicts in secular culture. But in the evangelical church the replacing of rational discourse with emotionalized assertions is not due to the *fact* that each side is shouting from irreconcilably different moral territory. They are not. Rather, it is because of the *conviction* of the traditionalists that this is so.

Guilt by Association: Liberalism, Gnosticism, and Feminism

When the issue of gender roles is conceived in terms of two opposite and extreme positions or "bandwagons," any belief espoused by one of the bandwagons will be seen to be part and parcel with all the other beliefs on that bandwagon. The modern secular feminist bandwagon endorses wider vocational opportunities for women and shared or equal authority in the home and society. It also endorses legalized abortion, homosexuality, and sexual promiscuity. Since the latter beliefs are clearly wrong from a Christian perspective, the former beliefs are assumed to be wrong as well; they are guilty by association.

But viewing equality for women in terms of equal vocational opportunity does not necessarily also entail viewing sexual "freedom" as an element of women's equality—any more than belief in Christianity necessarily entailed support of the Inquisition or the Salem witch trials. The sexual rights/abortion rights emphasis of modern secular feminism is not a logically necessary correlate of the idea of equal rights for women. Rather, women's equality is a true idea, which, at the hands of modern secular feminism, has become twisted and militantly misapplied, leading to an unbalanced extremism. But an invalid, extremist understanding and application of an idea, which is not necessarily demanded by or intrinsic to the idea itself, ought not be used as grounds to condemn the idea.

Guilt by association operates on the basis of superficial similarity alone and disregards the fundamental differences beneath the surface. Two ide⸗s may be linked in one system of thought, but may in another system of thought have no connection whatsoever. Modern secular feminist thought links "abortion rights" with women's equality, but pro-life feminist thought (such as evangelical feminism) finds the idea of women's equality to be incompatible with the idea of abortion rights.[1] Because contemporary secular feminism ascribes a more extreme meaning to the concept of women's equality than does evangelical feminism, the perceived consequences of equality are very different for the modern secular feminist than for the evangelical feminist.

The Charge of Liberalism

Similarly, liberal theology links the ordination of women with the ordination of practicing homosexuals, but evangelical feminism holds that the biblical justification for women's ordination does not imply the ordination of practicing homosexuals. The evangelical feminist argument in support of the ordination of women has fundamentally different premises than the liberal argument. The assumption of guilt by association ignores these fundamental differences. Because liberal denominations seem to justify the ordination of women and the ordination of practicing homosexuals for the same reasons, conservatives follow suit and condemn the ordination of both women and practicing homosexuals, as though they were a single issue rather than two separate issues requiring separate consideration.

Evangelicals who favor placing qualified women in positions of pastoral leadership are frequently charged with having a "low" view of Scripture. After all, liberal churches ordain women, and we *know* what *they* think of the Bible's authority (or lack thereof). The conclusion is hastily drawn that an advocacy of equal ministerial opportunity for women can *only* derive from a lack of respect for the Bible, and, conversely, that the only interpretation that respects biblical authority is the traditional one. Any deviation from traditional biblical interpretation is ipso facto "liberal." The possibility that an interpretation which allows for women in pastoral leadership may also arise quite legitimately from a "high" view of Scripture is not acknowledged. By this strategy, the issue is deflected from biblical interpretation to biblical authority.[2]

As Harvie Conn notes in his review of evangelical feminism, "the result of this narrowing of perceptions gives the 'traditionalist' more the appearance of a knee-jerk reaction agent."[3] Once evangelical feminism is identified with a low view of Scripture, the entire debate is effectively neutralized. No need remains to address the issues being raised by feminists in both the church and secular society, or even to consider the cultural and social factors which influence biblical interpretation—including traditional biblical interpretation.

Guilt by association may also be imputed to evangelical feminism because the hermeneutic it employs to justify women's equality seems similar to the hermeneutic employed by liberals who seek to justify the practice of homosexuality. Those who endeavor to reinterpret the Bible in such a way as to approve of homosexuality claim that the established, traditional view of what the Bible teaches on this subject is not based on the overall scriptural message of liberty and justice but is constructed on the basis of a few isolated proof texts. Biblical feminists claim a similar exegetical strategy for their position, as did the abolitionists of over a century ago. But comparing the evangelical movement to liberate women with the movement in the liberal churches to "liberate" homosexuals does not render evangelical feminism false any more than merely comparing it with the movement to liberate slaves renders it true.[4]

The truth or falsity of one biblical interpretation cannot be established by association or analogy with another. Just because some false doctrines *claim* to be supported by biblical principles rather than biblical proof texts does not mean that *every* doctrine that relies more on principle than proof text is false. If that were true, we would have to admit biblical justification for slavery.[5] The real question at stake is whether or not a particular traditional biblical interpretation is true to the biblical message. Each effort to break away from tradition must be evaluated on its own terms in order to determine whether the traditional or the newer interpretation is biblically justifiable.

Heresy by Association

Guilt by association can devolve into heresy by association. This too is the result of jumping to conclusions on the basis of superficial similarities alone. Charges of heresy by association entail the assumption that every way in which a heresy differs from orthodoxy is part and parcel of the heresy. In other words, all that the heretics have believed and done is seen as false, and all that the orthodox have believed and done is seen to be correct. This too is a bandwagon mentality. It refuses to acknowledge either the possibility that, where the orthodox have assimilated unbiblical cultural values into their theological tradition, they could very well be wrong, or the possibility that heretics may occasionally hit on a truth that the orthodox community somehow missed. All beliefs espoused by a heresy are not necessarily false—although, by definition, certain crucial core beliefs must be false.

Evangelical feminists are not only charged with being modern liberals who disavow biblical authority; they are also accused of subscribing to the ancient heresy of Gnosticism. Because Gnostics appear to have espoused some views or practices which superficially resemble some of the views and practices of evangelical feminism, and because Gnosticism is a heresy, some traditionalists have arrived at the conclusion that evangelical feminism is a Gnostic heresy. This conclusion, however, can endure only as long as the evidence and reasons for these supposedly similar views and practices remain unexamined.

Gnosticism is a heretical doctrine which challenged biblical orthodoxy early in church history. It consists of "a related body of teachings stressing the acquisition of 'Gnosis,' . . . the inner and esoteric mystical knowledge of ultimate reality. It discloses the spark of divinity within, thought to be obscured by ignorance, convention and mere exoteric religiosity."[6] Gnosticism appears to have come from "the work of heterodox Diaspora Jews" who blended an assortment of pagan beliefs into a mythology "based upon a repudiation of the God of the Hebrew Bible" and "a radical revision of biblical material."[7] Gnostic beliefs have recently been experiencing a resurgence among those inclined toward New Age thought.

Elaine Pagels's *Gnostic Gospels* has had no small influence in creating renewed interest in and admiration of Gnostic ideas. Pagels is inclined to idealize Gnostic spirituality, and she makes a number of claims concerning it which are not warranted and which have drawn fire from scholarly critics. One of these claims is that Gnosticism most authentically represents the teachings of Jesus Christ; orthodox Christianity, by contrast, constitutes a political perversion of these teachings.[8] Another of Pagels's claims is that the Gnostics were feminists. For this she has received criticism as well.[9]

Pagels's insistence that the Gnostics were feminists apparently has been highly influential in convincing some traditionalists that evangelical feminism is a Gnostic heresy. But while there may be some superficial similarities between some Gnostic and some feminist views and practices, the contention that the Gnostics were feminists is highly debatable. Even if the Gnostics were feminists, it does not follow that all feminists are Gnostics, certainly not that evangelical feminists are Gnostics.

What, then, are the views and practices of Gnosticism with which anti-feminists associate evangelical feminists? What were the Gnostic presuppositions behind these views and practices, and how do they differ from the evangelical feminist belief system?

It is not easy to determine what antifeminists have in mind when they accuse feminists of being Gnostics; frequently, they offer little or no evidence for the accusation. One gets the impression that the charge is made on account of the effect it creates rather than the theological ground on which it stands. Harold O. J. Brown, for instance, gives a resounding endorsement to *Recovering Biblical Manhood and Womanhood: A Response to Evangelical Feminism,* predicting that it "could prove as useful in refuting 20th-century Gnostic insanity as Irenaeus' *Against Heresies* was against the Gnosticism of the second century."[10] I could find no clue in the book as to why Brown speaks of evangelical feminism as "20th-century Gnostic insanity." Peter Jones refers to feminism in the church as "a neo-Gnostic revision of Christianity" in his effort to associate evangelical feminism with Gnosticism, liberal feminist theology, New Age pagan goddess religion, and most other varieties of modern feminism.[11]

The Gnostic View of God

Relying heavily on Elaine Pagels's ideas, Louis Brighton attempts to demonstrate that the ordination of women is a Gnostic heresy. He states that the Gnostic practice of ordaining women is grounded in the Gnostic view of God as both masculine and feminine. He seems to think this view of God is shared by evangelical feminists and contradicted by the orthodox Christian belief in a wholly masculine and entirely unfeminine God. He states that the Gnostic idea of a God with both masculine and feminine elements "is in marked contrast to both the canonical Scriptures and the orthodox church's belief, in which the feminine element is absent in both thought and symbolism of God."[12] And, of course, it would follow that the ordained leaders of a religion with a masculine God ought all be masculine themselves.

Brighton's assertions redound in error. The idea that the evangelical feminist concept of God bears any resemblance to the sexualized Gnostic notions of deity is patently false. Unlike the gods of Gnostic and other pagan heresies, the God of the Bible is not a sexual being. Reifying the masculine and feminine imagery of God in the Bible leads to a misunderstanding of God's essentially nonsexual nature. God is not male, nor is he both male and female. God is neither male nor female.[13]

It is also false to say that the biblical God is symbolized or described only in masculine and never in feminine categories. Curiously, Brighton backs up his understanding of the "orthodox" view of God with Elaine Pagels's statement concerning "the absence of feminine symbolism" for the "masculine" God of the Bible.[14] But this is Pagels's opinion, and Pagels is no orthodox Christian theologian. It seems that Brighton not only believes everything Pagels says about Gnosticism; he believes what she says about Christianity as well. Following her remark concerning the un-equivocal masculinity of the biblical God, Pagels acknowledges that "Jew-ish, Christian, and Islamic theologians today are quick to point out that God is not to be considered in sexual terms at all."[15] In other words, even Pagels recognizes that her view of the biblical God as male is not the offi-cial orthodox position. (Although it does appear to be the view of many traditionalist Christians who are otherwise orthodox.)

Brighton is also too eager to accept Pagels's idea that an equalitarian view of women and men should be inferred from the Gnostic writings, which "speak of God as a dyad who embraces both masculine and femi-nine elements."[16] As Kathleen McVey points out, such writings in them-selves prove nothing of the Gnostic view of male and female. "The rela-tionship between male and female elements in the dyad is the crucial issue. Since the male principle represents the spiritual realm and the female prin-ciple at worst the material realm, at best the spiritual elements in the material realm, all the gnostic cosmologies are ultimately patriarchal in conception."[17] Elisabeth Schüssler Fiorenza offers further evidence that Gnostic views of femaleness and maleness resemble the traditional more than the feminist.

> Gnosticism, we may conclude, employed the categories of "male" and "fe-male," not to designate real women and men, but to name cosmic-religious principles or archetypes. . . . In Gnosticism, the pneumatics, men and women, represent the female principle, while the male principle stands for the heav-enly realm: Christ, God and the Spirit. The female principle is secondary, since it stands for the part of the divine that became involved in the created world and history. Gnostic dualism shares in the patriarchal paradigm of Western culture. It makes the first principle male and defines femaleness rel-ative to maleness. Maleness is the subject, the divine, the absolute; female-ness is the opposite or the complementary "other."[18]

Gnosticism and Women's Ordination

Brighton also too readily accepts Pagels's assertion that "our evidence, then, clearly indicates a correlation between religious theory [that God is both male and female] and social practice [that women are socially equal to men]."[19] Not only is the evidence dubious for a Gnostic view of God as equally male and female, there simply is no evidence for a generally accepted Gnostic practice of according women equal social status with men. There are no Gnostic documents that provide any evidence of the Gnostic view of gender roles in society. The only historical sources on this subject are provided by the church fathers Irenaeus and Tertullian, who criticized Gnosticism. McVey notes that these sources are "discounted by Pagels when they describe behavior of which she disapproves but taken literally when the behavior is acceptable to modern feminist views."[20] Pagels questions the accuracy of Irenaeus when he states that the Gnostic Marcus recruited women for his sect by seducing them sexually, but she accepts as historical the reports of Irenaeus and Tertullian that Gnostics allowed women to perform some priestly functions.

The Gnostic writings themselves do not refer to a Gnostic custom of ordaining women to the priesthood, nor do they specifically offer a theological justification for doing so. We do not know whether Irenaeus's and Tertullian's reports of women acting as priests were indicative of isolated instances or of a widespread Gnostic practice of gender equality. Because the extant Gnostic writings do not discuss this practice, we can only speculate as to the theological reasons which may have been behind it.

An examination of Gnostic theology reveals no hint of similarity to the evangelical feminist theological basis for women in pastoral ministry. In the first place, the work of the Gnostic priest (as dispenser of myths and keeper of mysteries) is of an entirely different nature than that of the Christian pastor (as expositor of God's word and shepherd of God's people). In the second place, what appears to have been the Gnostic motivation for putting women in religious leadership is entirely different from that of evangelical feminism. Principally, evangelical feminists seek opportunity for qualified women to enter the pastoral ministry because they believe a person's sex ought *not* be a relevant factor in determining suitability for the pastorate. In Gnosticism, however, it appears that women were priests *because* they were women. There are two possible reasons why Gnostics might have placed women in positions of spiritual leadership.

In some strains of Gnosticism—as in other pagan religions—the feminine spiritual principle was exalted as a mediator of divine grace.[21] It would therefore be appropriate for women to serve as priests or spiritual mediators in these religions. Perhaps this was part of the rationale for Gnostic women acting as priests. Here, we can see some resemblance between modern radical feminist spirituality and ancient Gnostic and pagan views of the divine feminine. But the theology of evangelical feminism could not be further removed from religions which deify the feminine spiritual principle.

On the other hand, "some Gnostic groups exalted the feminine princi-ple as a divine, literary, or historical figure while they denigrated actual women."[22] The following text from the Gospel of Thomas illustrates the Gnostic tendency to view women as spiritually inferior to men. "Simon Peter said to them, 'Let Mary leave us, for women are not worthy of life.' Jesus said, 'I myself shall lead her in order to make her male, so that she too may become a living spirit resembling you males. For every woman who will make herself male will enter the kingdom of heaven.'"[23] Con-cerning this saying, F. F. Bruce comments, "The general rabbinic idea that women were incapable of appreciating religious doctrine . . . was rein-forced in Gnostic anthropology, where woman was a secondary and de-fective being."[24] Many Gnostic sayings reveal a strong element of misogy-ny and contempt for female sexuality.[25] For example, one Gnostic writer offers this exhortation: "Flee from the madness and the bondage of fe-maleness and choose for yourselves the salvation of maleness."[26]

Gnostics espousing this misogynist anthropology would consider the priesthood to be a male role which a woman could fill only by attempting to become like a man. Interestingly, this is also the view which tradition-alists hold toward women in the priesthood. J. I. Packer calls women pres-byters "substitute men."[27] Of course, this does not make Gnostics of Pack-er or other traditionalists. But in view of the traditionalist assertion that evangelical feminists are Gnostics, it is interesting to discover that what probably served as a theological basis for the Gnostic practice of ordain-ing women could much more readily be identified with traditionalism than feminism. At any rate, with such a strong current of misogyny in its the-ology, it hardly seems justifiable to accuse Gnosticism of being feminist, or feminism of being Gnostic.

"While the Gnostics essentially permitted women to serve in tradi-tional male roles, they were still bound to a sexist mentality in that they believed a woman had to become a male in order to realize the true spiri-tual benefits of Christianity."[28] Traditionalists today, of course, differ from the Gnostics in that they do not believe there is any need for a woman to improve herself spiritually by becoming male. Unlike both Gnostics and traditionalists, evangelical feminists do not believe that the role of reli-gious leadership is a male role which women fill only as "substitute men." Rather, evangelical feminists believe that women as women are no less spiritually qualified for leadership than men. Because leadership is not male but gender-neutral, women in leadership are not imitating men. Gnostics and traditionalists believe that leadership *is* male and that women in leadership *are* imitating men—but, again, Gnostics would seem to ap-prove of women occupying leadership roles, while traditionalists do not.

Gnostics have not been the only ones to assert that maleness is spiritual but femaleness is of the material realm, and that women are spiritually inferior to men and hence must in some sense become male in order to move up the ladder of spirituality. Some of the church fathers echoed these ideas. Origen stated, "What is seen with the eyes of the creator is masculine, and not feminine, for God does not stoop to look upon what is feminine and of the flesh."[29] Ambrose said, "She who does not have faith is a woman and should be called by the name of her sex, but she who believes progresses to perfect manhood. . . . She then does away with the name of her sex."[30] Jerome likewise believed that as "long as woman is for birth and children, she is different from man as body is from soul. But when she wishes to serve Christ more than the world, then she will cease to be a woman and will be called a man."[31]

The Gnostic view of women resembles traditional misogyny (absorbed from secular patriarchal culture by Christians throughout church history), but it bears no resemblance to evangelical feminism, which maintains, on the basis of Galatians 3:28, that all Christians are equally saved and equally heirs of God, regardless of their sex (or race, or socioeconomic status). As McVey puts it, "In short, heresy and feminism were not such good bedfellows as either Pagels or the modern Christian misogynists would have us believe."[32]

Gnosticism and Androgyny

Since Gnostic mythology is a potpourri of often contradictory elements, it should not be surprising that yet other Gnostic writings view sexuality as something that must be eliminated altogether. The following text from the Gospel of Thomas is illustrative: "Jesus said to them, 'When you make the two one, and when you make the inside like the outside and the outside like the inside, and the above like the below, and when you make the male and the female one and the same, so that the male not be male nor the female female . . . then you will enter [the kingdom].'"[33] But, as discussed earlier in relation to androgyny,[34] the elimination of sexual distinctions between men and women is certainly not on the agenda of evangelical feminism, nor is it compatible with most varieties of contemporary secular feminism. Nonetheless, some antifeminists persist in believing that androgyny is a central concern in all varieties of feminism, and that this renders feminism like Gnosticism.

Philip J. Lee perceives "striking similarities between the attitudes of the ancient gnostics and that of modern feminists."[35] Curiously, he refers to Saying 114 of the Gospel of Thomas ("women are not worthy of life") in support of these "striking similarities." Lee later refers to Saying 22 ("make the male and the female one") as evidence of the link between Gnosticism and feminism,[36] so apparently he sees as feminist the Gnostic idea of denying the sexual distinctions between male and female.

David Ayers, a contributor to the antifeminist manifesto *Recovering Biblical Manhood and Womanhood,* also appeals to the idea of androgyny in his assertion that evangelical feminists are Gnostics. Ayers speaks of "the 'new' feminist evangelicalism"[37] and explains in an endnote: "I put quotes around 'new' because feminist ideology bears a startling resemblance to the 'old' Christian gnostic heresy." He refers the reader to June Singer's *Androgyny: Toward a New Theory of Sexuality,* which he calls "a feminist work." He comments that Singer "celebrates this rebirth of gnosticism in the feminist resurrection of an androgyny ideal."[38] It is stretching the point to call Singer's book "a feminist work." It is even more far-fetched to view the concepts in her seventeen-year-old work as representative of feminist thought today. And the idea that Singer's occultic, Jungian theorizing somehow resembles "feminist evangelicalism" is beyond belief. There is no real resemblance—startling or otherwise—between evangelical feminist beliefs and the occultic peregrinations of June Singer's thoughts in *Androgyny.* All that is startling here is Ayers's refusal to acknowledge the obvious, fundamental differences between Bible-based evangelical feminism and Gnostic/occult mysticism.

Ayers also refers the reader to a vitriolic article on androgyny[39] which, while strongly biased toward a view of biology as destiny, nonetheless makes no mention of either Gnosticism or evangelical feminism and so fails to provide any support for Ayers's contention of a "startling resemblance" between the two.

The so-called androgyny of evangelical feminism and the "androgyny" of Gnosticism are similar only in the sense that both in some ways reject to some degree some traditional ideas of sexuality. But the similarity is merely superficial, because these two belief systems reject different aspects of traditional views for very different reasons. There is in evangelical feminism none of the androgyny which entails merging the male and the female so as to create a sexually undifferentiated androgyne—as Singer and some Gnostic writings seem to advocate. The assertion that such ideas resemble evangelical feminism could result only from profoundly misconstruing evangelical feminist teaching. The fact that *some* varieties of feminism and *some* strands of Gnosticism advocate *some* ideas of androgyny is an inadequate premise for the conclusion that *all* feminism—including evangelical feminism—is Gnostic.

Many antifeminists apparently understand a declaration of women's equality as a denial of women's sexuality; feminism, therefore, equals androgyny, or sameness of the sexes. This conclusion results from the traditional equation of women's sexuality with women's inferiority or inequality. *Status* differences between women and men are viewed as an integral part of the *sexual* differences between men and women. Granting women equality with men is therefore seen as tantamount to eliminating sexual distinctions between women and men. This is then deemed "Gnostic," despite the fact that all feminism does not advocate androgyny, all Gnosticism does not advocate androgyny, and all theories of androgyny are not Gnostic.

So, whether evangelical feminists are accused of being Gnostic heretics because they dispute the view of God as male or masculine, or because they allow women into traditional "male" leadership roles such as the pastorate, or because they do not adhere to all the rules for traditional gender roles, the attempt at heresy by association lacks even the remotest justification. Any significance that could be derived from superficial similarities is undermined by the radically different reasons behind the views and practices of Gnostics and evangelical feminists in regard to the role of women.

The willingness of some traditionalists to ignore crucial theological distinctions in their apparent eagerness to condemn evangelical feminism as a Gnostic heresy is not an argumentative strategy that they would like to have turned on their own views. Traditionalists do not appreciate it when their concept of male authority is likened to the tyrannical authority of the traditional patriarch. The difference between benevolent rulership and dictatorial rulership is a legitimate one and should be respected. The significance of this distinction, however, seems to pale beside the vast theological gulf separating Gnostic and evangelical feminist beliefs concerning God, creation, women, men, and the Bible.

Until the debate between evangelical feminists and traditionalists is confined to the actual issues at hand, without straying into superficial speculations of heresy, there will be no hope of either side even understanding the other, much less of coming to a resolution. It is essential that in this controversy we heed our Lord's instruction to "stop judging by mere appearances, and make a right judgment" (John 7:24).

Logic, Culture, and Controversy

The more divisive the issue and the more urgent the cause, the greater the tendency to abandon reason and resort to the rhetoric of the passionate and the sensational. Claims are exaggerated, assertions are undocumented, and accusations become extravagant. Unless those of us who attempt cultural analysis are aware of the many pitfalls that lie in wait, our conclusions will be more likely to reflect the bent of our own prejudices than an accurate and reasonable picture of the social landscape. This chapter will discuss some of the errors in thinking that tend to recur in discussions of the feminist/traditionalist issue.

Begging the Question

When the premise of an argument is unexamined and undefended, it can easily show up as a conclusion. If an argument's purported conclusion is simply the premise restated, the argument is circular and proves nothing. An argument which proceeds from the assumption that the opponent's position is false begs the question of whether or not the opponent's position *is* false.

As noted in relation to the issue of Gnosticism, traditionalists frequently accuse feminists of encouraging women to act like men, to usurp the role of the male, to become "substitute men." This sort of remark is often followed by something to the effect that "'true liberation . . . comes with humble submission to God's original design.' Indeed, the noblest achievement of *any* human being—male *or* female—is to discover God's design and fulfill it."[1] Such statements concerning God's order and original design for gender roles are persuasively couched in terms that seem to defy disagreement. Who is opposed to "true liberation"? Who would decline to be noble or to fulfill God's design? But these lofty pronouncements do not serve as an effective argument for the truth of the traditionalist position; they merely assume its truth. The traditionalist charge that feminists want to be "substitute men" is not a refutation of feminism; it is an accusation which presupposes that feminism is false.

If the traditionalists are correct in their conviction that God intended gender to be the fundamental factor determining a person's position in the spiritual and psychological arenas as well as the biological, then—and only then—is it a violation of God's order to cross over any of the traditional gender boundaries. But this contention must be shown to be true before it is used as an assumption from which to launch invectives at women who want to "act like men."

Larry Christenson sees feminism as a concerted effort to "impose another role upon women," a move he sees as motivated by "the idea that the only life worth living is a man's life."[2] Certainly it is wrong for a woman to act like a man rather than like a woman; the question is not the wrongness of such behavior, but what actually constitutes such behavior. Christenson begs this question. His denunciation of feminism is based on his premise that the feminist idea of how a woman should live is wrong because it constitutes a usurpation of the unique role of the man. In other words, his premise is no different from his conclusion. His reasoning is circular.

Elaine Storkey's response to Christenson is apt. "Feminists are not interested in living a man's life. The whole point is that they want to live an oppression-free *woman's* life."[3] If, as feminists contend, men have cornered certain rights that should be shared by both men and women, then the feminist goal is not to be like men. Rather, it is to break out of the stereotypical caricature of women and, instead, to be like women were truly meant to be. The feminist understanding of what those "certain rights" are and of what women are "meant to be" will differ, of course, depending on the feminist. But the contention that men need to share with women certain rights which they have been keeping for themselves is central to all feminist thought. If traditionalists wish to dispute this contention, they must do more than simply presuppose that it is false and then hurl anti-feminist accusations based on that presupposition.

The False Dilemma

Widely-held but erroneous assumptions have remarkable power to generate misunderstanding and forestall the resolution of disagreement. Such an assumption is the false dilemma. "The context of most present-day debate regarding women's 'place' has become a forced choice between two extremes. Though the range of opinion has varied widely, traditionalism and feminism have become the ideological poles which, to a large degree, have set the limits of creative discussion."[4] But these options do not exhaust the possibilities. There are more alternatives available than traditionalism and modern secular feminism. "Every time we hear a dichotomy, an 'either-or,' we should immediately look between the horns of the dilemma to see if there is any middle ground."[5]

The creating of false dilemmas is sometimes referred to as black-or-white thinking. If something is not black, it is white; if it is not white, it must be black. As a fellow once said to a friend, "Everything is either black or white with me; there is no gray matter." He was quite right; making everything a black-or-white issue does eliminate much of the demand for gray matter!

Black-or-white thinking is not always inappropriate, however. For example, an airplane is either on the ground or off the ground, and those two conditions are the opposite of one another. But black-or-white thinking is fallacious when it comes to the issue of gender roles; it assumes that a naked dichotomy exists between two mutually exclusive positions which are the opposite of one another. Yet, in reality, no such dichotomy exists. Opinions on gender roles range along a spectrum of possible positions, with evangelical feminism actually closer ideologically to traditionalism than to the radical feminism with which it is so readily associated.[6]

Speaking in philosophical terms, traditionalism and modern secular feminism stand in a contrary, not a contradictory, relation to one another. Contradictory statements cannot both be false; either one or the other must be true. For example, God either exists or he does not. But contrary statements *can* both be false, although they cannot both be true. A parent who declares to the children on a Saturday morning, "The whole family may go on a picnic, or no one may go on a picnic," would be uttering contrary, not contradictory, statements. There is another possibility besides the alternatives proposed. Some but not all of the family members could steal away on a picnic, in which case both statements would be shown to be false.

Unfortunately, the possibility that traditionalism and modern secular feminism might both fall short of the truth is ruled out by the black-or-white thinking which insists that there are only two options, one of which is entirely false and the other entirely true. All too often, arguments proceed from the assumption that if the other side is wrong at any point, one's own side must be right at every point. It is presumed that one has only to discredit the opposite position in order to "prove" the truth of one's own position. A corollary assumption is that if someone does not agree with your views at every point, he or she believes the exact opposite of what you believe on every point. If a person is not a traditionalist, he or she is assumed to be a feminist, and all feminists are assumed to reject *all* traditionalist values.

The black-or-white thinking of the false dilemma is prevalent not only in the church but in secular culture as well. As James Hunter observes, "In today's climate of apprehension and distrust, opinions that attempt to be distinctive and ameliorating tend to be classified with all others that do not affirm a loyalty to one's own cause."[7] Extremist activists readily identify anyone who is not wholly with them in their cause as being wholly against them. The middle ground and the moderate view have disappeared from the battlefields of the culture wars.

Someone with a moderate position will be classified with the conservative bandwagon by those on the radical bandwagon and will be deemed a radical by those on the conservative bandwagon. With opposing camps both doing the name-calling, one person or position may be affixed with several mutually contradictory labels. Traditionalists, therefore, would tend to categorize a book such as this one with radical secular feminism, while radical secular feminists would spurn such a book as unenlightened traditionalism. An academic who is a liberal feminist might be vilified by the radical academic feminists as a right-wing fascist.[8] Similarly, someone who does not support every effort of the "gay rights" activists is often deemed homophobic (irrationally fearful and hateful toward all persons of homosexual orientation). All these categorizations are absurd; they are the result of an anti-intellectual, emotionalized polarization of the battlefield. Such "thinking" disallows the mutual understanding and dialogue which are prerequisites to the resolution of conflict.

I believe the goal for Christians should be to articulate a theology of gender which is thoroughly biblical in principle. Such a theology would do more than simply baptize a secular cultural path with Christian rhetoric—whether it be (most commonly) traditionalism or (less commonly) modern feminism. But the effort to critique culture according to the timeless truths of biblical principles is not as easy and straightforward as the black-or-white thinking of the bandwagon mentality. A person who rejects the false dilemma and acknowledges a third option—a point of balance between the two extremes—doubles her apologetic load: she must hold out against errors on both the right hand and the left, with precious little support from either side!

"The Failure of Feminism"

The tendency of antifeminists to set up a false dilemma and to disregard all middle ground between traditionalism and modern secular feminism is exemplified in a *Newsweek* essay entitled, "The Failure of Feminism."[9] The author, Kay Ebeling, is a single mother who has decided that feminism is the "Great Experiment That Failed." She believes that feminism is the reason there are so many single mothers who have been abandoned by the fathers of their children, and who are therefore working to support their children themselves. Women have ended up with all the responsibility of parenthood, and men with none. So, Ebeling concludes, "feminism freed men, not women."

But is this conclusion justified? Is it feminism per se—the essential idea of women's equality—that has freed men not women, or is it that aspect of modern secular feminism which tends toward rampant divorce and sexual irresponsibility? The "ethic" of the sexual revolution, while concurrent with and endorsed by the modern secular feminist movement, is not integral to the fundamental feminist belief—shared by all varieties of feminism—that women as well as men should have the opportunity to choose their own vocation. Ebeling misdiagnoses the problem. She blames the fact that many mothers now have their own careers, for a problem that is actually caused by sexual irresponsibility and easy, frequent divorce.

Ebeling also contends that feminism has produced exhausted married women who stay up half the night doing housework because they are at work during the day. But what is responsible for this unhappy state of affairs? Is it the feminist idea that women can combine career with family or the selfishness of husbands and older children who thoughtlessly leave all the housework for Mom to do? Ebeling remarks that "women don't belong in 12-hour-a-day executive offices." (Presumably she means women with children.) But men who have children at home ought not work twelve hours every day either. Feminist women are not the only irresponsible, self-absorbed parents who are contributing to the problem.

Ebeling's proposed solution is that we abandon the idea of careers for women and return to having employed men supporting unemployed women and their children—"the way it was, pre-feminism." But to apply that "solution" to every family situation is uncreative and reactionary. We need not choose between "frenzied and overworked women often abandoned by men" on the one hand, and full-time motherhood for all married women on the other hand. A creative and responsible solution would address the real causes of the problem—namely, irresponsible sexual behavior and family members who won't do their share of work at home—and not simply blame feminism for encouraging some women to have both children and careers.

In maintaining that women should return to being unemployed mothers financially supported by their husbands, Ebeling commits the logical mistake of the false cause as well as the false dilemma. She seems to believe that the prevalence of women in the workplace is the cause of the prevalence of poverty-stricken single mothers. The fallacy of the false cause is also known as *post hoc ergo propter hoc* ("after this, therefore, because of this"). Because societal symptoms of family breakdown (such as poverty-stricken single mothers) increased *after* women entered the workplace in greater numbers, it is assumed that the family is disintegrating *because* women are working. This is a common assertion of traditionalists, and it results from the confusion of correlation with causation. A logical link—not merely a temporal connection—must be established between employed mothers and family breakdown before all working women can justifiably be directed back to the home.

It is curious that, although Ebeling denounces the effects of divorce for women and the idea of careers for mothers, she makes no mention of the clearly problematic consequences of non-marital sex, especially for women.[10] Although this certainly accounts for how a considerable number of single women came to be single mothers, Ebeling seems to accept such behavior as a social given, or at any rate does not make a point to condemn it.[11] To object to the employment of mothers as a source of difficulty for women, while ignoring the prevalence of sex outside of marriage, is to strain at a gnat and swallow a camel. The feminism which Ebeling claims has failed is a feminism which entails sexual irresponsibility. This by no means proves either the failure of evangelical feminism or the truth of traditionalism. To adapt a G. K. Chesterton witticism, one could say that feminism without sexual sin, that is to say, biblical feminism, "has not been tried and found wanting. It has been found difficult; and left untried."[12]

Ebeling's essay does not demonstrate the failure of feminism, but her own failure to distinguish between the good and the bad within feminist thought. This is characteristic of antifeminists. Instead of rejecting the bad and conserving the good in modern feminism, they perceive only the good in traditionalism and only the bad in modern feminism; these two opposites are then set up as the only alternatives. Another characteristic error is to confuse the idea of women's "right" to choose abortion, to indulge in non-marital sex, to get divorced at the slightest provocation, and to pursue a career at the expense of her children's welfare, with the idea of women's right to an equal education, equal employment opportunities, equal respect as a voice in the public sphere, and equal treatment under the law. The former is not necessitated by the latter, as demonstrated by the pro-family ethic of sexual responsibility espoused by nineteenth- and early-twentieth-century feminists.

James Dobson declares that Kay Ebeling's essay is the best testimonial he has read of the fact that the women's liberation movement is now defunct.[13] He is, in fact, so persuaded of its significance that he has reprinted it in its entirety in his newly revised *Straight Talk.* The chapter, "Whatever Happened to the Women's Liberation Movement?" consists entirely of Ebeling's essay. Dobson apparently believes—true to the tenets of the false dilemma—that this opinion piece demonstrates not only the failure of all forms of feminism, but also the truth of traditionalism.

Although one antifeminist guest column in *Newsweek* can hardly serve as definitive evidence that feminism is "defunct," it does point to a salient shortcoming in the modern feminist concept of equality. Because it has based the idea of women's equality on a false system of beliefs and has consequently misapplied the idea of women's equality, contemporary secular feminism has failed to achieve a society of justice and equity for both women and men. This failure of modern secular feminism is not due simply to its promotion of rights for women, but to its promotion of such rights for women to which neither women nor men have any real right—most notably sexual rights couched within the notion of the "right to privacy." The exercise of these false rights has included frequent no-fault divorce and sexual relations outside of marriage. These practices have resulted in single parents, usually women, living in poverty or near poverty—the situation to which Kay Ebeling so vigorously objects.

But the "failure" of modern secular feminism by no means justifies a rejection of the idea that both women and men should have equal opportunity to invest their lives in activities appropriate to their individual personhood, within a context in which rights are balanced with responsibilities. The *context* of equality between women and men is crucial to its success, as is the delineation of its limits. Modern secular feminism has failed to provide either the appropriate context or the reasonable limits of equality.

We must take into consideration the *reason* for the "failure" of modern secular feminism before we conclude what that failure "proves." If the reason for its failure is its rejection of the basic moral ideals of sexual integrity, marital monogamy, and mutual, self-giving love, then its failure can only be used to show the need for sexual integrity, marital monogamy, and mutual, self-giving love. Its failure cannot be used to demonstrate that, per traditionalist teaching, every married woman should become a vocational homemaker.

To reject modern secular feminism is not necessarily to embrace traditionalism. There is a third alternative, a middle ground, which takes from traditionalism a commitment to the family and from feminism the idea of women's equality—even as early feminism did a hundred years ago and evangelical feminism does today.

Confusing the Absolute and the Relative

The inability to recognize an alternative other than the two extremes of modern secular feminism and traditionalism seems often to be a result of the inability to distinguish between that which is absolute or unconditional (universal principles independent of historical happenstance) and that which is relative or conditional (social customs dependent on circumstances). In the face of the modern (liberal) push to relativize the absolute, the reactive (conservative) tendency is to absolutize the relative. So in their effort to preserve the ideal of marriage as a permanent and exclusive covenant between a woman and a man, conservatives are inclined to view as equally crucial the traditional roles of wife as subservient, unemployed homemaker and husband as authoritative, employed provider. A marriage that deviates from these roles is seen as falling short of what a marriage should be. The marital roles become as absolute as the marriage itself.

The tendency in hanging on to tradition is to retain that which ought not be retained. But in breaking from tradition, the equal and opposite error tends to occur, and things which ought not be rejected are summarily dismissed. So liberals, recognizing that the absolutizing of vocational roles for men and women is not warranted, proceed to relativize not only gender roles but sexual ethics and marriage itself. The marriage bond, for example, is changed from the unconditional "as long as we both shall live," to the conditional "as long as we both shall love." On the liberal bandwagon, all guidelines for behavior have been relativized. On the conservative bandwagon, rules are everywhere, absolute and unyielding.

When the relative is absolutized, peripheral issues become as crucial to the definition of biblical orthodoxy as the central core of Christian faith and morality. Deviation from these relative, peripheral concerns is therefore viewed as "heresy." But the feminist deviation from the traditionalist mandate that the wife stay at home while the husband goes to work is not of either the *magnitude* or the *nature* of the modern feminist deviation from the traditionalist mandate that the human right to life and the marriage covenant be respected. It is one thing to say that women as well as men ought to have some choice as to their vocation, and that married women don't necessarily have to stay at home while their husbands work full-time outside the home (provided, of course, that the children can be properly cared for). It is another thing entirely to absolutize women's "right" to vocational "choice" such that it rides roughshod over absolute moral principles such as the sanctity of the marriage covenant and the human right to life—including the right of a young, undeveloped, unwanted human life which interferes with its mother's chosen lifestyle.

Traditionalists assert that equality and vocational choice for women lead inevitably to rampant divorce, abortion, and family breakdown. But only absolutizing the relative good of personal choice and relativizing the absolute good of human life and marital fidelity—as contemporary secular feminism has done—inevitably leads to such social disaster. And the absolutizing of personal choice follows only from the world view of modern individualism (to which modern secular feminism subscribes), wherein the will of the individual is absolutized. It does not follow simply from the feminist conviction of women's essential equality with men. Because the Christian world view is grounded in belief in a God who transcends the individual, a truly Christian feminism balances the concerns of the individual woman with those of the family and community, placing both under God. It thereby avoids the error of traditionalism which, in placing priority on a woman's duty to her family, often swallows up the woman's personal interests, needs, and callings. It also avoids the error of modern feminism which exalts the woman's self-fulfillment above both God and family.

Shooting the Straw Woman

Caricature exaggerates the worst in the opponent's position and then ridicules that exaggerated view, giving the impression that the opponent's actual position has thereby been refuted. The creating of a caricature follows from the creating of a false dilemma. As James Hunter observes, "The most conspicuous way each side discredits its opposition is by portraying their opponents as extremists."[14] Once the assumption is made that all those who oppose one's own position are rabid extremists, ridicule through caricature comes easily and naturally.

Feminists are frequently caricatured by conservatives as angry, unshaven, loudmouthed, elitist, man-hating, and militant—fearsome and despicable creatures, to be sure. Rather than debating actual feminist ideas, traditionalists often set up a straw woman—loosely based on impressions received from the media or from random encounters with radical feminists. This straw woman is then attacked by ridicule. Gretchen Gaebelein Hull observes that "role-conscious people will often find it difficult to be open to new ideas. It is easier for them to caricature feminism and then to blame that caricature for various human problems than to be open to re-examining traditionalism."[15] Since biblical feminists are seen to be closely related to—if not virtually identical with—modern secular feminists, they too are quickly condemned by the caricature and rarely allowed opportunity to explain or clarify their position. But a cogent critique of culture is precluded when ridicule replaces reason. Unless our analysis is applied to the actual merits of an idea rather than to a caricature of the idea, we will never reach a knowledge of the truth.

Those who caricature feminism define feminism according to the characteristics of extremely radical feminism. This narrow definition does not result in non-radical feminists being deemed non-feminists (although that would be the opinion of the extremely radical feminists). Instead, it results in the sweeping condemnation of all feminists as they are lumped in with those who are extremely radical. This serves the assumptions of the false dilemma: one is either a traditionalist/antifeminist or an extremely radical feminist.

The caricature offers no option but to reject the ridiculous and to join the ranks of the antifeminists. Lloyd Billingsley, for example, describes the organizing principle of feminism as contempt for motherhood and obsession with abortion as the "rite of passage" or "sacrament" of the feminist religion.[16] He maintains that if feminists had gotten hold of the Virgin Mary, she would have been "led to believe that a desire to have children was a legacy of traditional, male-dominated society, a sexist belch from the past."[17] Mary's decision to go through with her pregnancy would have been "greeted by howls of derision from the feminist pews."[18] Billingsley's distress over the "holocaust" of abortion is certainly understandable. But his vitriol spills over to vilify any and all feminist thought, regardless of how reasonable or moderate it might actually be.

Another striking example of the use of caricature to ridicule feminism is found in Tal Brooke's *When the World Will Be As One*. In a chapter titled ironically "The Halls of Caricature," the author maintains that the feminist movement is intent on caricaturing all men as cruel abusers of women and children. For feminists to depict men in this way *is* a caricature. But to depict all feminists as depicting all men thus is also a caricature. In objecting to what he perceives to be the feminist caricature of men, Brooke responds with his own caricature of feminists. Speaking of the horrors of the "women's agenda," he declares:

> There are seminars and planning sessions on totally egalitarian marriages. It should be a world of emasculated men submitting to assertive women. . . . It will be a golden age of lesbianism and homosexuality and perhaps the banning of such evils as marriage. . . . There is a new ideal of androgyny. . . . Men would glory in their effeminacy, and women would become pseudomales. So many butch women have defaced what little genuine femininity they might have had. . . . The allies of these women have become the whispering, effeminate males who are either attracted to other men or who have become ashamed of maleness and who have conceded defeat to the feminist and lesbian causes.[19]

While there are probably such people with such attitudes in some sectors of radical feminism, it is unwarranted to characterize all feminism in this way without a single qualifying word. Moreover, it is inaccurate to say that androgyny creates "pseudomale" women who are more masculine than the "whispering, effeminate" men. Androgyny by definition refers to an equal mixture of feminine and masculine traits in both male and female persons; it does not refer to women adopting the temperament of the traditional male and men assuming the personality of the traditional female. It is also incorrect to characterize egalitarian marriages as "emasculated men submitting to assertive women." By definition, egalitarian means equal; it refers to a situation of mutuality and equality in which neither sex is dominated by the other.

In wars of ideas, people are prone to apply simplistic, one-dimensional definitions to certain trigger words, and then to use those words as weapons—without stipulating their definitions. Tal Brooke, for example, states that "some men are flying to Asia to get mates to whom they are attracted—feminine women who want to be wives."[20] The implicit meaning of both *feminine* and *wives* here is clearly "subservient." Yet the impact of this remark goes further than the simple statement that men who want subservient women for wives must leave America and go to Asia. Rather, the message of this statement is that "feminist" women have denied their womanhood; they have lost the uniquely womanly capacity to be wives. They have lost their femininity. This is serious ridicule. Few women—feminist or otherwise—desire to deny their womanliness and cease to be attractive to men. The unstated premise behind this remark appears to be that only subservient women are real women. If this premise were made explicit, the remark would have no power to ridicule feminists; it would simply be regarded as one man's rather narrow understanding of femininity. But because the premise is hidden and the "trigger words" are left undefined, it all sounds quite shocking and significant.

Another trigger word is *motherhood*. In general, motherhood is understood by traditionalists to be a full-time vocation, woman's primary calling; any other view of motherhood is considered a rejection of both motherhood and true womanhood. So it was that when students at all-female Wellesley College objected to having Barbara Bush as their 1990 commencement speaker, Rolf Zettersten concluded that "the students' rejection of Barbara Bush was also a rejection of the concept of motherhood." Rejecting motherhood, in Zettersten's view, is the essence of feminism. For Zettersten, the "twisted philosophies" of these "feminists" ultimately entail "reducing full-time moms to second-class status."[21]

But as the Wellesley students themselves made clear, they had no intention of rejecting either Barbara Bush or motherhood.[22] They simply considered it inappropriate to invite a woman as commencement speaker on the basis of her husband's accomplishments rather than on the basis of her own. (This does not mean Barbara Bush is not a wise and wonderful woman in her own right. But the fact remains that she was invited primarily because of her husband's position.) After all, a men's college would not invite a male commencement speaker simply because he was married to a woman of achievement. We would expect the students of a men's college to object to the implication that success for a man is attained by marrying a successful woman. It seems the Wellesley students were primarily trying to reject the sexual double standard and to be true to the Wellesley tradition (which, incidentally, predates modern feminism by over a hundred years) of teaching young women how to develop their own skills and life goals as individuals.

After dealing with the Wellesley students, Zettersten moves on to ridicule the female students at Mills College for not wanting the school to be open to male students. The caption under a photograph of wailing women reads, "A plane crash? An auto wreck? No, these women were just told they were going to have to share a college with men." In other words, their distress was ridiculously inordinate. Zettersten then explains that the reason they were so upset was "simply because the feminist agenda portrays men as abusers, aggressors and attackers," and the Mills students were in "a toxic sexist environment . . . where all males are viewed with suspicion." His "simply because" explanation betrays a view of feminism which is one-dimensional, biased, and simplistic. He caricatures feminists as "toxic" man-haters. He understands all feminists to be alike, with "lesbianism and abortion as tenets of their agenda."[23] The bandwagon mentality here effectively precludes any rational consideration of the legitimate reasons that favor all-women colleges.

In addressing the Mills College issue, columnist John Leo first remarks (as Zettersten does) on the apparent hypocrisy of women objecting to all-male colleges but insisting on preserving all-female colleges. But "having said all that," Leo feels "bound to say that . . . the Mills protesters have a strong case. . . . A fairly large body of evidence now indicates that women learn more, learn faster and emerge more confident at women's colleges than at coed colleges."[24] Apparently, some studies are showing that coeducational schools provide a more favorable learning environment for male students than for female students. This seems to be due to a number of factors, including the male readiness to elicit attention by speaking out in classes, the comparative lack of confidence among female students which inhibits their class participation, and the tendency of some teachers to assume that males are more achievement-oriented and intellectually competent than females. The result is that male students in coed schools are more likely to receive the attention and encouragement necessary for them to learn and succeed. Female students, on the other hand, are more likely to receive the confidence-building encouragement that they need in all-female schools.[25]

Zettersten notes that these factors were mentioned by the Mills protesters, but he dismisses such objections as feminist-induced male bashing. Yet the case for the female disadvantage at coed colleges—although not overwhelmingly conclusive at this point—is certainly deserving of more consideration than he gives it. It is just possible that the students at Mills College were motivated more by a desire for a good education than by a "feminist" contempt for men in general.

There are doubtless some students at both Mills and Wellesley who fit Zettersten's depiction of feminists as women who hate men and despise motherhood. It is to be hoped that such women will not labor for long under these convictions. But it is both unfair and inaccurate to smear all women who are bound for a destiny other than vocational homemaking with the same dirty "feminist" brush, especially when the brush obscures the important and complex issues of why a woman should receive an education and what it means to be a wife. Ridicule and caricature seize upon extreme incidents, such as occurred at Mills and Wellesley, and then present these incidents as being even more extreme than they actually are.

Billingsley's feminist fanatics, Tal Brooke's unattractive, "butch" feminists, and Zettersten's "new generation of feminists" who reject motherhood and scorn men, contrast sharply with the information in an article on feminism written at about the same time for a secular news magazine. This article reports that the young women in the new generation of feminists staunchly affirm women's rights but reject the label *feminist* because of its unfeminine connotations. "Hairy legs haunt the feminist movement, as do images of being strident and lesbian. Feminine clothing is back; . . . motherhood is in again. To the young, the movement that loudly rejected female stereotypes seems hopelessly dated."[26] The journalists who gathered the information for this article apparently found among the younger generation little or no evidence of Rolf Zettersten's, Lloyd Billingsley's, and Tal Brooke's feminists who despise men, motherhood, and marriage.

Misuse of Analogy

It is a common argumentative strategy to "prove" the truth of an idea by comparing it with a situation in which that idea does hold true. In other words, a metaphor often is enlisted in an attempt to prove rather than merely to illustrate a particular idea. But analogies, while helpful for clarifying, illustrating, or explaining a concept, are often insufficient for demonstrating the truth of a concept.

A staple belief of traditionalism is that, in the home, someone *must* be designated as the "final decision-maker." One reason frequently given for this belief is that in other areas of life it *is* necessary for one person to be in charge. "Because two captains sink the ship and two cooks spoil the broth," says James Dobson, "I feel that a family must have a leader whose decisions prevail in times of differing opinions."[27] Therefore, the husband must have authority over the wife. (Once it is established that someone must be in control, it seems to go without saying that that "someone" will be the man.) But a marriage is not much like either a ship or a kettle of broth. Simply because ships and kettles require one person in charge in order that the sailing and the cooking proceed as they ought is no reason to conclude that one person in a marriage relationship needs to be in charge of the other person in order for the relationship to be as it ought. What, after all, does cooking broth or sailing a ship have in common with relationships between people? And how would putting one person in a position of authority over another person help to foster loving, lifelong intimacy between those persons?

Married couples who profess to have a hierarchical family structure are nonetheless often loving and intimate. But their love and intimacy is not a result of the authority structure, it is in spite of it.[28] In a marriage between two people who love and submit to one another, a policy of mutual, rather than hierarchical, decision-making is more likely to produce not only harmony among family members, but decisions which are best for all concerned.[29] As my husband and I have learned from our own experience, mutual decision-making is also the surest way to hear from God so that we may obey his will for our lives. When decisions are made according to what the husband believes is God's will, the family is more likely to get off track than when husband and wife wait for God to confirm his will to both of them.

The emphasis on having a leader in a marriage is frequently a result of forgetting that marriage is first and foremost a relationship. Often the primary goals of marriage are viewed instead as the production of offspring and the running of a household. Such a view casts marriage in the light of a business or military operation which requires a CEO or commanding officer in order to function efficiently. It is therefore assumed that in order for the home and the marriage to function properly, the husband must be in charge of the entire operation.[30]

Another analogy which today is more often unspoken than spoken is that women are like children; consequently, they need care, leadership, protection, and provision in a way that the (male) adult does not. In earlier days this was a commonly accepted and frequently expressed view. The phrase "women and children" referred to one category, not two. The view of the "weaker sex" as childishly dependent upon and inferior to men lurks behind many of the reasons given in support of traditional gender roles.

Pointing out the misuse of analogy in such instances shows a weakness in the traditionalist argument for male authority; it does not in itself prove that male authority is unbiblical. It is possible that the Bible may require of us something for which we can find no logical argument—from analogy or otherwise. But it is not probable. Nor would such a biblical interpretation be particularly persuasive. Significantly, few if any traditionalists claim they see no reason for male authority other than that they believe the Bible teaches it. Most people who believe that the Bible mandates traditional gender roles have a number of extrabiblical arguments for why these roles are correct. The traditionalists' view of gender makes sense for them; it fits their view of women, men, marriage, and the world. The husband must be in charge because the home is like a business (or a ship, or a kettle of broth) and the wife is rather like a child in her need of guidance and leadership.

Motives and Means

Considerable confusion concerning the motives of evangelical feminists and traditionalists also muddles the issue. Traditionalists accuse feminists of wanting to demean and destroy marriage and the family; feminists accuse traditionalists of wanting to demean and destroy women. Such accusations are harmful for two reasons. First, discussion is fruitless as long as it remains on the ad hominem level of attacking the opponent's motives. Dialogue is helpful only when it concerns actual reasons and propositions. Second, feminists in the church do not want to destroy the family any more than traditionalists want to destroy women. Evangelicals—both traditional and feminist—share the same motive of wanting to provide a healthy, godly model of family life for Christians. The difference is not over motives but over means.

The means recommended for achieving a happy, godly life for men, women, and families differs between evangelical feminists and traditionalists because of their differing understandings of what men, women, and families are like and/or ought to be like. They view marriage differently, with traditionalists emphasizing rules and roles, and evangelical feminists mutual submission. Because the presuppositions of traditionalists (concerning what they understand to be innate differences between men and women) are often unstated or unproved, feminists may find the assertions based on these assumptions to be insulting to women. But it is not the traditionalists' intention to insult women; they really believe women are better off in traditional roles. The debate often becomes so emotionally charged that people forget they share a common motive with their "opponents." This common motive should instead be used to foster understanding and dialogue between the two viewpoints.

Of course, a good motive is no defense for wrong behavior. Good motives should be acknowledged where they are present but should not be used to obscure or excuse error. When a wrong belief is sincerely held or wrong behavior earnestly performed—even for good motives—the end result is functionally evil. In the wise words of Blaise Pascal, "Men never do evil so completely and cheerfully as when they do it from religious conviction."[31] But false beliefs and wrong behavior on both sides can be brought to light when the discussion centers on the real issues and avoids the many temptations to spurious and insulting criticism.

Social Change, Freedom, and Responsibility

Social change is never an unmixed blessing. Even when change is needful—and certainly there is always room for improvement in a fallen world—it is difficult. The old ways of doing things are frequently more convenient and orderly. Moreover, when social change comes and drives out old evils, it brings in new evils. Often the worst evil that change brings is an untempered extremism, a shooting over to the opposite end of the spectrum.

Few would deny that the freeing of East Germany in the last decade or the freeing of African-Americans from segregation practices in the civil rights movement of the 1960s were needful changes. Yet these good changes had socially disruptive consequences. Philip Yancey reports on some West Germans' comments to him about East Germans who migrated west for employment: "They didn't understand the work ethic: They showed up late, took no pride in their work, and could not master basic principles of pleasing the customer." In short, they had not learned to live with freedom; they had not learned that a free (unenslaved) life self-destructs without self-discipline. Yancey's observation was that this was "reminiscent of what I used to hear in the American South, when white employers first began hiring blacks."[32]

There is a parallel here with feminism. Women truly did need to be freed from their childlike status under male management in traditional society. After millennia without freedom, women in the twentieth century have received a sudden freedom. Now they too must learn the self-discipline that protects the unenslaved life from self-destruction. Society has been struggling awkwardly to deal with this new female freedom. The neat and tidy social order of the past has been replaced with social uncertainty and confusion. It is a time of adjustment—or, more precisely, maladjustment.

Historically, when oppressed members of a society suddenly receive freedom from subjugation, the social change is attended by disruption and dire predictions on every hand, even though the freedom itself is good and needful.

When women struggled to gain the vote, it was said that suffrage would destroy order and the family, for it would take woman out of her place. When abolitionists worked for the emancipation of blacks, it was said that the black people were unable to contribute to society in any way other than as laborers; freeing them would destroy order and trigger degeneracy in society. Instead of the predicted results, we have all reaped benefits from the abilities of blacks and women whose contributions would have been lost to us if they had been left to die in southern plantation cottonfields or bounded by kitchens and parlors.[33]

It was difficult and costly to enfranchise women and slaves; in a sense, American society is still struggling to cope with the implications and aftereffects of these actions. But because these changes were necessary, no one can justifiably regret that they were made.

The answer to the distress of social change is not a return to pre-liberation days. If the old ways are unfair to women, then we ought not continue in them, even if doing so would bring the benefits of social order and convenience. The answer, rather, is in learning the self-discipline and moral guidelines that will preserve our newfound freedom from the evils of unregulated extremism. We must weather the storm of change—keeping our wits about us and our spirits submitted to the truth that sets us free.

Endnotes

Introduction

1. Millard J. Erickson, *Christian Theology* (Grand Rapids, Mich.: Baker, 1983–1985; orig. pub. in 3 vols.), 26.

2. Ibid.

3. I will not be developing fully the biblical argument for equality in this book. This has been done in a number of other books, many of which are included in the reading list beginning on page 239.

Chapter 1: How Traditional Is Traditionalism?

1. The relative paucity of historical evidence concerning women's social position in Palestine and the Greco-Roman world during the time of Christ and the early church has allowed for some debate on the issue. However, the weight of opinion and evidence seems to be in favor of the view that the treatment of women by Jesus and the position of women in the early church ran counter to the contemporary cultures, in which women's roles were very restrictive and their status definitely inferior to that of men. See Millard J. Erickson, *The Word Became Flesh: A Contemporary Incarnational Christology* (Grand Rapids, Mich.: Baker, 1991), 577–93. See also Alvin John Schmidt, *Veiled and Silenced: How Culture Shaped Sexist Theology* (Macon, Ga.: Mercer Univ. Press, 1989), 163–212. The central thesis of Schmidt's book is that historically the church has been influenced by secular cultural views toward women.

2. See Margaret L. Bendroth, "The Search for 'Women's Role' in American Evangelicalism, 1930–1980," in *Evangelicalism and Modern America*, George Marsden, ed. (Grand Rapids, Mich.: Eerdmans, 1984), 122.

3. For discussion of this issue, see chapter 9.

4. David Lyon, *Sociology and the Human Image* (Leicester, England: Inter-Varsity, 1983), 167. Lyon takes his ideas in this section from Roberta Hamilton's *The Liberation of Women*.

5. See Dorothy L. Sayers, *Are Women Human?* (Grand Rapids, Mich.: Eerdmans, 1971; orig. pub. 1947 in Sayers, *Unpopular Opinions*), for a spirited defense of women's right to work outside the home, since industrialization has taken traditional women's work outside the home.

6. James Davison Hunter, *Evangelicalism: The Coming Generation*, chap. 4, "Fam-

ily: Toward Androgyny," coauthored by Helen V. L. Stehlin (Chicago: Univ. of Chicago Press, 1987), 84.

7. Louise B. Silverstein, "Transforming the Debate about Child Care and Maternal Employment," *American Psychologist* 46 (October 1991): 1026.

8. Hunter, 92.

9. From a speech by Elizabeth Stanton, read at the Waterloo convention August 2, 1848; quoted in Andrew Sinclair, *The Emancipation of the American Woman* (New York: Harper Colophon Books, Harper & Row, 1966), 257.

10. Sinclair, 121.

11. Una Stannard, *Mrs. Man* (San Francisco: Germainbooks, 1977), 51.

12. Ibid., 56.

13. Ibid., 60–61.

14. Alice Freeman Palmer, *Why Go to College?* (New York: Thomas Y. Crowell, 1897), 10–11.

15. Ibid., 9.

16. Ibid., 21.

17. Ibid., 19.

18. James C. Whorton, *Crusaders for Fitness: The History of American Health Reformers* (Princeton, N.J.: Princeton Univ. Press, 1982), 326.

19. Stannard, 65.

20. William C. Ringenberg, *The Christian College: A History of Protestant Higher Education in America* (Grand Rapids, Mich.: Christian Univ. Press, available from Eerdmans, 1984), 95–96.

21. Hunter, 90.

22. Palmer, 23.

23. Sinclair, 119.

24. Ibid., 356.

25. Ibid., 116–17.

26. Palmer, 21.

27. Ibid., 21–22.

28. Ibid., 19.

29. Charlotte Woodward's reminiscences written in 1920; quoted in Sinclair, 60.

30. "Give Me a Break: Advice for Working Mothers II," "Focus on the Family" broadcast, 8 May 1990.

Chapter 2: Today's Traditionalism

1. Andrew Sinclair, *The Emancipation of the American Woman* (New York: Harper Colophon Books, Harper & Row, 1966), 354–55.

2. James Davison Hunter, *Evangelicalism: The Coming Generation,* chap. 4, "Family: Toward Androgyny," coauthored by Helen V. L. Stehlin (Chicago: Univ. of Chicago Press, 1987), 90–91.

3. Brigitte Berger and Peter L. Berger, *The War over the Family: Capturing the Middle Ground* (Garden City, N.Y.: Anchor Books, Doubleday, 1983), 15–16.

4. For a brief survey of women's work from 1900–1960, see Douglas W. Carlson, "Discovering Their Heritage: Women and the American Past," in *Gender Matters:*

Women's Studies for the Christian Community, June Steffensen Hagen, ed. (Grand Rapids, Mich.: Academie Books, Zondervan, 1990), 105–9.

5. Marilyn I. Mollenkott, "'That One Talent Which Is Death to Hide': Emily Dickinson and America's Women Poets," in *Gender Matters,* 170.

6. Thomas Sowell, *Civil Rights: Rhetoric or Reality?* (New York: William Morrow, 1984), 99.

7. Ibid., 100.

8. Sinclair, 357.

9. Berger and Berger, 15.

10. Sinclair, 362.

11. Betty Friedan, *The Feminine Mystique,* Twentieth Anniversary Edition (New York: Laurel Books, Dell, 1983), 65.

12. Sinclair, 366.

13. Alice Freeman Palmer, *Why Go to College?* (New York: Thomas Y. Crowell, 1897), 22.

14. See Betty Friedan's well-documented chapter on education in *The Feminine Mystique,* 150–81.

15. Berger and Berger, 28.

16. Ibid., 26.

17. James Davison Hunter, *Culture Wars: The Struggle to Define America* (New York: BasicBooks, Harper Collins, 1991), 180.

18. Friedan, 49.

19. Kari Torjesen Malcolm, *Women at the Crossroads: A Path beyond Feminism and Traditionalism* (Downers Grove, Ill.: InterVarsity, 1982), 132.

20. Margaret L. Bendroth, "The Search for 'Women's Role' in American Evangelicalism, 1930–1980," in *Evangelicalism and Modern America,* George Marsden, ed. (Grand Rapids, Mich.: Eerdmans, 1984), 131.

21. Hunter, *Evangelicalism,* 76.

22. Ibid., 78.

23. Larry Christenson, *The Christian Family* (Minneapolis: Bethany Fellowship, 1970), 11.

24. Ibid., 127.

25. Ibid., 47.

26. Ibid., 127–28.

27. James C. Dobson, "Out of Focus—Masculinity and Femininity: More Ambiguous Than Ever," *Focus on the Family* (September 1991): 5.

28. Ibid.

29. Hunter, *Evangelicalism,* 96–97.

30. Dobson, 4.

31. Michael Brown, *The Christian in an Age of Sexual Eclipse* (Wheaton, Ill: Tyndale, 1983); quoted in Hunter, *Evangelicalism,* 265 n. 41.

32. W. Peter Blitchington, *Sex Roles and the Christian Family* (Wheaton, Ill.: Tyndale, 1984), 95; quoted in Hunter, *Evangelicalism,* 80.

33. Hunter, *Evangelicalism,* 113.

34. Mary Stewart Van Leeuwen, *Gender and Grace: Love, Work, and Parenting in a Changing World* (Downers Grove, Ill.: InterVarsity, 1990); see chap. 8, "The Case for Co-Parenting," 145–64.

35. Miriam Adeney, *A Time for Risking: Priorities for Women* (Portland, Ore.: Multnomah, 1987); see chap. 7, "Sharing Children: How to Nurture Your Child's Caregiver," 111–28.

36. Sinclair, 366.

37. Van Leeuwen, 170.

38. David R. Brubaker, "Secret Sins in the Church Closet," *Christianity Today,* 10 February 1992, 32.

39. On the correlation between traditional family structure and abusive relationships, see James Alsdurf and Phyllis Alsdurf, *Battered into Submission: The Tragedy of Wife Abuse in the Christian Home* (Downers Grove, Ill.: InterVarsity, 1989), and Margaret Josephson Rinck, *Christian Men Who Hate Women: Healing Hurting Relationships* (Grand Rapids, Mich.: Pyranee Books, Zondervan, 1990).

40. Hunter, *Evangelicalism,* 114; see also Berger and Berger, chap. 1, "Historical Evolution of a 'Problem,'" 3–21.

41. Hunter, *Evangelicalism,* 114.

42. Peter L. Berger, et al., *The Homeless Mind: Modernization and Consciousness* (New York: Random House, 1973), 202.

Chapter 3: Evangelicalism and the Rise of American Feminism

1. Douglas W. Carlson, "Discovering Their Heritage: Women and the American Past," in *Gender Matters: Women's Studies for the Christian Community,* June Steffensen Hagen, ed. (Grand Rapids, Mich.: Academie Books, Zondervan, 1990), 100.

2. Sir William Blackstone, *Commentaries on the Laws of England,* 4 vols. (Philadelphia, 1771–1772); quoted in Andrew Sinclair, *The Emancipation of the American Woman* (New York: Harper Colophon Books, Harper & Row, 1966), 84.

3. Sinclair, 4.

4. John Stuart Mill, introduction to *The Subjection of Women,* Wendell Robert Carr, ed. (Cambridge, Mass.: M.I.T. Press, 1970; orig. pub. 1869), xiii.

5. Henry Blackwell to Lucy Stone, 13 June 1853, Library of Congress; quoted in Sinclair, 47.

6. Henry Blackwell to Lucy Stone, 24 August 1853, Library of Congress; quoted in Sinclair, 47.

7. Elinor Rice Hays, *Morning Star: A Biography of Lucy Stone, 1818–1893* (New York: Harcourt, Brace & World, 1961), 108.

8. Ibid., 129.

9. *The History of Woman Suffrage,* vol. 1, Elizabeth Cady Stanton, et al., eds. (Rochester, N.Y.: Fowler and Wells, 1881), 260–61; quoted in Eleanor Flexner, *Century of Struggle: The Woman's Rights Movement in the United States,* rev. ed. (Cambridge, Mass.: Belknap Press of Harvard Univ. Press, 1975), 64.

10. Sinclair, 86.

11. John Stuart Mill, *On the Subjection of Women;* quoted in Elaine Storkey, *What's Right with Feminism* (Grand Rapids, Mich.: Eerdmans, 1986), 61.

12. John Stuart Mill, introduction to *On the Subjection of Women,* Everyman edition, viii; quoted in Sinclair, 53.

13. John Stuart Mill, introduction to *Subjection,* Carr, ed., xvii.

14. Albert Barnes, *An Inquiry into the Scriptural Views of Slavery* (Philadelphia: Perkins & Purves, 1846), 375; quoted in Mark A. Noll, *One Nation under God? Christian Faith and Political Action in America* (San Francisco: Harper & Row, 1988), 117.

15. Mary Stewart Van Leeuwen, *Gender and Grace: Love, Work, and Parenting in a Changing World* (Downers Grove, Ill.: InterVarsity, 1990), 239.

16. Cornelius Plantinga, "Partnership in the Gospel: Some Observations," lecture given at the Partnership in the Gospel Conference of the Committee for Women in the Christian Reformed Church, Grand Rapids, Michigan, November 1988, 18–19; quoted in Van Leeuwen, 239.

17. Donald W. Dayton, *Discovering an Evangelical Heritage* (New York: Harper & Row, 1976), 90.

18. Van Leeuwen, 236.

19. Albert Taylor Bledsoe, "Liberty and Slavery: Or, Slavery in the Light of Moral and Political Philosophy," in *Cotton Is King,* E. N. Elliot, ed. (New York: Negro Universities Press, 1969; orig. pub. 1860), 379–80; quoted in Willard M. Swartley, *Slavery, Sabbath, War, and Women: Case Issues in Biblical Interpretation* (Scottdale, Penn.: Herald Press, 1983), 49.

20. Alvin John Schmidt, *Veiled and Silenced: How Culture Shaped Sexist Theology* (Macon, Ga.: Mercer Univ. Press, 1989), 196–97.

21. See Letha Scanzoni, "The Great Chain of Being and the Chain of Command," *Reformed Journal,* October 1976, 16. See also Faith McBurney Martin, *Call Me Blessed: The Emerging Christian Woman* (Grand Rapids, Mich.: Eerdmans, 1988), 48–49.

22. Patricia Gundry, *Woman Be Free! The Clear Message of Scripture* (Grand Rapids, Mich.: Ministry Resources Library, Zondervan, 1977), 52.

23. Frederick Ross, quoted in Eugene D. Genovese, *"Slavery Ordained of God": The Southern Slaveholders' View of Biblical History and Modern Politics* (Gettysburg, Penn.: Gettysburg College, 1985), 19; quoted in Noll, 118.

24. Josiah Priest, *Bible Defense of Slavery* (Glasgow, Ky.: W. S. Brown, 1851); quoted in Schmidt, 33.

25. Noll, 125.

26. Bledsoe, 379–80; quoted in Swartley, 49.

27. Martin Luther, *Luther's Works,* vol. 46, Robert C. Schultz, ed. (Philadelphia: Fortress, 1967), 39; quoted in Faith McBurney Martin, 48.

28. "Tischreden" in *Luther's Works,* Walsch edition, 1743, vol. xxii, p. 2260; quoted in Andrew D. White, *A History of the Warfare of Science with Theology in Christendom,* 2 vols. (New York: George Braziller, 1955), 1:126.

29. Frederic W. Farrar, *The History of Interpretation* (London: Macmillan, 1886), preface, xviii, and Charles W. Shields, *The Final Philosophy* (New York: Scribner, Armstrong, & Co., 1877), 60–61; quoted in White, 1:127–28.

30. For a discussion of principles of biblical interpretation, see the section on "Biblical Feminists and the Bible" in chapter 7, pp. 111–15.

31. George M. Marsden, *Fundamentalism and American Culture: The Shaping of Twentieth-Century Evangelicalism: 1870–1925* (New York: Oxford Univ. Press, 1980), 83.

32. Sinclair, 223.

33. J. M. Craig, "Women's Suffrage Movement" in *Dictionary of Christianity in America,* Daniel G. Reid et al., eds. (Downers Grove, Ill.: InterVarsity, 1990), 1268.

34. Storkey, 149.

35. Miriam Schneir, ed., *Feminism: The Essential Historical Writings* (New York: Vintage, 1972), 82; quoted in Carlson, *Gender Matters,* 101.

36. Horace Bushnell, *Women's Suffrage: The Reform against Nature* (New York: C. Scribner & Co., 1869), 136; quoted in Schmidt, 159.

37. See Schmidt, 154–61.

38. Sydney E. Ahlstrom, *A Religious History of the American People* (New Haven, Conn.: Yale Univ. Press, 1972), 640.

39. *Christian History* 23 (1989): 29.

40. Ruth A. Tucker and Walter L. Liefeld, *Daughters of the Church: Women and Ministry from New Testament Times to the Present* (Grand Rapids, Mich.: Academie Books, Zondervan, 1987), 252–53.

41. Ahlstrom, 643.

42. Paul E. Johnson, *A Shopkeeper's Millennium: Society and Revivals in Rochester, New York, 1815–1837,* American Century Series (New York: Hill & Wang, 1978), 108.

43. Sinclair, 20.

44. Ahlstrom, 643.

45. Noll, 71.

46. *National Anti-Slavery Standard* (New York), 15 July 1841, 22; quoted in Keith E. Melder, *Beginnings of Sisterhood: The American Woman's Rights Movement, 1800–1850,* Studies in the Life of Women (New York: Schocken Books, 1977), 43.

47. Melder, 39.

48. Craig, "Women's Suffrage Movement," in *Dictionary,* 1267–68.

49. Marsden, 83.

50. David Lyon, *The Steeple's Shadow: On the Myths and Realities of Secularization* (Grand Rapids, Mich.: Eerdmans, 1987), 111–12.

51. George Grant, *Third Time Around: A History of the Pro-Life Movement from the First Century to the Present* (Brentwood, Tenn.: Wolgemuth & Hyatt, 1991), 100; emphasis mine. Please note that these criticisms of Grant's work are not intended to invalidate the overall merit of the book.

52. Ibid., 121.

53. Julia Ward Howe, "The Relation of the Woman Suffrage Movement to Other Reforms," *Transactions of the National Council of Women of the United States,* Washington, D. C., 22–25 February 1891, 242; quoted in Sinclair, 318.

54. Dayton, 91.

55. Van Leeuwen, 167.

56. Although the term *feminism* did not come into general use until early in the twentieth century, it is useful to refer to the women's rights movement in the nineteenth century as early feminism, in order to highlight the continuity, as well as the disparities, between it and the various forms of modern feminism.

57. Storkey, 92.

58. Barbara Dafoe Whitehead and David Blankenhorn, "Man, Woman, and Public Policy," *First Things,* August/September 1991, 29.

59. For more on this, see chapter 4.

60. See Tim Stafford, "The Abortion Wars," *Christianity Today,* 6 October 1989, 16–20. A booklet documenting the pro-life position of nineteenth-century feminists may

be obtained from Feminists for Life of America, 811 E. 47th St., Kansas City, Mo. 64110; (816) 753-2130.

Chapter 4: Evangelical Feminism: A Two-Century Tradition

1. *Annual Address of Miss Frances E. Willard, President, before the 19th National W.C.T.U. Convention, Denver, Colo., U.S.A., 1892* (Chicago, 1892), 6; quoted in Margaret L. Bendroth, "The Search for 'Women's Role' in American Evangelicalism, 1930–1980," in *Evangelicalism and Modern America,* George Marsden, ed. (Grand Rapids, Mich.: Eerdmans, 1984), 124.

2. Ruth A. Tucker, *Women in the Maze: Questions and Answers on Biblical Equality* (Downers Grove, Ill.: InterVarsity, 1992), 180.

3. Tim Stafford, "How Women's Missions Won the World," book review, *Christianity Today,* 8 August 1989, 50.

4. Ibid., 52.

5. For more information, see Janette Hassey, *No Time for Silence: Evangelical Women in Public Ministry around the Turn of the Century* (Grand Rapids, Mich.: Academie Books, Zondervan, 1986), from which much of the following was obtained.

6. Donald W. Dayton, *Discovering an Evangelical Heritage* (New York: Harper & Row, 1976), 90.

7. Mark A. Noll, *One Nation under God? Christian Faith and Political Action in America* (San Francisco: Harper & Row, 1988), 113.

8. Dayton, 88.

9. Ibid., 91.

10. Ibid., 88.

11. Edith Deen, *Great Women of the Christian Faith* (Westwood, N.J.: Barbour & Co., 1959), 378.

12. Ray Strachey, *Frances Willard: Her Life and Work* (New York: Revell, 1913), 208; quoted in Kari Torjesen Malcolm, *Women at the Crossroads: A Path beyond Feminism and Traditionalism* (Downers Grove, Ill.: InterVarsity, 1982), 124.

13. Hassey, 132.

14. Ibid., 33.

15. Ibid., 134.

16. Norman H. Murdoch, "The 'Army Mother,'" *Christian History* 26 (1990): 5.

17. Ibid., 5–6.

18. Amanda Smith, *An Autobiography: The Story of the Lord's Dealings with Amanda Smith* (Nobelsville, Ind.: Newby Book Room, 1972; orig. pub. 1893), 185; quoted in Malcolm, 125.

19. Dayton, 97–98.

20. Ibid.

21. Seth Cook Rees, *The Ideal Pentecostal Church* (Cincinnati: Knapp, 1897), 41; quoted in Ruth A. Tucker and Walter L. Liefeld, *Daughters of the Church: Women and Ministry from New Testament Times to the Present* (Grand Rapids, Mich.: Academie Books, Zondervan, 1987), 368.

22. Dayton, 98.

23. Hassey, 53.

24. Paul S. Rees, *Seth Cook Rees: The Warrior Saint* (Indianapolis: Pilgrim Book Room, 1934), 13; quoted in Malcolm, 126.

25. Copies of A. J. Gordon's "The Ministry of Women" are available from Christians for Biblical Equality, 380 Lafayette Freeway, #122, St. Paul, Minn. 55107.

26. A. B. Simpson, "Our Mother God," *When the Comforter Came*, 1911; quoted in Hassey, 16.

27. Hassey, 16.

28. Ibid., 110.

29. Lee Anna Starr, *The Bible Status of Woman* (Zarephath, N. J.: Pillar of Fire, 1955; orig. pub. 1926), 5.

30. Hassey, 88.

31. Ibid., 125.

32. Ibid., 44.

33. Ibid., 43.

34. J. Ellen Foster, "Work for Women," *The Institute Tie* 9 (February 1909): 483; quoted in Hassey, 183.

35. Arthur T. Pierson, *Catherine of Siena, an Ancient Lay Preacher* (New York: Funk & Wagnalls, 1898), 5; quoted in Hassey, 135.

36. Hassey, 27.

37. See *The Scofield Reference Bible*, C. I. Scofield, ed. (New York: Oxford Univ. Press, 1909, 1917), 9, 1224–25.

38. Bendroth, 131–32, 203 n. 30.

39. Ibid., 132.

40. Hassey, 93.

41. Dayton, 98.

42. Hassey, 142.

43. George M. Marsden, *Fundamentalism and American Culture: The Shaping of Twentieth-Century Evangelicalism: 1870–1925* (New York: Oxford Univ. Press, 1980), 79–80.

44. Ethelbert D. Warfield, "May Women Be Ordained in the Presbyterian Church?" *The Presbyterian* 99 (14 November 1929): 6; quoted in Bendroth, 123.

45. John R. Rice, *Bobbed Hair, Bossy Wives and Women Preachers* (Wheaton, Ill.: Sword of the Lord, 1941), 65, 68.

46. Ibid., 59.

47. Malcolm, 131. For a historical look at how opportunities for women in public ministry closed up gradually between 1920 and 1950, and how this closing up was prompted primarily by changing values in American society, see Michael S. Hamilton, "Women, Public Ministry, and American Fundamentalism, 1920–1950," *Religion and American Culture* 3 (Summer 1993): 171–96.

48. Stafford, 52.

49. A. J. Gordon, "The Ministry of Women," *World Missionary Review,* 1893; article reprint from Christians for Biblical Equality.

50. Tucker, *Maze*, 216.

Chapter 5: Modern Feminism: The Good News and the Bad News

1. Abraham Kuyper, *Women of the Old Testament, Fifty Meditations,* 2d ed., Henry Zylstra, trans. (Grand Rapids: Mich.: Zondervan, 1936), 5.

2. See Alvin John Schmidt, *Veiled and Silenced: How Culture Shaped Sexist Theology* (Macon, Ga.: Mercer Univ. Press, 1989), 115–18.

3. See Julia O'Faolain and Lauro Martines, eds., *Not in God's Image* (New York: Harper & Row, 1973), 120–22.

4. For a discussion of Gnosticism, see chapter 12.

5. "Our Bodies, Their Selves," *Newsweek,* 17 December 1990, 60.

6. See "1991 Health Guide: Top 10 Health Trends," *U.S. News & World Report,* 20 May 1991, 99.

7. Katherine Kersten, "What Do Women Want? A Conservative Feminist Manifesto," *Policy Review,* Spring 1991, 8.

8. For a defense of this argument in regard to the black civil rights issue, see Thomas Sowell, *Civil Rights: Rhetoric or Reality?* (New York: William Morrow, 1984).

9. Nancy Gibbs, "The War against Feminism," *Time,* 9 March 1992, 55.

10. Marilyn I. Mollenkott, "'That One Talent Which Is Death to Hide': Emily Dickinson and America's Women Poets," in *Gender Matters: Women's Studies for the Christian Community,* June Steffensen Hagen, ed. (Grand Rapids, Mich.: Academie Books, Zondervan, 1990), 182.

11. Dorothy L. Sayers, *Are Women Human?* (Grand Rapids, Mich.: Eerdmans, 1971; orig. pub. 1947 in Sayers, *Unpopular Opinions*), 36.

12. David Lyon, *The Steeple's Shadow: On the Myths and Realities of Secularization* (Grand Rapids, Mich.: Eerdmans, 1987), 110.

13. This is not to say that this is the *only* use to which abortion is put. Abortions for reasons of rape or incest or to save the life of the mother are certainly not in this category, but such cases are relatively rare compared with the total number of abortions.

14. Elizabeth Fox-Genovese, *Feminism without Illusions: A Critique of Individualism* (Chapel Hill, N.C.: Univ. of North Carolina Press, 1991); quoted in Suzanne Fields, "Tough-minded Feminism," book review, *First Things,* November 1991, 55.

15. Elaine Storkey, *What's Right with Feminism* (Grand Rapids, Mich.: Eerdmans, 1986), 170.

16. Irving Kristol, "Men, Women, and Sex," *The Wall Street Journal,* 12 May 1992.

17. See Schmidt, 44–46, 63–66, 132–36.

18. See Germaine Greer, *The Female Eunuch* (New York: McGraw-Hill, 1971).

19. The term *innocent* is a significant qualification. The right to life is not itself absolute, as a person may forfeit his or her right to life by taking the life of another human.

20. Tim Stafford, "The Abortion Wars," *Christianity Today,* 6 October 1989, 18.

21. For documentation of nineteenth-century feminist anti-abortion views, see Mary Krane Derr, ed., *"Man's Inhumanity to Woman, Makes Countless Infants Die": The Early Feminist Case against Abortion* (Kansas City, Mo.: Feminists for Life, 1991).

22. Guy M. Condon, "You Say Choice, I Say Murder," *Christianity Today,* 24 June 1991, 22–23.

23. Sally Carmody Keeney, "Feminists for Life," *Life in Oregon,* July 1991, 5. See also Kay Castonguay, "Pro-Life Feminism," *Political Woman,* Summer 1986, 11–15, as reprinted in a Feminists for Life of America brochure. More information and resources

concerning pro-life feminism may be obtained from Feminists for Life of America, 811 E. 47th St., Kansas City, Mo. 64110; (816) 753-2130.

24. Daphne de Jong, "Feminism and Abortion: The Great Inconsistency," in *Pro-Life Feminism: Different Voices*, Gail Grenier Sweet, ed. (Lewiston, N.Y.: Life Cycle Books, 1985), 56.

25. See Martha Bayles, "Feminism and Abortion," *The Human Life Review*, Summer 1990, 41–42. See also Aline Rousselle, "Body Politics in Ancient Rome," in Pauline Schmitt Pantel, ed., *From Ancient Goddesses to Christian Saints*, vol. 1 of *A History of Women in the West* (Cambridge, Mass.: Belknap Press, Harvard Univ. Press, 1992), 307–8.

26. An excellent such attempt was made by a number of men and women of diverse political and religious perspectives in a full-page *New York Times* advertisement, July 1992. See "A New American Compact: Caring about Women, Caring for the Unborn," *First Things*, November 1992, 43–45, for a reprint of this document.

27. See Marvin Olasky, "Victorian Secret: Pro-Life Victories in 19th-Century America," *Policy Review*, Spring 1992, 30–37.

Chapter 6: Varieties of Feminist Thought

1. For discussion along these lines, see chapters 5 and 7.

2. Rosemarie Tong, *Feminist Thought: A Comprehensive Introduction* (Boulder, Colo.: Westview Press, 1989), 2.

3. Suzanne Fields, "Tough-minded Feminism," book review, *First Things*, November 1991, 56. See also Katherine Kersten, "What Do Women Want? A Conservative Feminist Manifesto," *Policy Review*, Spring 1991, 8.

4. See Carol Gilligan, *In a Different Voice: Psychological Theory and Women's Development* (Cambridge, Mass.: Harvard Univ. Press, 1982).

5. Many variations of Marxism have developed since Marx first advanced his ideas. Probably few today are as utopian as this "original" version.

6. For a secular presentation of varieties of feminist thought, see Tong. For a Christian analysis, see Elaine Storkey, *What's Right with Feminism* (Grand Rapids, Mich.: Eerdmans, 1986).

7. See Junda Woo, "Feminist Legal Theory Enters Business Arena," *The Wall Street Journal*, 4 June 1992, B1, for evidence of the radical feminist influence in this area.

8. Tong, 3.

9. The idea that women are viewed as the "Other" is credited to Simone de Beauvoir in her pivotal feminist work, *The Second Sex*, 1949; English trans. 1953.

10. Storkey, 106.

11. Kay Leigh Hagan, "Orchids in the Arctic: The Predicament of Women Who Love Men," *Ms.*, November/December 1991, 31.

12. Christina Hoff Sommers, "Feminism and the College Curriculum," *Imprimis*, June 1990, 2. Christina Sommers is a liberal feminist who teaches philosophy at Clark University and is noted for her criticism of academic feminism. See also Stephanie Riger, "Epistemological Debates, Feminist Voices: Science, Social Values, and the Study of Women," *American Psychologist* 47 (June 1992): 730–40, for an interesting critique of different feminist epistemological approaches to scientific method and the study of gender.

13. Alison Jaggar, *Ms.*, October 1985, 50; quoted in Christina Hoff Sommers,

"Should the Academy Support Academic Feminism?" *Public Affairs Quarterly* 2 (July 1988): 102.

14. Cynthia Fuchs Epstein, *Deceptive Distinctions: Sex, Gender, and the Social Order* (New Haven: Yale Univ. Press, and New York: Russell Sage Foundation, 1988), 19, 21. A similar point is made in Barbara G. Walker, "Science: The Feminists' Scapegoat?" *Skeptical Inquirer* 18 (Fall 1993): 68–72.

15. Epstein, 23.

16. Brigitte Berger, "Academic Feminism and the Left," *Academic Questions,* Spring 1988, 6–15; quoted in *Genesis,* 9 April 1990, 6.

17. For a review of different feminist theological beliefs, see David W. Diehl, "Theology and Feminism," in *Gender Matters: Women's Studies for the Christian Community,* June Steffensen Hagen, ed. (Grand Rapids, Mich.: Academie Books, Zondervan, 1990).

18. Archaeologist Marija Gimbutas, *The Language of the Goddess* (Harper & Row, 1989), is representative of this line of approach.

19. Naomi R. Goldenberg, *Changing of the Gods: Feminism and the End of Traditional Religions* (Boston: Beacon Press, 1979), 3, 25.

20. *WomanSpirit,* Summer 1976; quoted in Alison Lentini, "Circle of Sisters," *SCP Newsletter,* Fall 1985, 14.

21. Faith McBurney Martin, *Call Me Blessed: The Emerging Christian Woman* (Grand Rapids, Mich.: Eerdmans, 1988), 34.

22. H. R. Rookmaaker, *The Creative Gift: Essays on Art and the Christian Life* (Westchester, Ill. Cornerstone Books, 1981), 30.

23. Gretchen Gaebelein Hull, *Equal to Serve: Women and Men in the Church and Home,* A Crucial Questions Book (Old Tappan, N.J.: Revell, 1987), 83.

24. Storkey, 125–26.

25. W. A. Visser't Hooft, *The Fatherhood of God in an Age of Emancipation* (Geneva: World Council of Churches, 1982), 55. Similar objections to goddess worship may be found in (briefly) Dale Youngs, "What's So Good about the Goddess?" *Christianity Today,* 16 August 1993, 21; and (more extensively) Tikva Frymer-Kensky, *In the Wake of the Goddesses: Women, Culture, and the Biblical Transformation of Pagan Myth* (New York: Fawcett Columbine, 1992).

26. For critical treatments of the historicity of the feminist belief in a prehistoric matriarchal culture of the earth goddess, see Mary Lefkowitz, "The Twilight of the Goddess," *The New Republic,* 3 August 1992, 29–33; Olivia Vlahos, "The Goddess That Failed," *First Things,* December 1992, 12–19; Stella Georgoudi, "Creating a Myth of Matriarchy," in Pauline Schmitt Pantel, ed., *From Ancient Goddesses to Christian Saints,* vol. 1 of *A History of Women in the West* (Cambridge, Mass.: Belknap Press of Harvard Univ. Press, 1992).

27. Donald K. McKim, *What Christians Believe about the Bible* (Nashville, Tenn.: Thomas Nelson, 1985), 139.

28. Elizabeth Cady Stanton; quoted in McKim, 142.

29. Carol A. Newsom and Sharon H. Ringe, eds., *The Women's Bible Commentary* (Louisville, Ky.: Westminster/John Knox Press, 1992), xiii, xv, xviii.

30. Ibid., 4.

31. Ibid., 7.

32. Elisabeth Schüssler Fiorenza, "The Will to Choose or to Reject," in *Feminist In-*

terpretation of the Bible, Letty M. Russell, ed. (Philadelphia: Westminster, 1985), 125–36; quoted in *Gender Matters,* 32.

33. Although, as this chapter has shown, there are many different kinds of feminism, I use the term "modern secular feminism" to designate, in general, those aspects of feminist thought characteristic of feminist spokespersons outside of evangelical feminism. This designation is for convenience more than for precision, in that a primary purpose of this book is to distinguish evangelical feminism from all other types of feminism. "Modern secular feminism" is "modern" in that it is marked by the unique aspects of feminism which have developed since 1960; it contrasts with nineteenth- and early twentieth-century feminism. It is "secular" in that, unlike evangelical feminism, it is premised on the tenets of secular culture rather than on basic biblical principles.

Chapter 7: Evangelical Feminism Compared with Other Views

1. Elaine Storkey, *What's Right with Feminism* (Grand Rapids, Mich.: Eerdmans, 1986), 178.

2. Ruth A. Tucker, *Women in the Maze: Questions and Answers on Biblical Equality* (Downers Grove, Ill.: InterVarsity, 1992), 182.

3. It should be noted that, although the traditionalist doctrine curtailing the teaching role of women in the church depends on the translation of this term as "authority," the biblical feminist interpretation does not depend on arriving at an alternate translation. Regardless of whether or not the issue is authority, this passage can justifiably be understood to have a limited, culturally specific application—as F. F. Bruce and many other evangelical biblical scholars have concluded. See "F. F. Bruce: A Mind for What Matters," interview with W. Ward Gasque and Laurel Gasque, *Christianity Today,* 7 April 1989, 24–25. For a discussion of the translation of *authentein,* see Richard Clark Kroeger and Catherine Clark Kroeger, *I Suffer Not a Woman: Rethinking 1 Timothy 2:11–15 in Light of Ancient Evidence* (Grand Rapids, Mich.: Baker, 1992), 84–104.

4. Gordon D. Fee, *The First Epistle to the Corinthians,* New International Commentary on the New Testament (Grand Rapids, Mich.: Eerdmans, 1987), 492, 502. See pp. 518–22 for Fee's treatment of 1 Corinthians 11:10.

5. For a synopsis of the exegetical and translational difficulties in 1 Corinthians 11:2–26; 14:33b–36 and 1 Timothy 2:8–15, see Sanford Douglas Hull, "Appendix II: Exegetical Difficulties in the 'Hard Passages,'" in Gretchen Gaebelein Hull, *Equal to Serve: Women and Men in the Church and Home,* A Crucial Questions Book (Old Tappan, N.J.: Revell, 1987), 251–66. For an evangelical feminist treatment of a number of key passages, see Gilbert G. Bilezikian, *Beyond Sex Roles,* 2d ed. (Grand Rapids, Mich.: Baker, 1986).

6. Millard J. Erickson, *Christian Theology* (Grand Rapids, Mich.: Baker, 1983–1985; orig. pub. in 3 vols.), 122.

7. "F. F. Bruce: A Mind for What Matters," 25.

8. Erickson, 124. See also pp. 112–25, for a helpful discussion of the difference between "liberal" and "conservative" approaches to deriving doctrine from Scripture and for an overview of interpretive principles.

9. For more on the evangelical feminist hermeneutic, see Kroeger and Kroeger, chapter 1, "Approaching the Bible with Faith," 29–40; Robert K. Johnston, "An Evangelical Impasse: Women in the Church and Home," *Reformed Journal,* June 1978, 11–14; and W.

Ward Gasque, "The Role of Women in the Church, in Society, and in the Home," *Crux,* date and page unknown. These resources are available from Christians for Biblical Equality, 380 Lafayette Road S., Suite 122, St. Paul, Minn. 55107-1216; (612) 224-2416.

10. Mary Stewart Van Leeuwen, *Gender and Grace: Love, Work, and Parenting in a Changing World* (Downers Grove, Ill.: InterVarsity, 1990), 239. See also Tucker, 110–11, 123–25.

11. Mark A. Noll, *Between Faith and Criticism: Evangelicals, Scholarship, and the Bible in America,* 2d ed. (Grand Rapids, Mich.: Baker, 1991), 207.

12. Storkey, 152.

13. For an evangelical treatment of the issue of homosexuality, see John R. W. Stott, *Decisive Issues Facing Christians Today,* rev. enl. ed. of *Involvement* in 2 vols. (Old Tappan, N.J.: Revell, 1990), chap. 16, "Homosexual Partnerships," 336–64. See also Stanton L. Jones, "The Loving Opposition," *Christianity Today,* 19 July 1993, 19–25.

14. See Randy Frame, "The Evangelical Closet," *Christianity Today,* 5 November 1990, 57. Note also the inset on Klyne Snodgrass of North Park Seminary in Chicago, regarding his belief that women's ordination is supported biblically but homosexuality is not.

15. Susan T. Foh, *Women and the Word of God: A Response to Biblical Feminism* (Grand Rapids, Mich.: Baker, 1980), 18–19.

16. Tucker, 203.

17. The annotated bibliography in Richard Boldrey and Joyce Boldrey, *Chauvinist or Feminist? Paul's View of Women* (Grand Rapids, Mich.: Baker, 1976)—compiled at the beginning of the modern resurgence of evangelical feminism—contains no less than twelve evangelical feminist works authored *prior* to the rise of modern feminism in the 1960s.

18. See Janette Hassey, *No Time for Silence: Evangelical Women in Public Ministry around the Turn of the Century* (Grand Rapids, Mich.: Academie Books, Zondervan, 1986), 110.

19. Ron Rhodes, "The Debate over Feminist Theology: Which View Is Biblical?" *Christian Research Journal,* Summer 1991, 21.

20. For a discussion of this point, see the section on "Non-Traditional Evangelical Traditionalism" in chapter 2.

21. See the list of permissible activities for women in John Piper and Wayne A. Grudem, eds., *Recovering Biblical Manhood and Womanhood: A Response to Evangelical Feminism* (Wheaton, Ill.: Crossway Books, 1991), 58.

22. James C. Dobson, "Out of Focus—Masculinity and Femininity: More Ambiguous Than Ever," *Focus on the Family,* September 1991, 4.

23. Cynthia Fuchs Epstein, *Deceptive Distinctions: Sex, Gender, and the Social Order* (New Haven: Yale Univ. Press, and New York: Russell Sage Foundation, 1988), 233. Epstein's book is a sociological refutation of this view of sex differences.

24. Reay Tannahill, *Sex in History* (New York: Stein and Day, 1980), 85–97.

Chapter 8: The Feminist Bogeywoman

1. Mary Pride, *The Way Home: Beyond Feminism, Back to Reality* (Westchester, Ill.: Crossway Books, 1985), 4. Pride is here quoting Mary Daly, *Beyond God the Father: Toward a Philosophy of Women's Liberation* (Boston: Beacon Press, 1973), 96.

2. Ibid.

3. Ibid., 9.

4. Christian Book Distributors catalog, 1991 and 1992; emphasis mine.

5. Elaine Storkey, *What's Right with Feminism* (Grand Rapids, Mich.: Eerdmans, 1986), 114.

6. Faith McBurney Martin, *Call Me Blessed: The Emerging Christian Woman* (Grand Rapids, Mich.: Eerdmans, 1988), 13.

7. Ruth A. Tucker and Walter L. Liefeld, *Daughters of the Church: Women and Ministry from New Testament Times to the Present* (Grand Rapids, Mich.: Academic Books, Zondervan, 1987), 399.

8. Ruth A. Tucker, *Women in the Maze: Questions and Answers on Biblical Equality* (Downers Grove, Ill.: InterVarsity, 1992), 225–26.

9. This is especially the case with doctrinal issues such as the roles of women and men in the church. Where the more central doctrines are concerned—those crucial, core beliefs of Christian orthodoxy outlined in the early creeds and officially professed by virtually every Christian denomination—tradition serves as a reliable, although not infallible, guide to biblical truth.

10. Blaise Pascal, "Preface to the Treatise on the Vacuum," Great Books of the Western World, vol. 33 (Chicago: Encyclopaedia Britannica, 1952), 358.

11. See Susan Foh's review of *Recovering Biblical Manhood and Womanhood* in *Christianity Today*, 8 April 1991, 49–50.

12. David J. Ayers, "The Inevitability of Failure: The Assumptions and Implementations of Modern Feminism," in *Recovering Biblical Manhood and Womanhood: A Response to Evangelical Feminism*, John Piper and Wayne A. Grudem, eds. (Wheaton, Ill.: Crossway Books, 1991), 312, 523 n. 3.

13. For a response to the charge that evangelical feminists are Gnostics, see chapter 12.

14. William Weinrich, "Women in the History of the Church: Learned and Holy, But Not Pastors," in *Recovering Biblical Manhood and Womanhood*, 279.

15. *Recovering Biblical Manhood and Womanhood*, xiv.

16. Ibid., 406.

17. Ibid., 471.

18. "Biblical Masculinity and Femininity," "Focus on the Family" broadcast, 9 & 10 March 1992.

19. Naomi R. Goldenberg, *Changing of the Gods: Feminism and the End of Traditional Religions* (Boston: Beacon Press, 1979), 4.

20. Mary A. Kassian, *The Feminist Gospel: The Movement to Unite Feminism with the Church* (Wheaton, Ill.: Crossway Books, 1992), 220; Pride, 5.

21. Kassian, 226–27.

22. "Biblical Masculinity and Femininity," "Focus on the Family" broadcast, 10 March 1992.

23. Ibid.

24. Mary Stewart Van Leeuwen, *Gender and Grace: Love, Work, and Parenting in a Changing World* (Downers Grove, Ill.: InterVarsity, 1990), 36.

25. Tucker, *Maze*, 221.

26. Nicholas Wolterstorff, "Between the Times," *Reformed Journal*, December 1990, 20.

27. Storkey, 178.

28. "The Search for the New Ideal Man," ABC-TV special, 22 April 1992.

29. The variety of feminist views concerning gender differences and gender roles is discussed in chapters 6 and 7.

30. For an example of this approach, see Ayers, 312–31.

31. Andrew Sinclair, *The Emancipation of the American Woman* (New York: Harper Colophon Books, Harper & Row, 1966), 239.

32. Christianity Today Institute, "Women in Leadership: Finding Ways to Serve the Church," *Christianity Today,* 3 October 1986, 6–I.

33. John R. W. Stott, *Decisive Issues Facing Christians Today,* rev. enl. ed. of *Involvement* in 2 vols. (Old Tappan, N. J.: Revell, 1990), 257.

34. Christianity Today Institute, 7–I.

35. See Pride, 9–10.

36. Kassian, 210.

37. Ibid. Kassian quotes Virginia R. Mollenkott, *Women, Men, and the Bible* (Nashville, Tenn.: Abingdon, 1977), 95.

38. See chapters 6 and 7 for more on the differences between evangelical feminism and varieties of modern feminism.

Chapter 9: Cultural Discernment: The Contemporary versus the Conservative

1. Alvin John Schmidt, *Veiled and Silenced: How Culture Shaped Sexist Theology* (Macon, Ga.: Mercer Univ. Press, 1989), 230.

2. Ibid., 1.

3. S. Scott Bartchy, "Power, Submission, and Sexual Identity among the Early Christians," in *Essays on New Testament Christianity: A Festschrift in Honor of Dean E. Walker,* C. Robert Wetzel, ed. (Cincinnati: Standard Publishing, 1978), 52.

4. For discussions of the last two movements, respectively, see Mark A. Noll, "Rethinking Restorationism—A Review Article," *Reformed Journal,* November 1989, 15–21; and Garry D. Nation, "The Restoration Movement," *Christianity Today,* 18 May 1992, 27–31.

5. Noll, 18. In this article reviewing several books on the subject, Noll describes the authors' assessment of the Churches of Christ movement.

6. Nation, 31.

7. See Douglas R. Groothuis, *Confronting the New Age: How to Resist a Growing Religious Movement* (Downers Grove, Ill.: InterVarsity, 1988), 47–58, for a discussion of these three biblical themes of cultural engagement.

8. Noll, 16.

9. For discussion of this point, see chapter 6, pp. 99–101.

10. Faith McBurney Martin, *Call Me Blessed: The Emerging Christian Woman* (Grand Rapids, Mich.: Eerdmans, 1988), 52.

11. Schmidt, 224.

12. Robert M. Bowman, *Orthodoxy and Heresy: A Biblical Guide to Doctrinal Discernment* (Grand Rapids, Mich.: Baker, 1992), 61.

13. For a development of this idea, see Arthur F. Holmes, *All Truth Is God's Truth* (Grand Rapids, Mich.: Eerdmans, 1977).

14. Herbert Spencer; quoted in A. J. Hoover, *Don't You Believe It! Poking Holes in Faulty Logic* (Chicago: Moody Press, 1982), 63.

15. Nicholas Wolterstorff, "Between the Times," *Reformed Journal,* December 1990, 17.

16. See Donald W. Dayton, *Discovering an Evangelical Heritage* (New York: Harper & Row, 1976), 3.

17. Gilbert G. Bilezikian, "Hierarchist and Egalitarian Inculturations," *Journal of the Evangelical Theological Society* 30 (December 1987): 421.

18. C. S. Lewis devised the term "chronological snobbery" and applied it to the modernist contempt for tradition, but the concept applies equally well to the traditionalist contempt for modernity.

19. See chapters 3 and 4.

20. For more on views on women's roles in the nineteenth century, see chapters 1, 3, and 4.

21. Dale A. Johnson, *Women in English Religion, 1700–1925* (New York: Edwin Mellen, 1983), 122; quoted in Ruth A. Tucker, *Women in the Maze: Questions and Answers on Biblical Equality* (Downers Grove, Ill.: InterVarsity, 1992), 218.

Chapter 10: Emotional Resistance to Evangelical Feminism

1. Nicholas Wolterstorff, "Between the Times," *Reformed Journal,* December 1990, 18.

2. S. Scott Bartchy, "Power, Submission, and Sexual Identity among the Early Christians," in *Essays on New Testament Christianity: A Festschrift in Honor of Dean E. Walker,* C. Robert Wetzel, ed. (Cincinnati: Standard Publishing, 1978), 52.

3. Joseph Farah, "TV's Assault on Families Is No Joke," *Focus on the Family,* January 1990, 9–11.

4. Christianity Today Institute, "Women in Leadership: Finding Ways to Serve the Church," *Christianity Today,* 3 October 1986, 7–I.

5. *Focus on the Family,* January 1991, back cover.

6. Connie Marshner, *Can Motherhood Survive? A Christian Looks at Social Parenting* (Brentwood, Tenn.: Wolgemuth & Hyatt, 1990), 22, 76.

7. See Mary Stewart Van Leeuwen, *Gender and Grace: Love, Work, and Parenting in a Changing World* (Downers Grove, Ill.: InterVarsity, 1990), 113–15.

8. *Traditional* is not the same as *traditionalist.* Chapters 1 and 2 distinguish truly traditional social customs, which held sway for many centuries in Western society, from those that date from the nineteenth century and are advocated by today's traditionalists.

9. Tal Brooke, *When the World Will Be As One: The Coming New World Order in the New Age* (Eugene, Ore.: Harvest House, 1989), 140.

10. Bartchy, 53.

11. Alvin John Schmidt, *Veiled and Silenced: How Culture Shaped Sexist Theology* (Macon, Ga.: Mercer Univ. Press, 1989), 63–64. See also pp. 44–46 and 132–36 for a discussion of this attitude in ancient cultures.

12. Elaine Storkey, "Men and Women as Images of God." A talk given in March 1991 at Bethel College and Seminary, St. Paul, Minn. Tape available from Christians for Biblical Equality.

13. Patricia Klein, et al., *Growing Up Born Again: A Whimsical Look at the Blessings and Tribulations of Growing Up Born Again* (Old Tappan, N.J.: Power Books, Revell, 1987), 106.

14. Bartchy, 52.

15. Van Leeuwen, 118–19.

16. "The 700 Club," 3 May 1991.

17. See p. 114 for why this teaching is unbiblical.

18. *Headship* as traditionally defined, that is. Evangelical feminists believe that it is exegetically and theologically more appropriate to understand the biblical use of *head* with respect to the husband as a metaphor for life-source rather than for authoritative ruler.

Chapter 11: "Culture Wars" and the Traditionalist Fear of Feminism

1. James Davison Hunter, *Culture Wars: The Struggle to Define America* (New York: BasicBooks, Harper Collins, 1991), 42.

2. Ibid., 44.

3. This is my observation, not Hunter's. Although he is an evangelical, he does not write here as an evangelical but as a sociologist; he therefore does not draw out the implications of his theories for Christians.

4. Hunter, 44–45.

5. Ibid., 43.

6. Ibid., 107.

7. Ibid., 122.

8. Hunter claims that those who believe in biblical authority will naturally believe that men and women differ in "psyche" as well as roles and spiritual callings. But this belief is extrapolated from a traditionalist interpretation of Scripture; it is not overtly taught in Scripture. Nowhere does the Bible speak of psychological differences between men and women. Basing the prohibition of homosexuality on this highly debatable "biblical" view of male/female differences weakens rather than strengthens the biblical position on homosexuality. The prohibition of homosexual behavior ought simply to be grounded in the incontrovertible biblical principle of marital fidelity between a man and a woman (Gen. 2:24) and the specific biblical texts which clearly condemn homosexual behavior.

9. Hunter, 122–27.

10. Ibid., 44.

11. Although traditionalists would doubtless contest that they favor men over women, it *is* favoritism to give men the choice of all ministries and occupations, but to limit women to the subordinate ones—which, for women gifted in intellectual and/or leadership abilities, are generally the least challenging and interesting roles.

12. As will be shown below, a majority of the religiously orthodox do *not* necessarily adhere to traditional gender roles, but I am assuming here, for the sake of argument, that they do.

13. For an interesting study of the cultural context and the exegetical implications of the temperance movement for evangelicals, see John L. Merrill, "The Bible and the American Temperance Movement: Text, Context, and Pretext," *Harvard Theological Review* 81, no. 2 (1988): 145–70.

14. Even though the Bible ought not be construed as specifically forbidding the con-

sumption of alcoholic beverages, I do think that, because of the biblical mandate to exercise self-control and consideration for others and the widespread death and destruction which alcohol is wreaking on modern society, a Christian could easily and reasonably decide upon abstinence from alcohol as the most morally responsible option.

15. Hunter, 96, 338 n. 65, 339–40 n. 68. My observations are generalizations which don't necessarily hold true for each religious subgroup within the orthodox and progressive camps; that is, 47 percent (less than a majority) of orthodox *Protestants* took the "liberal" position disagreeing with husbandly authority, and 31 percent (less than a majority) of progressive *Jews* had a conservative view of pre-marital sex.

16. Ibid., 132, 304–5.

17. Ibid., 305.

18. Ibid.

19. Ibid., 131.

20. Ibid., 130.

21. Ibid., 131.

Chapter 12: Guilt by Association: Liberalism, Gnosticism, and Feminism

1. For more on this, see chapter 5, pp. 78–87.

2. For further discussion of the traditionalist charge that evangelical feminists do not respect biblical authority, see the section on "Misunderstanding Evangelical Feminism" in chapter 7.

3. Harvie M. Conn, "Evangelical Feminism: Some Bibliographical Reflections on the Contemporary State of the 'Union,'" *Westminster Theological Journal* 46 (1984): 104–24.

4. See the section on "Misunderstanding Evangelical Feminism" in chapter 7 for more on the homosexual issue.

5. See the section on "Abolitionism and the Church" in chapter 3.

6. Douglas R. Groothuis, *Revealing the New Age Jesus: Challenges to Orthodox Views of Christ* (Downers Grove, Ill.: InterVarsity, 1990), 74.

7. Richard Clark Kroeger and Catherine Clark Kroeger, *I Suffer Not a Woman: Rethinking 1 Timothy 2:11–15 in Light of Ancient Evidence* (Grand Rapids: Mich.: Baker, 1992), 148–49.

8. For a refutation of this claim made by Pagels and others who propound a New Age revisionist view of Jesus, see Groothuis, chapters 4 and 5.

9. See Kathleen McVey, "Gnosticism, Feminism, and Elaine Pagels," *Theology Today* 37 (January 1981): 498–501.

10. John Piper and Wayne A. Grudem, eds., *Recovering Biblical Manhood and Womanhood: A Response to Evangelical Feminism* (Wheaton, Ill.: Crossway Books, 1991), back cover.

11. Peter Jones, *The Gnostic Empire Strikes Back* (Phillipsburg, N.J.: Presbyterian and Reformed, 1992), 53. This book is probably the most apt example I have found of relying upon guilt by association, the bandwagon mentality, and highly emotionalized alarmism in an attempt to argue against feminism in any form. Jones describes what he perceives as "the present evangelical landslide capitulation to various forms of contempo-

rary feminism" as "the unwitting adoption and imposition on Scripture of an alien ideology [i.e., 'the Gnostic empire'] bent upon the annihilation of orthodox Christianity" (63). Although I do not respond directly to Jones's work in this chapter, the evangelical-feminist-as-gnostic arguments I address are basically the same as those Jones employs.

12. Louis Brighton, "The Ordination of Women: A Twentieth-Century Gnostic Heresy?" *Concordia Journal*, January 1982, 14.

13. For a discussion of this issue, see chapter 6, pp. 101–2.

14. Elaine H. Pagels, *The Gnostic Gospels* (New York: Random House, 1979), 48.

15. Ibid.

16. Ibid., 49.

17. McVey, 500.

18. Elisabeth Schüssler Fiorenza, "Word, Spirit and Power: Women in Early Christian Communities," in *Women of Spirit: Female Leadership in the Jewish and Christian Traditions,* Rosemary Radford Ruether and Eleanor McLaughlin, eds. (New York: Simon & Schuster, 1979), 50.

19. Pagels, 60.

20. McVey, 500.

21. Kroeger and Kroeger, 70–73.

22. Ibid., 172.

23. The Gospel of Thomas, Saying 114, in *The Nag Hammadi Library in English,* trans. Thomas O. Lambdin, James M. Robinson, ed. (San Francisco: Harper & Row, 1988), 138. The Gospel of Thomas is not regarded as authentic by conservative biblical scholars.

24. F. F. Bruce, *Jesus and Christian Origins outside the New Testament* (Grand Rapids, Mich.: Eerdmans, 1974), 153–54.

25. Kroeger and Kroeger, 173.

26. Zostrianos 8.1.131.5–8, in *The Nag Hammadi Library in English,* 430.

27. J. I. Packer, "Let's Stop Making Women Presbyters," *Christianity Today,* 11 February 1991, 18.

28. Alvin John Schmidt, *Veiled and Silenced: How Culture Shaped Sexist Theology* (Macon, Ga.: Mercer Univ. Press, 1989), 201.

29. Selecta in Exodus 17.17; quoted in Schmidt, 43.

30. Evangelius Secundum Lucum 10.161; quoted in Schmidt, 201.

31. Commentarius in Epistolam and Ephesios 3; quoted in Schmidt, 201. The word *wishes* appeared as *wished* in Schmidt, which I assumed to be in error and therefore corrected for the purpose of clarity.

32. McVey, 501.

33. The Gospel of Thomas, Saying 22, in *The Nag Hammadi Library in English,* Robinson, ed., 129. Brackets were in the Robinson edition.

34. See the section on "The Androgyny Alarm" in chapter 8.

35. Philip J. Lee, *Against the Protestant Gnostics* (New York: Oxford Univ. Press, 1987), 138.

36. Ibid., 213.

37. David J. Ayers, "The Inevitability of Failure: The Assumptions and Implementations of Modern Feminism," in *Recovering Biblical Manhood and Womanhood,* 312.

38. Ibid., 523 n. 3.

39. Allan Carlson, "The Androgyny Hoax," *Persuasion at Work,* March 1986.

Chapter 13: Logic, Culture, and Controversy

1. Ron Rhodes, "The Debate over Feminist Theology: Which View Is Biblical?" *Christian Research Journal,* Summer 1991, 26. Rhodes is here quoting Elisabeth Elliot.

2. Larry Christenson and Nordis Christenson, *The Christian Couple* (Kingsway Publications, 1978), 141; quoted in Elaine Storkey, *What's Right with Feminism* (Grand Rapids, Mich.: Eerdmans, 1986), 115–16.

3. Storkey, 116.

4. Margaret L. Bendroth, "The Search for 'Women's Role' in American Evangelicalism, 1930–1980," in *Evangelicalism and Modern America,* George Marsden, ed. (Grand Rapids, Mich.: Eerdmans, 1984), 123.

5. A. J. Hoover, *Don't You Believe It! Poking Holes in Faulty Logic* (Chicago: Moody Press, 1982), 35.

6. For a development of this idea, see chapter 7, pp. 121–27.

7. James Davison Hunter, *Culture Wars: The Struggle to Define America* (New York: BasicBooks, Harper Collins, 1991), 160.

8. This has been the experience of philosopher Christina Sommers, who was referred to in chapter 6.

9. Kay Ebeling, "The Failure of Feminism," *Newsweek,* 19 November 1990, 9.

10. For a discussion of how "sexual liberation" has hurt women and undermined feminism, see chapter 5, pp. 76–78.

11. Ebeling does not even condemn extramarital sex in the more-conservative-than-*Newsweek* publication *The Human Life Review* ("Feminists Are Not Funny," Spring 1991, 33–42), although she makes clear in that article that she became pregnant with her second child while unmarried. She does, however, make a good case against abortion as a "solution" for unplanned pregnancies.

12. "The Unfinished Temple," *G. K. Chesterton: Collected Works,* 28 vols. (San Francisco: Ignatius Press, 1987), 4:61; quoted in Gary DeMar and Peter J. Leithart, *The Reduction of Christianity: A Biblical Response to Dave Hunt* (Fort Worth, Tex.: Dominion Press, and Atlanta, Ga.: American Vision Press, 1988), 122–23.

13. James Dobson, *Straight Talk: What Men Need to Know, What Women Should Understand,* rev. ed. (Dallas: Word, 1991), 186.

14. Hunter, 144.

15. Gretchen Gaebelein Hull, *Equal to Serve: Women and Men in the Church and Home,* A Crucial Questions Book (Old Tappan, N.J.: Revell, 1987), 58.

16. Lloyd Billingsley, *Religion's Rebel Son: Fanaticism in Our Time* (Portland, Ore.: Multnomah, 1986), 105.

17. Ibid., 101.

18. Ibid., 102.

19. Tal Brooke, *When the World Will Be As One: The Coming New World Order in the New Age* (Eugene, Ore.: Harvest House, 1989), 139–40.

20. Ibid., 141.

21. Rolf Zettersten, "The New Feminists," *Focus on the Family,* July 1990, 23. This criticism of this particular article should not be taken as a criticism of the entire "Focus on the Family" ministry. The efforts undertaken by this ministry on behalf of families and children, and against such social problems as abortion, divorce, pornography, and statist intervention in religion and family life are certainly commendable.

22. See Gloria Borger, "Behind the Wellesley Flap," *U.S. News & World Report*, 28 May 1990, 32.

23. Zettersten, 23.

24. John Leo, "The Smart Case for Women's Schools," *U.S. News & World Report*, 11 June 1990, 21.

25. For more on loss of self-esteem in female students at coed schools, see the following: ibid.; Peter Freiberg, "Self-esteem Gender Gap Widens in Adolescence," *APA Monitor*, April 1991, 29; Leslie Miller-Bernal, "College Experiences and Sex-Role Attitudes: Does a Women's College Make a Difference?" *Youth & Society* 20 (June 1989): 363–87; and Mary Crawford and Margo MacLeod, "Gender in the College Classroom: An Assessment of the 'Chilly Climate' for Women," *Sex Roles* 23 (1990): 101–22.

26. Claudia Wallis, "Onward, Women!" *Time*, 4 December 1989, 81.

27. Dobson, 184.

28. For further thoughts along these lines, see the final section of chapter 2.

29. For an excellent discussion of the practical ways in which a marriage of equality works out, see Patricia Gundry, *Heirs Together: Mutual Submission in Marriage* (Grand Rapids, Mich.: Ministry Resources Library, Zondervan, 1980), 135–63.

30. For more on this idea, see Gretchen Gaebelein Hull, *Equal to Serve*, chap. 8, "Crucial Choices," 146–77.

31. Blaise Pascal, *Pensees*, 895, Great Books of the Western World, vol. 33 (Chicago: Encyclopaedia Britannica, 1952), 347.

32. Philip Yancey, "What a Truckload of Deutsche Marks Cannot Do," *Christianity Today*, 19 November 1990, 72.

33. Patricia Gundry, *Woman Be Free! The Clear Message of Scripture* (Grand Rapids, Mich.: Ministry Resources Library, Zondervan, 1977), 33.

For Further Reading

General

Gundry, Patricia. *Woman Be Free! The Clear Message of Scripture.* Grand Rapids, Mich.: Ministry Resources Library, Zondervan, 1977. 112 pp. A concise, "classic" exposition of the biblical case for women's equality.

Hagen, June Steffensen, ed. *Gender Matters: Women's Studies for the Christian Community.* Grand Rapids, Mich.: Academie Books, Zondervan, 1990. 304 pp. A collection of essays by professors (mostly from The King's College, Briarcliff Manor, New York) giving a Christian feminist perspective on various areas of academic study. Helpful, interesting material—but perhaps a bit too "trendy" in places.

Hull, Gretchen Gaebelein. *Equal to Serve: Women and Men in the Church and Home.* A Crucial Questions Book. Old Tappan, N.J.: Revell, 1987. 302 pp. Defines biblical feminism as the belief that women and men should have equal opportunity to serve in both church and society—this contrasted with the secular feminist emphasis on equal rights and the traditionalist emphasis on prescribed roles.

Malcolm, Kari Torjesen. *Women at the Crossroads: A Path beyond Feminism and Traditionalism.* Downers Grove, Ill.: InterVarsity, 1982. 215 pp. This book gently points the reader toward a biblical balance between the two extremes of secular culture. Especially valuable for its insight into women's roles throughout church history and its personalized approach encouraging women to make Christ their first love.

Martin, Faith McBurney. *Call Me Blessed: The Emerging Christian Woman.* Grand Rapids, Mich.: Eerdmans, 1988. 180 pp. A gold mine of insight and information ranging over many aspects of the women issue, including biblical and church history, theology, and biblical studies.

Sayers, Dorothy L. *Are Women Human?* Introduction by Mary McDermott Shideler. Grand Rapids, Mich.: Eerdmans, 1971. 47 pp. A reprint of Dorothy L. Sayers's two lectures on the subject of womanhood and the difference it does and does not make. Trenchant, witty, and thoroughly delightful to read!

Tucker, Ruth A. *Women in the Maze: Questions and Answers on Biblical Equality.* Downers Grove, Ill.: InterVarsity, 1992. 276 pp. A clear and readable response to questions frequently asked concerning the "gender" of God, the significance

239

for women of the creation and fall, the Old Testament and Jewish culture, the New Testament and women, the role of women in church history, and issues relating to feminism in contemporary society.

History and Social Science

Brown, Ann. *Apology to Women: Christian Images of the Female Sex.* Leicester, England: Inter-Varsity, 1991. 192 pp. An overview of how women have been perceived throughout church history, with an emphasis on Christian writing and art.

Cook, Kaye V., and Lance L. Lee. *Man and Woman, Alone and Together: Gender Roles, Identity, and Intimacy in a Changing Culture.* Wheaton, Ill.: BridgePoint, Victor Books. 288 pp. A self-help approach by two psychologists, encouraging men and women to adopt the values of flexibility, tolerance, respect, and responsibility in their relations with one another.

Hassey, Janette. *No Time for Silence: Evangelical Women in Public Ministry around the Turn of the Century.* Grand Rapids, Mich.: Academie Books, Zondervan, 1986. 254 pp. A historically documented account of the evangelical support for women in preaching and teaching ministries a century ago in the United States.

Hubbard, M. Gay. *Women: The Misunderstood Majority.* Contemporary Christian Counseling. Irving, Tex.: Word, 1992. 274 pp. Written primarily for counselors by a psychologist, this book helps people "understand women" without the cultural mythology that tends to pervade traditional treatments of women's psychology; it also deals with gender research and the significance of sex differences.

Schmidt, Alvin John. *Veiled and Silenced: How Culture Shaped Sexist Theology.* Macon, Ga.: Mercer Univ. Press, 1989. 238 pp. A thorough exposition of how theologians throughout church history have been influenced by the sexist beliefs of secular culture.

Storkey, Elaine, *What's Right with Feminism.* Grand Rapids, Mich.: Eerdmans, 1985. 186 pp. An overview and critique—from a Christian perspective—of the history and beliefs of the major schools of feminist thought. The book concludes with a biblical, historical, and sociological case for evangelical feminism.

Van Leeuwen, Mary Stewart. *Gender and Grace: Love, Work, and Parenting in a Changing World.* Downers Grove, Ill.: InterVarsity, 1990. 278 pp. A Christian psychologist's analysis and insights concerning the issue of gender differences and gender roles. An excellent, well-informed, and evenhanded treatment of the subject. A bit academic in places.

Biblical Studies

Bilezikian, Gilbert G. *Beyond Sex Roles: What the Bible Says about a Woman's Place in Church and Family.* 2d ed. Grand Rapids, Mich.: Baker, 1986. 340 pp.

Evans, Mary J. *Woman in the Bible: An Overview of All the Crucial Passages on Women's Roles.* Downers Grove, Ill.: InterVarsity, 1984. 160 pp.

Keener, Craig S. *Paul, Women and Wives: Marriage and Women's Ministry in the Letters of Paul*. Peabody, Mass.: Hendrickson, 1992. 350 pp. This treatment of the biblical texts on women is notable for the author's in-depth knowledge of the cultures of biblical times and the significance of such for determining Paul's intended meaning in these passages.

Kroeger, Richard Clark, and Catherine Clark Kroeger. *I Suffer Not a Woman: Rethinking 1 Timothy 2:11–15 in Light of Ancient Evidence*. Grand Rapids, Mich.: Baker, 1992. 253 pp. A minister and a classicist offer new insights and evidence concerning the cultural context of 1 Timothy and its bearing on the meaning of the passage traditionally understood to deny women the opportunity to teach or preach in the church.

Mickelsen, Alvera, ed. *Women, Authority and the Bible*. Downers Grove, Ill.: Inter-Varsity, 1986. 304 pp. A compilation of addresses presented at the Evangelical Colloquium on Women and the Bible, October 1984, concerning issues in the biblical understanding of women's roles in the church and home.

Spencer, Aida Besançon. *Beyond the Curse: Women Called to Ministry*. Nashville, Tenn.: Thomas Nelson, 1985. 223 pp.

Marriage and Vocation

Adeney, Miriam. *A Time for Risking: Priorities for Women*. Portland, Ore.: Multnomah, 1987. 182 pp. An encouragement to women to say "yes" to what really matters, to risk pouring out their energies for the kingdom of God.

Gundry, Patricia. *Heirs Together: Mutual Submission in Marriage*. Grand Rapids, Mich.: Ministry Resources Library, Zondervan, 1980. 192 pp. A well-balanced and well-reasoned case for mutual submission in marriage that is biblical, sensible, and workable.

Shenk, Sara Wenger. *And Then There Were Three: An Ode to Parenthood*. Scottdale, Penn.: Herald Press, 1985. 219 pp. A Christian feminist's reflections on the meaning of marriage and motherhood, and the ultimate value of family and relationships.

Wang, Bee-Lan C., and Richard J. Stellway. *Should You Be the Working Mom? A Guide for Making the Decision and Living with the Results*. Elgin, Ill.: Lifejourney Books, David C. Cook, 1987. 173 pp. A thoughtful yet practical treatment of the issue of employment for mothers, written by an educator and a sociologist.

Wright, Linda Raney. *A Cord of Three Strands*. Old Tappan, N.J.: Power Books, Revell, 1987. 256 pp. A very readable defense of biblical equality for women in the home and the church.

Feminism and Abortion

Derr, Mary Krane, ed. *"Man's Inhumanity to Woman, Makes Countless Infants Die": The Early Feminist Case against Abortion*. Kansas City, Mo.: Feminists for Life,

1991. 46 pp. A collection of anti-abortion essays by nineteenth-century American feminists, with historical commentary by the editor.

Sweet, Gail Grenier, ed. *Pro-Life Feminism: Different Voices.* Lewiston, N.Y.: Life Cycle Books, 1985. 234 pp. A collection of essays by pro-life feminists on a variety of women's issues. Not written from an explicitly Christian perspective, but should be helpful for pro-life Christians interested in employing persuasive arguments against those who believe legalized abortion is a necessary prerequisite for women's liberation.

Subject Index

243

Scripture Index

Genesis
1–115, 118
1:26–27–5, 139, 155
1:28–149
2–115, 118
2:24–118, 234 n. 8
3:14–19–58
3:16–73, 109, 115
19:8–37

Leviticus
19:3–100

Deuteronomy
5:16–100
18:9–13–103
21:18–100
32:18–102

Judges
19–37

Proverbs
31–4

Isaiah
42:14–102
46:3–4–102

49:15–102
66:13–102

Matthew
19:8–100
23:37–102
28:18–20–113

Mark
7:8–131

Luke
10:38–42–100
11:27–28–57, 100

John
4:7–26–100
7:24–197
13:14–16–113
15:13–101

Acts
2–55
10:34–155
17:27–28–101

1 Corinthians
11:3–16–112, 113
11:11–12–68

14:34–35–113

Galatians
3:26–28–155
3:28–1, 35, 36, 52, 57,
   115, 139, 195

Ephesians
5:23–120

1 Timothy
2:5–114
2:11–15–113
2:12–112, 120

Hebrews
7:21–24–114

1 Peter
2:5–9–114
3:1–113

1 John
4:1–6–99, 103

Revelation
5:10–114
20:6–114